Praise for *Cruel Harvest*

"A story that seizes the reader's attention . . . the reader can't look away."

—*Publishers Weekly*

"Fran Grubb's childhood odyssey is a shatteringly dark tale of despair. But that's not the end of her captivating life story. Each page of *Cruel Harvest* reveals a remarkable journey of rescue and redemption. Your heart will be moved as you witness Jesus' power to deliver, forgive, reconcile, rebuild, and love."

—Denalyn and Max Lucado

"A deeply harrowing story, told with compassion and simplicity, by an extraordinarily brave writer."

—Anjelica Huston

"*Cruel Harvest* is an incredible story of survival and forgiveness. Fran's ability to survive brokenness as a child and even into adulthood and then to overcome those experiences through faith and forgiveness is a true testament to the power of God's love for each of us. Everyone can be inspired by her story."

—Sheila Walsh, author of *God Loves Broken People* and Women of Faith speaker

"Against all odds, Fran survived her trip through the 'valley of the shadow of death.' I loved reading this story of deliverance. Thank you for the reminder that God can turn our mourning into dancing!"

—Gracia Burnham, former hostage and author of *In the Presence of My Enemies*

"It is hard endorsing *Cruel Harvest* with just a few words. I want everyone to know how powerful her story is and how many lives it can help change, and is currently changing. Ever since reading Fran Grubb's story I have used it to help numerous clients that are victims of childhood violence. Every woman has commented on her faith and how her book has given them hope! We are putting the book in our library for all the ladies to read."

—Vicki Mason, Primary Crisis Interventionist, Women's Crisis Services of LeFlore County, Poteau, Oklahoma

"This was a wonderful book. We could feel the faith of the child throughout every page. We highly recommend *Cruel Harvest.*"

—DeWayne and Rebecca Hicks, founders of Courage to Change Ministries, Greenville, Arkansas

"*Cruel Harvest* will touch your heart clear through to your soul! I guarantee that you won't be disappointed and you won't be able to put it down."

—Pastor Ray Witherington, Midnight Cry Ministries / Restoration Revival Center Church, Townville, South Carolina

Cruel Harvest

A MEMOIR

FRAN ELIZABETH GRUBB

THOMAS NELSON
Since 1798

NASHVILLE DALLAS MEXICO CITY RIO DE JANEIRO

Published in Nashville, Tennessee, by Thomas Nelson. Thomas Nelson is a registered trademark of Thomas Nelson, Inc.

Thomas Nelson, Inc., titles may be purchased in bulk for educational, business, fund-raising, or sales promotional use. For information, please e-mail SpecialMarkets@ThomasNelson.com.

Library of Congress Cataloging-in-Publication Data

Grubb, Fran E.
Cruel harvest : a memoir / Fran Grubb.
p. cm.
ISBN 978-1-59555-505-2
1. Grubb, Fran E. 2. Grubb, Fran E.—Family. 3. Sexually abused children—United States—Biography. 4. Kidnapping victims—United States—Biography. 5. Migrant labor—United States—Biography. 6. Abusive men—United States—Biography. 7. Fathers—United States—Biography. 8. Escaped prisoners—United States—Biography. 9. Dysfunctional families—United States—Case studies. I. Title.
CT275.G787A3 2012
973.92092—dc23
[B] 2012004553

Printed in the United States of America

12 13 14 15 16 QG 6 5 4 3 2 1

To the Creator and giver of all good gifts: I love you and I know that I owe this book to you. I give you all the glory, honor, and praise for every sentence printed in this story. This book is yours, not mine.

To Wayne, whose love, support, and encouragement has kept me going year after year, through the churches, tent revivals, nursing homes, and prisons, and who keeps me laughing.

For all the times I may have forgotten to say thank you for carrying equipment, singing harmony, reading the Bible, navigating before the GPS, your wonderful sense of humor even after three meetings a day, and for never losing hope. Thank you!

Thank you for throwing out all the rules about love, listening to your heart and proving there are no rules or limits to unconditional love.

To Wayne, who has the heart of a child and the courage of a lion. Can I ever show you how much you mean to me? I hope this dedication is a start.

Cruel Harvest was written for all the adults and children who find themselves asking, "Why?" I pray you find the answer in these pages. God knows your name and has written your name on his hand!

(Isaiah 49:16; John 10:3)

Contents

Prologue

His fist shattered the glass panel of the back door the instant I turned the lock to keep him out.

His fiery, red face, twisted with unbridled rage, glared at me from outside the glass top half of the kitchen door. The only thing separating us was the jagged windowpane.

I stood still for just a second, frozen in shock as I looked into his evil, angry eyes. Shards of glass exploded inward toward me, some cutting into my forearm and head, the rest falling to the kitchen floor. He reached his calloused hand through the broken window to unlock the door. My shock was quickly replaced by fear, and I ran through the house to get to the front door as though the devil himself were chasing me. He was!

It was 1963 in Benton Harbor, Michigan. I was fourteen, and this little house was one of the best I'd lived in during my childhood. It had three rooms set in a line like train cars: the kitchen in the back, a bedroom in the middle, and a small living room at the front. I tore through that dark house as fast as I could, slamming into the front door. I had locked it only minutes earlier to keep him out. Now he was in the house with me and I could hear his footsteps and feel the rasp of his enraged breathing. I had only seconds to slide the bolt back, throw the door open, and leap from the house as if it were burning down behind me.

The front door opened to an old wooden porch with a sagging tin roof. Snow blanketed the front yard, rising up to cover the bottom two steps leading off the rotted decking. I jumped, my legs sinking a foot and a half into the drift. The cold air cut through the ragged clothes I wore. I remembered my coat was inside, but so was he. There was no going back in.

Millie and her young daughter, Mary Anne, were standing by our old car in the snow-covered front yard. A tattered cardboard box of blackened pots and pans lay beside it. I had dropped them before running back into the empty house, hoping the sound of clattering pans, lids, and pots would be an alarm in the still night and somebody would come to save me.

I heard him crashing through the house behind me just as I sailed off the porch. Little Mary Anne came chasing after me into the yard. The moon shone so brightly off of the snow that I could see her big, dark eyes pleading with me to take her along. She screamed my name as I dashed past her. She did have her jacket on, but at five years old, the snow was up to her waist in some areas and I worried she would get lost.

"Millie, grab your daughter!" I yelled.

I never slowed down as I turned away from the dirt road that ran in front of the house and plowed through the deep drifts to reach the covering of the woods at the side of the house. Clumps of snow fell from the pine branches in the yard; ice rolled down the back of my dress and burned my cheeks like fire. I knew that if I stopped, the pain would be much worse when he got his hands on me. I had no doubt that he would kill me just as he had killed my baby sister eight years earlier.

Mary Anne screamed again, louder this time. Her little voice echoed harshly through the night. It tore at my heart. A part of me regretted running off because I knew I was leaving that little girl behind. I could only hope that her mother would take care of her. For me, it was too late. I had to do it now. The decision had been made, and there was no turning back.

As her mother dragged Mary Anne back to the car where she had left the baby, I heard Daddy running behind me. I did not dare turn around but I was sure he was way too close. If he got his hands on me, I was finished. He was not a big man, but he was strong, especially when he was in a rage.

I was young enough to stay just ahead of him, jumping through the high snow. The muscles in my legs were burning like fire. As I finally reached the tree line and dove into the woods, the pine branches raked against my already cut forehead and arms. My blood left a faint red trail behind. I could only hope he couldn't see it.

Once in the shadows of the pine trees, I slowed down to catch my breath. My chest heaved, and I doubled over, trying to listen above the sound of my own breathing. My heart pounded in my ears. I couldn't hear him, but when I straightened up and looked through the canopy, I could see him. He stalked back and forth through the heavy drifts. When he got near the tree line, though, he hesitated. For some reason he did not plunge into the woods behind me. I don't know what made him stop, even to this day.

Standing still, staring out at him as he paced like a hungry lion, the cold seeped into my bones. I had to start moving, or I'd be in trouble. As quietly and as carefully as I could, I inched along the edge of the woods in what I hoped was the direction of the main road.

I stumbled. My foot hit something big buried in the snow, and I fell across a huge, old, hollowed tree lying on its side. The front of my dress ripped, and the splintered wood tore holes in my knees. To my ears, my fall sounded like an avalanche crashing down the side of a mountain. I was so sure he'd heard; I froze in my tracks. My exposed skin was pressed against the ice and the bark of the fallen tree. I listened, and what I heard froze me far deeper than any snow could.

"Get out here, *now*, or I'm gonna kill you," he hollered.

He continued to pace. "Frances! I'm coming in there, and I'll find you! You hear me?"

I held my hand over my mouth, trying to hide the sound of my breathing. My entire body was shaking. I knew he was telling the truth.

Through the pine branches, by the rays of moonlight striking the side yard, I saw him stop his pacing. His arms hung by his side, limp. I swore he was looking right at me. I clenched my teeth together so they wouldn't chatter.

When he called out again, his voice had changed.

"Come on out now, Frances." He spoke the way a man is supposed to speak to a child, maybe even a little too sweet. "Nothing is going to happen. Come on out now."

That tone of voice made me feel the pain. My body was dangerously near frostbite already. My calf was stuck to the frozen wood and my heart could not stop hammering in my chest.

At the same time, that tone made me remember. He had made promises before. I thought about Mary Anne. She had changed so much since her mother had married him. When I first met her she was a funny, happy little girl, laughing and playful. Now, she barely spoke. I was leaving her behind, possibly to share in the terrors I had experienced in the past. I knew that, and I felt awful about it. But my choice had been made, no matter what voice he used. I knew it would only be worse if I turned back now.

As I watched, my eyes wide and brimming with freezing tears, he lunged toward the woods. Something kept him back. Lurching like a crazed animal, he started his pacing again. I could see his body tensing up, his hands balled into hard, pain-dealing fists. The past crashed down on me like a tidal wave. My doubts shattered.

Millie called out. "Come on, leave her out there. We gotta get going before somebody hears us."

Then, while he continued to holler at me, he unbuckled his belt. Pulling it free from the loops, he lashed at the frozen tree branches.

"I'll kill you! I'll find you, just like I did last time. But this time I'll kill you! So help me God, you won't get away from me!"

It wasn't an idle threat. No matter how much I had hoped for help, it was not on the way. I was a migrant child, alone. I could disappear, and no one would know the difference. The rest of my family had escaped. I was the last one under Daddy's power. And no matter what, I would break free or die trying.

Chapter 1

Family

When I was nine years old, Daddy abducted me from an orphanage in South Carolina. It was 1958, and he had just escaped from a California prison where he had been serving a sentence for raping my oldest sister, Brenda, and attempting to murder my mother. For years he abused me in every way he could. At one point, my family consisted of two parents, three sisters, and two brothers. By the time I was fourteen years old, they had all escaped one way or another. Everyone but me.

My decision to write down my story began with my husband's encouragement. He felt I could help others as well as myself by public speaking. I started slowly, revealing intimate details at speaking engagements with the hope that my life would help others. I was amazed when hundreds of people, every place I went, wanted to hear more. After a few years of traveling, speaking at churches, prisons, women's meetings, rehabilitation clinics, and orphanages, sharing my story with the audience and talking to men and women who had gone through similar experiences, I was certain he was right. Many men, women, and even children had never discussed their abuse before. I experienced how hearing what I went through helped people work out the troubles in their own lives. This is why I want to tell about these events in such detail—why I don't want to hold back. It's the beginning of healing for others.

One day, my husband, Wayne, drove me to a doctor's appointment. It was a nice spring day, so he decided to sit in the car and wait for me. When we left the house, he had grabbed my writings off the table and brought them with him to read. Why he chose to do that, I am not sure, but I found it touching that he cared enough to read my words again for at least the third time. He's a quiet man, polite and gentle in his ways, tall and handsome in my eyes. Meeting him is one of the many amazing blessings I have been awarded in my life.

Wayne began to read when I got out of the car.

"Wow, Honey. Are you going to read that again?" I asked, smiling down at him.

"It'll give me something to do while I wait," he said, glancing through it and smiling as I shut the door.

I left Wayne and attended to my appointment. I cannot even remember what I was there for. What I can remember is walking back out to our car and finding Wayne, still sitting in the same place I had left him, with tears rolling down his cheeks. He turned and looked at me when I got in the car and closed the door.

"Are you crying because of what you read?" I asked.

Wayne didn't say anything. I slid into my seat and gave him a hug. We sat together in the parking lot as tears ran down his face.

"Don't worry about it, Honey," I whispered softly. "That was a long time ago."

Wayne smiled, but there was determination behind his eyes. I could tell he had made a decision, and that he was up to something.

I had lived my adult life without any family other than my two children and Wayne. I remember wishing I could be like everyone else and have brothers and sisters and parents. I would have settled for a great aunt. When Christmas or other holidays came around, I celebrated, but there was always something missing. It was almost as if my family had not existed; as if they had become just what I feared they would—a story.

Wayne had siblings, aunts, uncles, and a mother and father, and they treated me with kindness. I was happy for him. Still it made me sad to see the family pictures he had hanging up all over our house. It was so different for me. I had forgotten what my sisters looked like.

Wayne knew how I felt, and on his own he decided to do something to grant my wish. He decided to find my family. A few weeks after my doctor's appointment, he came to me with a phone number for my sister Brenda. I had not seen her in almost forty years.

Making the call was very difficult. I didn't know what to expect. Maybe, I thought, she'd want to leave the past dead and buried. I couldn't blame her for that. But instead, she invited Wayne and me to her home for Thanksgiving dinner.

We arrived at Brenda's home in Mobile, Alabama, and were welcomed with hugs and tears from her children and grandchildren. They had a beautiful home, full of laughter and life; Brenda was raising three of her grandchildren. When I first walked in the door, the aroma of turkey, stuffing, pies, and gingerbread was like a fantasy come true for me. I felt at home, as our childhood home should have been.

Her kitchen was warm and cozy even though it was open to the rest of the house. The cabinets were cherrywood, and she had white, starched-lace doilies on the top shelves. An antique butter churn stood beside an old milking stool, and a large Raggedy Ann doll sat on the stool. Brenda stood on the tile floor by the stove in her bare feet. When I walked into the kitchen and saw her for the first time in decades, she had a spatula in her hand and wore a wide, white apron, folded and tied around her middle. "Hello, Sissie." I whispered the nickname I had grown up calling her. She crossed the kitchen floor in two strides and wrapped her arms around me. We hugged, and I felt I had found peace. It was what I dreamed coming home would feel like.

I stared at my sister, taking her in as if she were the embodiment of the years I'd lost. She hadn't changed that much. Her sweet face was still very pretty, but now she had gray hair with touches of silver. She had gained some weight, which made me think about our hunger as children.

We pulled up chairs to the kitchen table and began catching up with each other and sharing our life events. All around us, her children and their spouses, her grandchildren, my husband, and people I didn't know yet filed through a buffet line she had set up on her long kitchen counter, filling their plates with baked ham, roast turkey, cornbread stuffing, macaroni and cheese, sweet potatoes, apple dumplings, and corn on the cob. Brenda loves to cook, and she loves to see people eat. Children crowded around the table with their plates filled, others wandered off to the dining room, and some took their food to the family room. All the while, Brenda waited to eat until everyone in the house had settled.

As we sat with our plates, talking just loud enough to be heard, a young man came to the back door of Brenda's house. He seemed to be in his early twenties—a good-looking boy. He walked right into the kitchen without knocking.

"Do you have any eggs we can borrow?" he asked. He opened her refrigerator and started gathering what he wanted as though it happened all the time.

Brenda stood up and introduced me to her young neighbor and invited him and his wife to come and eat with us. He politely declined, saying they would stop by later. She handed him a bowl for the eggs, they exchanged a few kind words, and the boy walked back out of the house. Awhile later, someone else came by to borrow another

Thanksgiving ingredient. I leaned over to one of Brenda's daughters, my niece.

"It's like she's running a grocery store," I said, smiling.

I laughed and chatted with my sister and her family, and Brenda held my hand, but I noticed she never laughed herself. Although she was kind, she didn't seem happy, and she never really smiled with her eyes. I was bubbling over with pure delight, but there was a somber air about Brenda, even as she served and comforted everyone else. I could tell she was happy to see me, but it never showed in her face. She just never let loose a single chuckle. I avoided the subject of the past; it seemed that she had been scarred so badly and affected in a way far deeper than I could ever know.

Still, watching Brenda share with everyone deeply touched me. Later that night, while I was still thinking about Brenda's kindness, I bumped into one of her sons while getting some tea from the refrigerator. After looking at me for a second, my nephew said, "I've never seen my mama smile the way you do. I've never seen her look happy."

There was no way to tell how much he already knew. I determined that was up to his mom to decide, so I vaguely referred to the tough childhood she'd endured and led him back to the family. We talked the night away on happier subjects.

Time flew by. I can honestly say that up to that point, it was like nothing I had experienced before. On that night I felt the first inkling of being part of something bigger. The feeling only grew as family members sleepily peeled off to go to bed. In the end, it was just Brenda and me at the dining room table. Although her voice was gentle and sweet, she still did not smile.

"You remember that train?" Brenda asked.

I shuddered. The memory sent a chill through me. I shifted in my seat and nodded.

"You were so afraid of the trains." Brenda almost whispered, as though unsure of how I would react.

I remembered. I did *not* want to talk about it, but I didn't want to interrupt or be disrespectful to my sister either. I had succeeded in shutting out many of the horrid, mind-numbing memories and could finally fall asleep without waking up screaming. Many of the memories had faded into the past; a part of my mind let me pretend it was a dream. I sure didn't want to bring them back up.

I could tell Brenda needed to talk, though. I tried to sit still and not let her see how uneasy I was as she took me back to our childhood.

Chapter 2

The Train

Smoke rose up from the dying campfire; a single wisp hit the trestles above and disintegrated like fragile glass thrown against the rusting iron. We had just finished another long, exhausting day picking apples. I was hungry again. Even at five years old, I could not stop thinking about food. Whenever I was allowed to eat, I swallowed it up fast, every bite, but I never felt full. That night, dinner was a little bruised apple I had snuck back to the camp from the farmer's orchard. I had hidden it in the pocket of my dress, a treasure to eat once everyone went to bed.

Sitting on a gravel bank, I could hear the soft trickle of moving water; it was barely enough to be called a stream. I stayed as still as I could, trying to fade into the ground and the gravel and the bridge trestles above. I sat on the bank away from our campsite and would not move until Brenda came to tell me it was bedtime. I knew something ugly and wrong was happening between my Daddy and oldest sister. I saw the way he groped at her chest as she tried to rush past him. I knew there was something horribly wrong with the way he touched her, and when she cried it hurt me too.

We were the only pickers left now, and everything was quiet that night. At five years old, I still did not understand the abuse that happened when the family bedded down. But I already had an unvoiced uneasiness when my dad was near. It was something evil, hidden in shame.

I didn't know to what extent he abused Brenda at that time, but I was to learn from firsthand experience as I passed from childhood to adolescence. Often, my cries at night, wrenched from the depths of my soul, brought me back to those nights when Daddy made Brenda cry.

She was only thirteen then, but I cannot remember a time that she did not take care of me.

That evening, sitting on the gravel bank, I saw her face in the flickering light of the fire. Her eyes were red, her cheeks puffy from crying. She greeted me with loving words, but she did not smile. Instead, she led me in my bare feet across the gravel to where a frayed green woolen army quilt spread out across the ground. My little brother was already lying down. Susie and Nellie were there, too, and Susie was sitting up. Brenda told me to wait there so she could wash my face, patting my arm as she walked away.

Nobody spoke for fear of our dad hearing us. Susie touched my blond curls. My brother stirred but did not make a sound. Then Brenda was back with that awful washcloth in her hand. I squirmed.

"Hush now," she whispered.

I saw the water from the spring dripping off the moldy gray cloth. Even before it got near my face, the smell made me want to run. I reeled, throwing my hands out to stop it from touching my face. I knew Brenda meant well, but that cloth smelled horrible. We didn't have soap, and everyone in the family washed with this same cloth. It made me sick to smell it, much less have it touch my face.

Brenda would have none of it. Not harshly, but firmly, she grasped my chin and cleaned the day's filth from my forehead. Even when she was done, the smell stuck to me as if it was lodged in my sinuses. After she got me tucked in beside the others she went back to the spring. I lay quietly watching as Brenda tried to wash what looked like a slip and her ragged underwear in the little stream below. She didn't have any soap, but she scrubbed at the tattered clothes, dunking them with restrained fury under the rocky streambed. This was much like any other night.

The morning came too fast. Before I even realized I had fallen asleep, a hand shook me awake. I grumbled and shook the hand off.

"Be quiet and get up," Brenda whispered in my ear. "We're leaving."

I sat up. It was still dark out, the sunlight just barely peeking above the tree line to the east. Our camp was in chaos. The soot-blackened pots and pans were lying on the rocks, strewn by the open fire. Our army blanket was in a heap, and my little brother, Robbie, was lying on the bare ground where he had rolled off in the middle of the night. Some of the few clothes we had to wear hung on trees drying; others had fallen to the ground. A few empty bean cans were tossed near the cold campfire that had gone out during the night.

Brenda moved away, joining my mother. Together, they gathered up what few belongings we had and prepared to tie them up inside the green army blanket. Mama hadn't combed her dark hair, and it fell across her face in tangles. Brenda was quiet as usual, but she moved quickly, picking up everything in the camp and stacking it on the blanket we used for our bed. My little brother's blond curls brushed his shoulders; he could have passed for a girl except for his ragged overalls and a white shirt that had turned grey from not being washed. His knees stuck through his frayed pants, and his brown brogan shoes were two sizes too large and had no laces, which made him fall down a lot. He snuggled up to me. I could see my own fear mirrored in his large blue eyes. It mixed with a nearly overwhelming wish to sit still and not leave this spot. If I stayed in this spot and let them leave me here, I would never have to run to catch another train or see my mama hurt or hear Brenda cry.

Daddy would have none of that. He barked out harsh words, and my mother and Brenda tried to pick up their already harried pace. The sun continued to rise and, as the daylight pushed back the night, Daddy got angrier. I sat completely still and refused to move. I hoped if I stayed still enough, nobody would notice and I wouldn't have to run with them to that dreaded, black monster.

It was not to be. My dad grabbed me by the collar of my dress and dragged me out of camp. The rest of the family followed as quickly as they could. That was when I heard the distant whistle of what, in my mind, seemed to be an approaching monster.

As I begged my little legs to hurry, I saw the trail of gray smoke coughing out of the coal-black locomotive. Its whistle sounded again, echoing over the Blue Ridge valley. Its mighty engine whined as it fought to pull its heavy load up the winding mountain.

"Get down," Daddy growled.

By that time, my sisters had caught up to me. We crouched close to the ground beside the bushes running along the orchard we had worked the day before. The dawn light spread darker shadows across the gloom. We tried to disappear into them as the train slowly rolled past, so close that the engineer could have seen us if he was looking. The smell of burning coal made it nearly impossible to catch my breath.

This particular train passed our campsite every day. Daddy had watched it daily, and he learned that it moved slowly. Due to the steep slope of the mountain, the train was famously called the Virginia Creeper. He knew that, and he also knew that an empty boxcar followed the tender car.

"Now!" he yelled.

At the sound of his voice, we made a break for that boxcar. My eyes locked onto the metal ladder that hung down past the opening; I knew I would have to grab it to pull myself inside. I was small for age five, and undernourished, so I was more the size of a three-year-old. The icy morning air tugged at my stringy blond curls and pierced my tattered clothes. All I could think about, though, was that metal ladder rung. If I couldn't grab it, those giant iron wheels would suck me under and tear me up worse than any imaginary monster.

My sisters passed me as though I were standing still. Unlike me, they had shoes, and I could hear the stones crunching under their soles. They may have wanted to scoop me up and carry me with them, but nobody in my family would defy Daddy in that way. He expected everyone who could walk to be an adult. To try it without a direct order from Daddy would not even cross their minds. With all my attention focused on that bar, all I could do was watch as they grabbed it, one after another, and hauled themselves onto the wooden floor of the boxcar. I cried out for Mama, but she didn't answer. The crushing sound of the Virginia Creeper filled my world like a dark and dangerous cloud.

My legs betrayed me and I started losing ground. My breathing grew more and more frantic. All I could do was look for something lower to the ground, some part of the train I might grab hold of that could save me from being left behind. All the while, that train's engine thumped and roared in my ears, confusing my thoughts, and terror radiated out of the pit of my stomach.

Brenda's face poked out from the dark hull of the boxcar.

"Hurry, Frances!" she screamed, reaching her hand out to me.

Mama and Daddy were ahead of me. Daddy had my brother, who was only a toddler, stuck under his arm like a sack of potatoes. As the train inched ahead, slowing to maybe five miles per hour, he threw my brother into the car. I heard Robbie crying from inside.

Daddy cursed as Mama grabbed the handle and disappeared into the boxcar. My dad followed Mama aboard and hollered at my brother, who was still crying. A second later Daddy appeared, leaning out of the car and looking me in the eye.

"Grab my hand, now!" he yelled.

I kept trotting, but my eyes darted nervously from his hand to the tracks. Eventually, the train would pick up speed, and I would be left behind. My family was disappearing before my eyes.

I looked ahead at Daddy's hand. If I lunged and missed, I'd fall. The train would be gone, and I would be left alone. A worse thought struck me in that instant. What if I missed the train and my family had to jump off? If I caused us to miss a free ride, I knew how bad the beating would be. With that thought, I leapt forward, straining to reach Daddy's callused hand.

I missed. Splayed out, I landed on the rocks, scraping my elbows and knees. My momentum caused me to roll toward those giant iron wheels. Luckily, the train had slowed down again, and I was able to stop myself from rolling underneath.

When I looked up, terror swept over me. I saw Daddy leap from the boxcar. His boots landed in the rocks and sent a cloud of dust and pebbles flying back at the train's wheels as he stormed toward me. His face was dark with fury; his small blue eyes burned.

I bent my head down and shut my eyes as tightly as I could. I felt him yank me into the air. He swung me around and into the boxcar. I hit the floor and immediately crawled across to the other side, deeper into the shadows, to get away from his anger. When I reached the far wall, I leaned against the metal door along with my sisters. Daddy jumped back onboard, spouting curses and angry words directed at me.

Brenda was near me, and I found some comfort in her presence as we huddled there. My body hurt, especially the scrapes on my elbows and knees. The train jerked as it picked up speed and started down the mountain. I rubbed at my arms, swallowing back the tears.

Chapter 3

Murder

Our new home outside Stilwell, Oklahoma, was a small shack—typical housing for migrant workers like us. Twenty of these shacks sat in a line on the farmer's land, each about forty feet apart. The farmer had thirty or so tents set up, too, and it was first come, first served. Everyone wanted a shack; though they had no running water and very little furniture, at least they had floors. The canvas tents had dirt floors and only flaps in the front to allow in a breeze, making them very hot inside.

The shacks were weathered grey, and some of the floors and doors, never having been painted, had rotted from the sun and rain. Even though floors were a luxury, you would have to sprinkle water from a bucket onto them before sweeping or you would just about choke to death from the dust clouds. Thick dust lay heavy on everything in the settlement. There were no locks for the doors, but at least there was a shutter on each side of the shack that you could prop up with a stick to let the air in. As for a toilet, there was one outbuilding at the far end of the line of shacks, about twenty feet from the last one. The farmer had dug a deep hole and built a box over it with a round seat cut out of the top. A small wooden building, about three feet by three feet, gave you privacy. Toddlers crawled around and played in the dirt, and there was one pump—where all the families got their drinking water—set up at the end of the camp opposite from the toilet. The desolate, lonely area sat in the middle of nowhere, miles from town.

We had arrived in time to get a shack. Although often these buildings had just one room, this one had two. Each room was about ten feet by ten feet. The back room had homemade bunk beds, nailed into the wall, with old bare wire springs instead of mattresses. In the forties and fifties, wire springs were used instead of box springs. The farmers usually provided a set of springs with cotton-packed mattresses covering them, but the migrant pickers took the mattresses because they could be rolled up and loaded onto the top of their automobiles when they moved. They left only the stiff, wire springs. When we got there, Mama found some cardboard to put over them because the springs were rusty, and if one of our hands fell down in between the wires while we slept, it would get cut up. Then she laid some of our dirty clothes on top of the cardboard to make up for the missing mattress. I would have preferred sleeping on the floor, but we followed my Daddy's instructions to the letter. He insisted everyone sleep together. He had to have total control over every aspect of our lives, and not even a simple decision to lie on the floor would go unnoticed by him.

The front room had a two-burner stove. On one end of the stove was a glass jar of kerosene. A line went from the jar to both burners. It looked a lot like the Coleman cookstoves that you take camping, but more old-fashioned, bigger and bulkier. Our shack also had a small table and one chair. Sometimes the previous residents of these shacks would leave a water bucket or broom behind. If we didn't have one, Mama would borrow one from one of the other migrant workers. Keeping our little area clean was important to Mama, and she tried hard, in spite of the overwhelming dust.

Our first night, Daddy and Mama did not speak. Daddy left the shack and went to get drunk somewhere, and Mama's mood immediately lightened.

"Anyone want some bean patties?" she asked.

Seeing her smile, we got excited. We surrounded her as she mashed up the pinto beans left over from dinner, added flour, and formed them into thin patties like hamburgers. She dropped the bean patties into hot grease in a deep iron skillet. I watched the patties as they sizzled in the pan and turned golden brown. When they were done, she removed each one and laid it on a towel to cool.

While we ate, Mama told us a story about a princess and a frog. Every opportunity she had, Mama tried to lift our spirits and give us hope. She had a kind, lighthearted spirit, and I never heard her speak ill of anyone. After the story, she started dancing around the old wooden table, trying to make us laugh as we stuffed her bean patties into our mouths. Her body rose up and down and she popped her hand on her open lips, making sounds like an Indian doing a war dance. Daddy often called her a squaw because of her Native-American ancestors, but it never seemed to bother her, and she made us all laugh as she danced around the room.

Taking a last bite, I jumped up and joined her. Soon, all five of us were hopping and hooting around the small shack. We must have danced for an hour before she declared it bedtime. Mama put the four younger kids down with smiles on our faces. Still excited, I lay on the bunk and listened to her and Brenda speaking softly in the front room. They talked for a long time before Brenda came to bed.

At some point in the night, my daddy came home. I woke up and heard his voice. He and Mama were set up to sleep in the front room near the stove. I remember hearing his footsteps coming into our room. I can still smell his whiskey breath. He bent over Brenda's bed. I heard harsh whispering; then it stopped. It sounded like two people leaving the room, but I was already falling asleep again, filled with a deep sense of unease.

The next day, as the sun just touched the horizon, Mama woke us. There was no breakfast and we had slept in our clothes, so fresh out of bed, Daddy took us straight to the fields to pick cotton. The fields were so long and wide that you could hardly see from one end to the other.

I imagine that little had changed since the Dust Bowl years. We worked from sunup until sundown. Workers would occasionally shuffle over to a fifteen-gallon milk can filled with tepid water, sharing one tin dipper between them. There were woods on one side of the field, a convenient latrine for us to use during the long workday. A large wagon, about thirty feet wide and fifty feet long, was parked in the middle of the cotton field. It was our job to fill its wire-sided bed with the day's harvest. The foreman stood in the wagon at the center of the field handing out canvas sacks of various sizes to put the picked cotton in. My sisters and I had done this before. We scurried up to the wagon and tried to find the smallest sacks. Brenda gave me the shortest one; I was so small, I couldn't drag a bigger one around the field for the whole day.

I took the bag and slung it over one shoulder, following Daddy to our row. Each family started to pick at one end of a row, and they didn't wander from that area until the cotton was pulled from every bole. Daddy would choose the area, and each of us, except Robbie and me, would have his or her own row. I tried to stay in front of Brenda, because if I left too much cotton, the farmer would holler. If the farmer hollered at me, I'd pay hundredfold when Daddy got me home that evening.

The stalks had to be cleaned with no trace of cotton left in the dry brown boles. I glanced over my shoulder; Daddy was behind me. He was looking at me, a frown on his face because I wasn't bent over picking. By the time I was twelve, I had to meet a quota of between ninety to a hundred pounds each day or he would beat me. When I was very small, though, my only requirement was that I had to keep working and not stop. Usually we poured my sack of cotton into my Daddy's to keep the field boss from knowing how little I was able to pick.

The cotton grew in stalks, sometimes up to four feet high. Smaller stalks grew off the main one, and at the end of each of these sat a dry brown bole filled with a puff of cotton. Picking cotton was the worst work I can remember. By the time the cotton was ready for picking, its three-inch-long green pods had opened up to expose the cotton, the boles drying to a hard, deep brown, with four or five needle-sharp points on each end. That day, as I reached my hand down to pluck the cotton out from the center, one of those points cut into my hand and drew blood. I dropped the cotton into my sack and did not pause to put my finger into my mouth. Instead, I forced myself to move on to the next bole, and the next prick. Everyone's hands bled when they picked cotton, and a few drops of blood were not unusual. Sometimes, at the end of the day, my hands would be so sore that I would pump water onto the ground and press my fingers into the cool wet mud to ease the pain.

As my fingers bled in the field, I heard the rumble of a large engine. I knew immediately what made it. I'd seen the source before, and I often thought of it. Every morning, I had a new plan for its arrival. As the sound of the engine grew nearer, I busied myself, moving down the line of cotton as if double-checking our work. The road was only about a hundred feet away. Slowly I bent down and pulled a tuft of cotton out of its spiny shell. A flash of yellow appeared in the corner of my eye. I stood, dropping the cotton and frantically pressing my tangled hair down flat with both hands. I brushed at the dust and dirt on my dress and stood up as straight and tall as I could.

I turned to face the school bus as it rolled down the dusty road toward me. I stepped closer to the road, spitting on my hands and using them to clean the dirt off my face, only succeeding in smearing the grime around in circles. I tried hard to make myself presentable.

"You gotta stop this time," I whispered.

My bare foot tapped the dirt with anticipation as the bus came closer and closer. I thought it slowed, and my heart raced with excitement. But it wasn't so. The bus full of kids flew past me on its way to school. I saw pairs of eyes looking down from those square windows; they belonged to girls and boys with clean clothes and shining faces. The bus passed me by—again.

Could the driver not have seen me?

Day after day I had contrived to stand closer to the edge of the road. Finally, this day, I realized that the bus driver could see the truth in my tangled hair and ragged dirty dress. He knew I did not belong in school, that I never would. Tears sprang to my eyes when I pictured myself walking up the bus stairs and sitting in one of those green benches. But I closed my eyes tight, trying to push the thought away. At the sound of Daddy's voice hollering my name, I scrambled back to the line.

As that day went on, the picking got sparser. More than once, I saw Mama and Brenda huddled near each other, speaking in hushed tones. I still had that same unease from the night before. Mama and Brenda never whispered alone or took a chance by talking in the fields. But Daddy didn't seem to notice that day. I knew something awful was going on in my family, something worse than the beatings my mama had to endure. I knew it, but I couldn't admit it until I was older.

"Down!" Daddy called out.

I saw Brenda and Mama react as if they'd been caught dancing with the devil. Daddy, though, was pointing up toward the road. I glanced in that direction and saw the car parked beside the fields. A man in a tan uniform was standing outside the vehicle. He had a pair of binoculars to his eyes, and he was peering in our direction.

I knew what this meant. The man was a truant officer. He was checking the fields to see if any kids were being held out of school.

My Daddy growled his order again. I tried to obey, but my heart would not let me. School was the one dream I held inside. I wanted more than anything to go to school with the children on that bus, to learn as they did, read books, and someday write down the wonderful stories that Mama told us. I stood still, looking at that man, hoping he would find me and take me to where I belonged. The sun reflected off the spyglass. *He'll see me for sure.*

Something hit the back of my leg, and I crashed to the ground. I rolled over and looked up into the burned red face of Daddy. He stood over me, his hands balled into tight powerful fists.

"I told you to get down," he snarled.

He opened the top of his cotton sack, pushing it toward my head. I quickly climbed inside. The dust and heat were suffocating, but the beating I would get if we got caught would be much worse. After a few moments he kicked at me through the sack.

"Ok. Get out," he barked.

I crawled out of the sack, and he left me there. I didn't have to get up off the ground to know that the truant officer was gone.

After working the fields all day, we walked slowly back to the shack. Daddy did not stay long. He yelled at us for not working hard enough, but soon left us alone. We all knew he was going out to get drunk. Although it was a relief to have him gone for a while, we also knew what state he'd be in when he returned. So there was a darkness to our moods.

Many times when he came back roaring drunk, he wanted to fight. Mama usually bore the brunt of his moods. Sometimes he came back already bloody from fighting, and then he would keep us all awake hollering and cursing. Everyone in our family was afraid of him whether he was roaring drunk or sober. Other times, he got satisfaction from pouring some of his whiskey over our food and forcing us to eat it. If we got sick, we would get beaten with his belt or fist.

After he left that night, Mama opened up a can of pork and beans. She sat us in a circle on the floor to eat and told us a story. Her voice was soft and full of love—and something more. I can guess now that it was longing.

"Things ain't always been the way they are now. I wish ya'll could have met my mama and papa. All men ain't mean like your daddy. I want you to remember that. My papa loved me."

A tear slid down her cheek as she talked. "We lived in South Carolina. My papa had a dairy farm, and fourteen men worked for him. Mama cooked buttermilk biscuits and chicken. We had a long table in the front room of the house, and Mama rang the dinner bell at six every morning. That was to let the workers know they could come in and eat breakfast with us after the milking was done."

Mama leaned forward, cocking her head to one side as if to make sure nobody was there to hear except us children. Then she continued.

"One day this young man about nineteen years old came in to eat at the table with us, and I couldn't keep my eyes off him. Papa's foreman had hired him the night before. Papa said he was a 'no-good,' and I remember hearing him tell Mama to keep me and my sisters 'away from that one,' cause Papa had 'a feelin' about him. Papa was real protective of his girls, and he hired Nanny Taddie, the retired schoolteacher, to come to the farm and teach us to read and write. Papa wanted us to do our learnin' from home rather than sending us to school."

Mama seemed uneasy as she talked now, and she got up several times to look out the front of the cabin door. She went on to tell us about the first time she slipped away and met Daddy.

"I didn't know anything about life back then." She looked sad. "This young boy, Broadus, didn't have any parents, and I felt sorry for him. I was sixteen, and Papa didn't let us date. The foreman told me Broadus had showed up hungry, asking for work. He was hired to do the milking for his room and board. Oh boy, was he good lookin' back then. And he could talk a milk cow into giving milk without puttin' his hands on her."

On her way back to us, Mama turned the lamplight lower. "He just swooped me out of my shoes and my dress. If Papa had known it, he would have killed Broadus, but by then it was too late. I was crazy about him. I loved my Papa, but Broadus had won my heart, body, and mind."

As Mama continued, I hung on her every word. It was very rare to be given the opportunity to listen to her talk about her parents, or any of her family for that matter. I did not want to miss a single word she said. Considering where the conversation would go later that night, though, I think she was lost in that moment, contemplating the impossible.

"Papa caught us late one night in the hayloft together. I think if I hadn't stood between them, Papa would have killed Broadus. I made my choice, and Papa disowned me. Papa declared I was no longer his daughter, ordered me never to set foot on his land again. He let me take my Bible and the clothes on my back. That Bible is all I have of him now. I guess I broke his heart."

Mama quietly wiped tears, then stopped suddenly as if she had heard something. She looked at all of us gathered around her. Fear was back in her soft, dark eyes and the sound of her voice. "You must never, ever tell one word of what I've told you here tonight."

The truth is that Daddy began to bully Mama the first day of their new life together. They went to Texas, but instead of working in the oil fields, he got a job for the two of them in the cotton fields. Because of one mistake my mother made when she was a young girl, she would spend the next seventeen years of her life in regret.

My daddy started to beat her if any man in the fields looked at her. By the time Brenda was born, my mother was so cowed down and brainwashed from fear that she obeyed him like a prisoner. It just got worse when they began to have more children. Mama gave birth to her first child, my oldest sister, Brenda, ten months after she met daddy. The following year, another daughter, Susie, was born. Two years after Susie, she gave birth to her first son, Jimmy, who would eventually be sold to Uncle Mose and his wife, Gracie.

Mama stopped talking and, with a soft gesture of her hand, she sent Brenda out to get us ready for bed. The old smelly washcloth came out, but I was too tired to put up a good fight. Brenda got us all into the bed we shared, and she went back to the front room. Instead of sleeping, though, I quietly got up. I wanted to play jacks. So I pulled out my little rubber ball, one of my few prized possessions, and ten small round rocks I kept in my dress pocket. I had no jacks, but the rocks worked fine.

I was sitting on the floor in the back room, half playing my game and half listening to the hushed words coming from the front room. Light flickered in from the kerosene lamp there, and the acrid smell of the other lamp Brenda had blown out still filled the air. She and Mama were talking softly.

As I played, I inched closer to the doorway. Soon I was able to make out their words. What I heard made me more frightened than I had ever been before.

"I can't take it any longer," Brenda said. Her voice sounded strange, as if she were choking on her own words.

Mama made a soft noise as if in agreement. I could tell she was trying to comfort her.

"We'll find a way out, Brenda. I've tried. You know I've tried. But last time, he almost killed us. I'm still carrying the scars."

"What about the others? You know who's next. I can't let that happen. I won't!" Brenda hissed.

Mama's voice was barely more than just air. "What can we do?

What can *I* do? There's no way to stop him. I've put rat poison in his food. I've left, and he found me and nearly killed me the last time. How long was it before I could open my eye?"

The room was silent for a moment.

"I stole his claw hammer," Brenda whispered. "I hid it behind the back of the cabin."

I stopped playing jacks and held the ball tightly in my hand.

"Keep your voice down, please, Honey," Mama said.

"I'm never gonna let him touch me again. I'd rather be dead," Brenda said.

"Lord, help us," Mama whispered. "May God forgive me."

"I'm gonna do it, Mama," Brenda said.

"I know," Mama said. "We should have done it long ago."

"I'm going to pull that hammer out tonight. I'm gonna put the hammer under the bed."

Mama's foot scuffed against the floor. Brenda paused for a second, then continued.

"Once he starts snoring, I'm gonna hit him in the head with that claw hammer. I'm gonna bash in his skull. I'm gonna hit him and hit him. That's what I'm gonna do. I'm going to kill him!"

Chapter 4

A Child's Innocence

I jumped up as the little ball dropped from my hand and rolled across the plank floor. My bare feet scattered the pebbles I used for jacks.

"Oh no! Mama, no! No!"

The words came pouring out of my mouth before I realized I had spoken. I had to keep Mama and Brenda safe, and I felt in my soul that this could only end badly. At the same time, my young mind could not wrap around what I had heard Brenda say.

I burst into the front room, seeing Mama sitting on the only chair and Brenda huddled close by her on the floor. Their faces looked pale in the lamplight. I saw fear and desperation in their eyes.

"Please don't kill Daddy! Please don't do it," I cried.

Tears streamed down my cheeks as I ran up to Mama. They both stood up quickly, and Brenda reached out for me. I jumped back before she could touch me. Mama shot her a nervous glance and then tried to put a smile on her face when she looked down at me.

"Calm down, Frances," she whispered. "You're gonna wake everybody up."

"You can't! You can't do murder!" I wailed.

Brenda hung her head and stared at the floor. Mama tried to reason with me.

"It's okay . . . it's okay," Mama said.

"I'll tell him. If you kill him, I'll tell him. I will!"

Mama saw how scared I was. Brenda did not seem to want to say anything. Mama sighed deeply and pulled me to her side. She looked very serious as she spoke to me.

"We were just playing, Frances. Just talking. That's all. Go back to bed and I promise you nothing is gonna happen to anybody."

I wanted to believe her, so it did not take much more convincing than that. I inched closer to Mama and she held me in her arms. She pulled me down and I snuggled into her lap, my fingers finding a rough fold of her cotton dress. I patted it as my heartbeat gradually slowed back to normal. All the while, Brenda did not say a word. After a while Mama carried me back to the room we slept in and laid me on the bed, tucking me under the blanket next to my sisters and Robbie.

My mama patted my head and softly started to tell me a story. It was the Indian princess and the frog, and it brought back the night we had danced around the shack. I fell asleep feeling a little better. I do not know how long I slept, but my eyes shot open when the front door opened and Daddy's curses filled the cabin. As I often did, I reached out for Brenda where she usually slept beside me. She was not there.

As my hand darted about looking for my sister, Mama screamed. I heard the thud and groan of Daddy striking her. Squeezing my eyes shut, I tried my hardest to pretend it was all a bad dream. The cursing and the pounding continued, and Susie's hand found mine under the covers. Robbie crawled up quickly from the foot of the quilt and wrapped both of his little arms around my waist. He nearly squeezed the breath out of me but I hardly noticed in my fear. We were all afraid to move or speak.

The beating was worse than ever before. It went on and on until I thought I'd get physically sick. I tried to blot out Mama's screams and his maniacal curses and accusations.

"Please Broadus, stop, please," she pleaded, but soon her words were silenced, and I heard her body fall to the floor. I shook and cried until my tears dried up, but my body was racked with sobs.

I prayed. I screamed inside my head. I poured out my grief and fear until the cabin fell silent. The final prayer on my lips before I fell into a fitful sleep was, "Please let me escape the ugliness and horror and see something pretty in this life. Please take care of my mama."

The next morning I awoke to find Daddy and Brenda packing up our meager belongings and placing them in the old car he'd swindled away from someone. We were moving again, going to another camp. Mama was too weak to even get up out of her bed. To my surprise, Daddy let her be. He must have known that he'd broken her ribs and her nose, which was swollen and slanted to one side. I could not stop staring at her as she drifted in and out of consciousness.

As was often the case, she needed medical attention but would not receive it. He would make her prove her loyalty before taking her to the hospital; he waited until he was satisfied that she would not turn him in to the authorities. So she traveled in pain. The cotton had been picked, and Daddy was on the hunt for more work. After several weeks Mama had recovered enough to be alert, I overheard her mention our Uncle Mose.

We were headed toward Greenville, South Carolina. When I found out we were actually going to Uncle Mose's house, I was elated. Uncle Mose was Daddy's brother. He was the complete opposite of Daddy. None of his brothers were mean like he was. My Uncle Mose was a kind man, large and quiet with the air of someone who understood the land and farming in a way that had been lost a century before. As we parked the car and walked nearer to his house, we could not hide our excitement. I skipped down the sidewalk, and even Brenda's gaze lifted from the ground. She did not smile, though.

Daddy swung at me, landing a blow to my shoulder. I stumbled but kept my feet. He looked around to see if anyone was in their yard, watching us. He saw no one.

"Stop running and wait for me, Frances. And understand this." Daddy gripped Mama by the arm. His blue eyes burned like fire. "If any one of you says anything while we are there, I will kill you."

I could see his knuckles turning white as he squeezed her. She whimpered but then went silent. I looked up at her face. Her pretty features were drawn thin. I wanted to reach out to her, to comfort her, but I could feel Daddy's eyes on me and cowered away.

We walked the last hundred yards in silence. Uncle Mose came outside. When Daddy saw him, he strode forward, a charming smile splitting his face.

"How are you, brother?" he said, extending a hand in greeting.

Uncle Mose nodded. "Good. You?"

Even at five I could sense the suspicion behind my uncle's tone. He glanced at Mama, who just stared at the ground. Uncle Mose knew something about my daddy that I did not. The two had been in Civilian Conservation Corps camp together when they were young men. The program, called CCC for short, began in 1933 as part of the New Deal, set up by President Roosevelt to create jobs. Young men could join and the government would put them to work planting trees and creating parks and wildlife refuges.

One day, my uncle saw my daddy get in a fight with a man at the camp. It was a vicious battle, and the other man got Daddy to the ground. Grabbing him by the hair, he slammed Daddy's head into the concrete over and over again. When the other man walked away, my daddy's head was busted open. My uncle swore he saw pieces of Daddy's brain on the sidewalk.

I don't tell this story as an excuse for my daddy's behavior and temperament. My uncle, though, thought his brother was a different man before that day. Maybe something happened to his head that caused him to change. Maybe the evil inside Daddy had been there all along. I'll never know.

"We won't be a bother, Mose," my daddy said as my uncle looked him over. "Just looking for a better car, and then we'll be off. I have a job lined up in Oklahoma. Good one too."

"Mmm hmm," my uncle said.

At that point my cousin Jimmy appeared; at least I thought he was my cousin. I would learn much later that he was actually my brother, and he would go on to play a large part in my search to reunite my family later in life. In truth, my daddy had sold him to my aunt and uncle for five dollars, recorded in the courthouse in Greenville, South Carolina, with a bill of sale. He forced Mama to sell baby Jimmy because he believed she had been unfaithful and Jimmy was not his child. Daddy's belief was totally unfounded. Mama was never allowed to go anyplace alone, much less consort with other men, but when Daddy got something in his head, there was no changing his mind. I remember noticing how Mama almost touched Jimmy on occasion, but only now can I begin to understand her loss. It reminded me of a story in the Bible when Moses' mother was forced to give her son away to save his life. I realize now that my mama went along with daddy to save Jimmy. With my uncle, he would be safe and have a life apart from her sad one.

At Uncle Mose's house, the adults faded into the background for me. I became a kid again, playing and laughing in the yard with the boy I didn't realize was my older brother. This was a rare taste of freedom, to run and play without fear. On top of that, my uncle's wife, Gracie, cooked us all dinner. In the largest cast-iron skillet I'd ever seen, she would fry Irish potatoes and serve us pinto beans with ham hocks boiled in a two-gallon pot. I can still taste her cornbread, baked in another cast-iron skillet until it was golden brown. And I can remember Mama watching us eat and play with a smile on her face when Daddy was out of the house for a while. Life at my uncle's house must have been what a normal life was like for a child my age. But I didn't know what normal meant.

We slept in a bed with sheets and took warm baths in a big claw-footed tub when we visited my uncle's house. We had hot meals and ate twice a day. Playtime was all day, and my daddy never dared touch Mama in anger. I wished it could last forever.

Then daddy bought another car. It was a jalopy that seemed to be held together by chicken wire and clothespins. Daddy was good with his hands, and all throughout my childhood, he kept sputtering old wrecks running by what seemed like sheer force of will—until he could sell it to some poor unsuspecting soul and buy another one.

In the late 1950s, you could shake a man's hand and it was like signing a contract. Most people were honest; nobody locked their doors back then. Daddy gave a local used car dealer the money we had earned from working on the farm for several weeks as a down payment, but when the next payment came due, we were hundreds of miles away. He did this often. Making out his own bill of sale, he would then trade the car he had for a less expensive one, a deal the owner of the car lot was eager to seal. Once he got the title to the older car, he'd promise to send his title the following week to the dealer for the one he "owned." Of course he never did.

My dad felt he needed a different car. The car we arrived in had blown a head gasket the day we reached South Carolina, and traveling by train was getting harder to do without someone seeing us. He could not let us get caught. He knew if the train conductors saw us riding in a boxcar, they might merely throw us off, but they could also call the sheriff. Daddy could not allow that. Even then before his arrest, I could sense his fear of the police. It seemed strange to me that a man who could be so mean, a man who would not hesitate to fight another man twice his size, would show any fear. But he did, and it was a fear that followed him throughout his life. His terrifying demeanor changed at even the mention of the police. I found out later that he had been locked up and the arresting officer had beaten him severely with a billy club to the point he had to be hospitalized. That may have been why he feared the police the way he did.

When Daddy showed up with that rattletrap car, we had to pack in like a bunch of sardines and go to our next destination. It tore at my five-year-old heart to have to leave. I wanted more than anything to stay and share the life of my lost brother.

As soon as our car pulled out of my uncle's driveway and out of sight, Daddy's hand shot out, slamming into the side of my mother's face without warning.

"You tramp!" my Dad screamed.

We all sat in the backseat afraid to move, knowing what was coming. Drops of deep red blood ran down Mama's chin. She reached up to dab at her face and he slapped her again.

"Don't even move, you witch!" He ordered. "I ought to kill you for flirting with my brother like some floozy!" Mama was crying, trying to choke back the sobs. "As soon as I find a place to pull this car over I'm gonna teach you to show me proper respect."

Mama said not a word. Her hair hung in her eyes, but she did not make a move to brush it away. It was as if she was trying to wish away the words and the anger—and what she knew was coming next.

"I should have never taken you from your slack-jawed parents. Nobody else would have you. Now look what I got."

I could see his leathery neck and his cheek full of stubble. His skin turned redder and redder as his voice rose.

"You're no woman. I seen how you strutted around in front of my brother. Crossing your legs so he could see up your dress. You wanted to make a fool out of me, didn't you?"

Mama tried one time to deflect the words Daddy was using against her. As usual, he was working himself up into a lather that would soon turn into a rage. Her efforts to change the subject only made him worse.

"Broadus," she said. "Look at that mountain. I ain't seen nothing so pretty, have you?"

"Shut your mouth, you pig! I'll tell you when you can speak! I'm gonna *show* you, and this time you're gonna learn to keep your snaggletooth mouth shut!"

"Honey." She tried again to get his attention off of her. "Did you see those deer over by that oak we just passed? They weren't near as big as the one you and Mose shot and skinned. You sure do know how to fix deer meat."

Daddy ignored her attempt, instead cursing her until he was sweating and his hands were shaking from anger. He drove faster and faster. I prayed, *Dear God, please let a policeman come by and save Mama.*

He cursed and threatened and howled the most awful words at her, but she did not flinch. Daddy pounded the steering wheel with his fist, accusing Mama with obscene lies he made up in his head. Suddenly and without warning, the car came to a screeching halt on the side of the road. Daddy burst out of his door and stormed around the front of the hood.

Mama mewed down deep in her throat, a sound like nothing I had ever heard. She softly cried, "No, Broadus, please don't hit me." Then her door was ripped open. Daddy's large hand reached into the car and his fingers latched into Mama's hair. He dragged her out onto the grassy bank by the road. All the while, he was screaming those awful words and spitting out cusses at her.

At first, I just sat there, terrified to move, as Daddy literally dragged Mama up the bank and toward a line of trees a few hundred feet from the road. Mama tried to walk, but he yanked her along so fast that she could not stay on her feet. She lost her shoes, but he kept dragging her and hitting her in the head with his fist. She was a small, frail woman, beautiful with long dark hair and a dimple in her chin like mine. She pleaded with him, but you could see that Daddy could not wait to get her in those woods.

Once they were out of sight, the bloodcurdling screaming started. It sounded as though Mama was going to die. I slid off the backseat onto the floorboard. I lay facedown, pressing my hands to my ears as hard as I could. No matter how hard I squeezed, I could not block out the sounds of Mama's pleading. I wished it could be me. In my heart, I would gladly have taken the beating for her.

Mama was a ray of light. When Daddy wasn't around, she was lots of fun, and she told me fairy tales every night except the times when he had beat her up so bad that she couldn't talk. She taught me to say my nighttime prayers when I first began to speak. I don't ever remember Mama being anything but kind to me, and I loved her dearly.

When Daddy hurt her, it felt as though a part of me would die. Sometimes she would have to go to the hospital to get her ribs set or stitches in a cut that would not stop bleeding on its own. He would buy her candy as an offering to keep her from telling the doctors how she got hurt. It was always chocolate-covered cherries—her favorite. He would force her to eat his guilt offering before allowing her to get medical treatment. It made me physically sick to see how bad she hurt, her mouth swollen and bleeding, and yet knowing she couldn't get medical treatment until she ate his candy.

I made a vow, lying on the floorboard in the car that day, that I would take my mama far away, and we would live in a beautiful house like in one of her fairy tales. I would not let anybody *ever* hurt her again.

Time stretched out. The beating went on longer than such a thing seemed possible. Then, finally, the woods went silent. The car was quiet. I remember being thankful the screaming stopped, but as the seconds went by, my relief was replaced by fear. It was one of the first times I thought that Mama might be dead. It was too quiet.

Daddy walked out of the woods first. His pace had slowed and his face was no longer red. He looked like a man who had just come back from working hard out in the fields. There was blood on the back of his hands. Mama eventually struggled out of the trees. One of her eyes was swollen closed and blood dripped onto the front of her dress from a slashing cut that ran across her chin. I learned later that he had taken out his knife and cut where her dimple had been.

By the next morning I knew something was different about that beating Mama endured. When I saw Daddy, I noticed right away that it must have been worse than most. He was doting on her, touching her hair and laughing like they were newly in love. He piled us into the car. I was afraid at first to get in, but he put his hand on my back and pushed me toward the door. I was confused, and his kindness to Mama did nothing to soften the fear. In fact, it made the feeling more ominous.

We drove for miles that morning and all through the night. We rode in silence, every one of us afraid to speak. Mama slept with her head against the passenger-side window, and we only stopped for gas. I assumed we were on the run again, but early the next morning he pulled onto a tree-lined road. I saw a sign but did not recognize it for what it was—the entrance to a park. I leaned forward, gripping Susie's hand as I pressed my nose against the window.

What I saw that day was beauty that only God could create. I had prayed for peace and to escape ugliness and horrors of this migrant life, and God showed me beauty beyond my imagination! I had no idea we were in California, so I didn't know the giant trees surrounding our car were redwoods. At the park's entrance, my heart nearly stopped. We were approaching the biggest tree I had ever seen with a hole through its base, and I could hardly breathe as we drove right through the middle of it! The sight was astonishing to me—trees so wide and tall that I thought they might swallow the car. Lush green ferns covered the ground between the trunks like the rolling surf of a green ocean. A light fog hung just above the leaves like the whitecaps of breaking waves.

Daddy pulled off at one of the open picnic areas.

"Wilma." He nudged Mama. "You feel like going for a walk?"

Her eyes wide, Mama got out of the car in awe of her surroundings. He had bought her another box of chocolate-covered cherries, and she clutched it to her chest like a security blanket. The scarlet of the box matched the angry wound on her chin. I think he was afraid Mama might actually die from the beating he'd given her, and that he would end up in prison for it.

"You kids go play in the park for a while," he ordered. "I'll blow the horn when it's time for you to come back."

We all looked at each other, not knowing what to do. Wide-mouthed, we watched as he led her into the woods. Mama shuffled along behind him as if she were half asleep.

For a few moments I sat in the car, watching the spot where my parents had disappeared around the bend of a path. I think we all knew what was happening. Daddy did it all the time. He would beat Mama so bad, and then buy her a cheap box of chocolates. He knew he had gone too far the night before and he was trying to make sure she did not turn him in. It worked too.

Eventually, my sisters got out of the car. One by one, they wandered off as if lost in the fog. My little brother glanced at me, but then hurried to join them. I was left alone among those mammoth trees. For some reason, I could not move at first. Instead, I watched the path, hoping to see Mama reappear. I was afraid that maybe Daddy would beat her up again in those woods and I'd never see her again.

Time passed and I realized all of my family was out of sight. I could only think of Mama, so I climbed into the front seat where she had been sitting. I took a deep breath, breathing in the scent of her. Her Bible was on the floor at my feet. I picked it up, clutching it to my chest, and continued to stare out into the dazzling green of the surrounding forest. It felt as if that wave of fog might come and crash over me, washing me away forever.

Nothing happened. The moment passed, and I reached out to open the car door, still holding Mama's Bible close to my heart. Once outside, I walked the opposite direction from where my siblings had gone, looking for a moment of peace and quiet and rare time alone.

As I followed a path deeper into the forest, sunlight cut through the fog in amazing bands of white. They dappled the ground and lit my way into what seemed to me like a land from one of the beautiful fairy-tale stories Mama told me when Daddy was out at night.

I followed a wooden walk lined with yellow, purple, and bloodred wildflowers. The path led to a rock bridge spanning a lazy creek that wound between the giant trees. I imagined I lived there in a small cabin that had window boxes filled with flowers. All the animals would come to visit me and the world would be peaceful. The dream gave me comfort. I lost track of how long I wandered in that majestic park.

Once across the creek, I stepped from the trail. I sat down under one of the redwoods and placed Mama's Bible on my lap. The green canopy above seemed to be miles over my head; I felt tiny. Sunlight cut through the branches and leaves like the spokes of a wheel rolling across the heavens. My hands wrapped around the Bible, and I felt a presence with me, close, like a soft blanket wrapped around my shoulders.

I could not read, but I opened the Bible and followed the words with my eyes. Mama knew how badly I wanted to learn, and she soothed my longing with the promise that God heard my prayer. She said the words in the Bible are all good and she promised me that God would understand if I was not able to read them. She assured me that one day I would learn to read. Until then, I could make up words that were good and pretend I was talking to God. So I *read* what I thought the page would say.

"God is with me every day," I read. "I am not alone. God knows who I am and He cares when I am hungry or afraid. God looks down from heaven and He sees all the children who need Him."

In that moment I felt light as a feather, floating on the breeze as it wrapped around those giant tree trunks. I could hear the words I pretended to read on the pages, words that the Lord put in my heart. They were words used by God to reassure a frightened child. As I sat on the grass under the giant trees holding Mama's Bible, I knew I had been touched in some way.

My freedom among the redwoods ended far too soon. I had to return to the life my daddy gave us. Mama recovered, or at least physically recovered, from the beating that almost killed her. When Daddy finally took her to a hospital in California days later, he told the doctors that she had not shut the car door all the way and had fallen out while they were driving at forty miles per hour. No charges were issued. The doctor wrapped up Mama's ribs and sewed the wound on her chin. Her dimple was gone, replaced by an angry, jagged scar. The deeper scars, however, were hidden inside.

Mama changed after that beating. She tried to please Daddy with an urgency that bordered on desperation, and she stopped touching me and the other children. I felt hurt and confused as she distanced herself from us, and my mind returned to that night she and Brenda had talked of killing him. If I had let them, the beating never would have happened. I could have saved her all the pain and misery. The guilt was so heavy that I felt I was choking from it.

When we left the redwoods, Mama left a part of her behind. She was not mean to us, but she did not dance or sing or read any longer.

Her wonderful fairy tales ceased, and she did not tuck me in at night. Along with my guilt, a new feeling burned inside me—hate. I hated my daddy for what he'd done to her. At the same time, I felt even more guilt for that fact. *How can I hate my own daddy? There must be something wrong with me.* It started a vicious circle that haunted me for a good part of my life.

We traveled on in the old jalopy, the five of us packed in the backseat, too afraid to talk or play. We were on our way to another hot farm back in Oklahoma, returning to the dusty, dreary work that we despised. After spending a week with Uncle Mose and two days at the redwood forest, it made the Oklahoma cotton fields seem drearier. Once we were settled in yet another migrant camp and Daddy was sure that Mama would not turn him in, the evil inside came out again. One evening, after we'd all returned to the shack at the close of a backbreaking day of work with no food at all, he handed Mama some money.

"Take them out to get some ice cream," he said.

My heart raced and my mouth watered. We children looked at each other, our eyes excited and hungry. When I looked up at Mama, I sensed something was not right, but the thought of ice cream kept me from heeding the warning. I had only had ice cream once before at my uncle's house, and we were so hungry.

As we skipped to the car, the first sign of trouble became clear. I heard Daddy over my shoulder.

"No, you stay."

I spun around, panicked that he meant me. Instead, he had a hand on Brenda's shoulder, and his fingers looked to be digging into her flesh. His face looked flush and his eyes glassy. Mama stopped.

"Get out," he hissed at her.

Mama didn't move. It was as if her body, standing in one place, shook in two different directions. Fear told her to get into the car. Her maternal instincts told her to stay. Daddy pushed Brenda back away from the door of the shack, and he stepped forward threateningly. Mama flinched and hurried us into the car.

"Be gone for an hour," he ordered.

Mama didn't say anything. Nellie and Robbie were talking about the ice cream. I was, too, but I kept looking at Mama as we drove to the gas station. Susie sat in the front seat with Mama.

Mama led us inside the Dairy Queen, and we stood in line. Each of us got a cone with one scoop of vanilla. By today's standard, it was small. To us, it was the greatest treat we could imagine.

That first lick was like heaven. The creamy sweetness took my taste buds by surprise. I smiled in delight and let the coldness turn warm before swallowing it down. Mama got us back in the car and started off. She headed away from the cabin.

After a few more licks, I thought again about Brenda. She was alone with Daddy, and she didn't get any ice cream. I decided I would save the rest of mine for her.

Mama kept driving around. It felt like we were going in circles, and eventually I realized that we actually were. All I could do was watch as my ice cream melted. I tried keeping it in the cone, but trails of milky white ran down its edges. I used my dress to wipe up the part I couldn't lick off.

The sun set, and still we did not go home. The hour started to feel like a month.

"Are we going back home?" I finally asked.

She did not answer. I don't even know if she heard me, she seemed so lost in thought. Finally, hesitantly, Mama pulled to a stop outside the shack. Before she could say anything, I burst out of the car and ran to the door with the melted cone still dripping down my arm. I pulled the door open, and the truth hit me like a fist to the stomach.

The first thing I noticed was the smell. It was sickeningly musky and hung in the air like an accusation. Darkness had descended outside, and a single lantern burned in the shack. It lit Brenda, cowering on the floor at the corner of the table, whimpering like a wounded animal. Her long, brown hair hung in front of her face in bloody strands, and her clothes were torn and soaking wet. Her face was bruised and swollen.

I stood in the doorway staring at her, and a realization without words crashed into my young mind. I can remember the feeling of the melted vanilla ice cream that had run down my arm, dripping to the floor of the shack. I finally understood what it was that Daddy had torn from Brenda. It was her innocence.

Mama understood right away. Maybe she had known since he sent us out to get ice cream. What she knew, and I did not, was that this was not the first time Daddy had hurt Brenda. Mama brushed Brenda's hair as she passed by her and I watched Brenda shrink from her touch. Mama got the younger kids put down to bed on our usual pile of cardboard and dirty clothes. Brenda followed, quietly and unwashed. I always slept next to Brenda, so when Mama left us, I reached a hand out, scared but determined. I touched Brenda and she did not shy away. All I could think to do to make her feel better was rub her back. I did that, and I felt her sobs.

"I love you, Sissie," I whispered. "No matter what."

Brenda cried all night, and I rubbed her back lightly, as you might a baby. After a while my arm ached, but I would not stop. I almost fell asleep, but I forced myself awake again. With all my soul I wanted to take the pain from Brenda, and this was the only way I knew to relieve some of it.

In that darkness, as I reached out to comfort my sister, I realized something else. I lost my innocence that night as well. Unlike Brenda's that was ripped violently away, mine melted like the ice cream cone I'd tried to save for her.

Several months later our family situation took a new turn. Mama started gaining weight, and she seemed different, but we were so busy it took awhile for me to notice. One day, out in the field, I asked Brenda.

"What's wrong with Mama?"

Brenda didn't say anything at first. I looked up and found her staring off into the distance. Then, in a soft voice, she spoke.

"She's gonna have a baby, honey."

I did not understand at first. But I was getting older, so it didn't take me long.

"We're gonna have a baby brother or sister?" I asked.

Brenda nodded. I jumped to my feet. Unable to stand still, I pranced in place.

"Oh, I hope it's a sister," I said. "Wouldn't that be wonderful?"

Brenda petted my hair as she looked to where Daddy worked a few hundred feet away. "Let's get back to work."

Chapter 5

Baby Girl

The season changed as the baby grew in my mama's belly. Her feet swelled, and she got tired quickly when working out in the fields. I was almost seven. It was the first time I could remember seeing this miracle. I decided it was to be a girl, and I could not wait to meet my baby sister.

Cotton season in Oklahoma was over, and Daddy put us on the move again. Daddy continued in what was a cycle of jobs that crossed the country in conjunction with the harvests. This time he made a deal for another car and drove us north. We eventually stopped in Manistee, Michigan. He arrived too late, and the farmer had already hired all the workers he needed. We were not permitted to move into one of the migrant worker shacks. The weather was turning cool, so he moved us into a single-wide trailer outside of town.

Our new home, though there was nothing really new about it, sat on a lonely piece of land overgrown with flowering weeds and bushes the size of an average tree. I clearly remember the look and feel of a small window in the front of the trailer. It cut a hole in the rickety front door and was covered in a layer of greasy dust, adding a haze to the view of the outside. The dirt and gravel driveway twisted about a hundred yards to the one lane road out front. The remains of a long untended apple orchard backed up to the trailer.

The trailer itself was ten feet by sixty feet and smelled of mildew and oil. The linoleum had worn down to the subfloor in spots, and there was no electricity. Instead, kerosene lamps provided the only light at night, and Mama cooked on an oil stove. I was excited, though, when I found we had running water.

The trailer was somewhat furnished. It had a single threadbare sofa that was missing a leg and wobbled when you sat on it, which I thought was funny. There was a table in the kitchen with chrome legs and two red vinyl chairs that were in pretty good shape. Each end of the trailer had a small bedroom. The kitchen and living room were in the middle, and we children slept in the bedroom on the opposite end of Mama's room. We still didn't have beds, but we laid down cardboard and piles of dirty clothes for softness and warmth. We still had the green wool army blanket that all of us shared.

As we settled in the trailer, I became even more aware of the changes that had come over the family. We didn't start off the next day working at a farm. Instead, when the sun barely peeked over the horizon, I heard Daddy leave. I laid on the floor, not daring to move until car tires crunched down the rocky drive.

The other children stirred about the same time. We knew when Daddy was moving around and when he wasn't. No one said anything, though. I didn't get up right away even after the car had clearly left. It was peaceful just knowing we were alone.

After a while, it seemed that the only movement was the birds calling from the overgrown orchard behind the trailer. Finally, I got up and walked out of the room the children shared. The sunlight made horizontal lines across the thin kitchen as it cut through the dingy windows. Mama busied herself cleaning.

No matter what conditions were forced upon us, Mama always tried to make it clean. She never stopped tidying and sweeping.

Finding her hard at work was not strange to me. Instead of bothering her, I went about playing with my most precious possession: my paper dolls. During our travels from camp to camp, I had found several old magazines and a Sears catalog. I pulled the pages out, folded them in half, and tore along one half of a silhouette, making a perfect little person, arms and legs outstretched. Susie, who was the brightest of us, showed me how to tear out dresses for the girls and pants for the boys. I tore a small tab out on each side of each garment so that the clothes would stay on the paper dolls when the tab folded over.

I played by myself for hours, pretending each doll had a name. The mama and daddy were nice, and all the children were happy. Nobody was hungry. Every once in a while, I would look up or make a noise, hoping Mama would notice me. She never looked my way, but kept on cleaning things even if it looked as though she'd cleaned them already.

Eventually, everyone was up. Brenda went about helping Mama, but I don't remember them talking much. I went outside to play with Nellie and Robbie. Nellie and I did not get along very well. Most often, we would end up fighting and cutting any game short. I think it was because we were so close to the same age.

When I finally got too frustrated with Nellie to play anymore, I went back inside. Daddy's absence left an air of relief and excitement. The house lightened when he was gone, as would Mama. I found Brenda, Susie, and Mama inside reading some old magazines. I wanted to play, but Brenda and Susie wouldn't talk to me. When I made my presence known, only Brenda looked up, so I chose her as the target of my seven-year-old ways.

"Stop reading and let's play," I said.

Brenda glanced up just long enough to give me a glare.

"Stopped-up-nose-Brenda, read, read, read," I teased.

Those were the worst words I could think to say. Daddy's absence gave me courage, so I took the game to its next step. I darted to where my sister sat on the floor and snatched her magazine away, giggling.

"I got your magazine, ole read-a-lot-Brenda."

I waited in front of her just a second to see what she was going to do. When she got up from the broken couch, I raced, giggling, out the door to the front yard. Then I heard the door swing open behind me, and Brenda gave chase, calling out to me with a good-natured warning.

"I'll get you Frances!"

I ran as fast as I could. Brenda tried, but she couldn't catch me. This made the game all the more fun for both of us. Even Brenda was laughing when I finally relented. I handed her the magazine and she laid it on the dry grass. She took me by my two hands and started to twirl me through the air—a game I loved!

I remember feeling so happy in that moment. The air blew my already unruly hair into my eyes as the ground spun below me. I laughed, knowing what would come next. The game was called *statue*. When Brenda eased me toward the ground and let go, I tried to fight the dizziness and freeze in place.

"Statue!" Brenda called out.

The idea was to stay the way you landed when the person turned you loose. I stumbled to one knee and put my arms out like I was still holding on to her. I would not move until Brenda said, "free." Then we did it again and again until I felt like the world spun whether I did or not. The dizzier I got, the more I liked it. We were laughing so loud that the others heard us and came running to join in the fun. Brenda set up a game of red light, green light. We played for some time, all of us enjoying the rare taste of freedom. Eventually, even we tired of the games and headed back inside together.

Brenda went back to her book. Before the beating she took, Mama would have been right in the middle of our game, laughing louder than the rest of us. Not this time. I found her sitting in one of the kitchen chairs. She seemed to be staring off into nothing. I moved over to where she sat and climbed up onto her lap. I expected warm arms to embrace me. Instead, it was like climbing onto a fallen tree. Mama did not touch me. She did not even acknowledge I was there. I ended up rolling right off her and sliding to the floor.

Rising to my knees, I looked up into Mama's face. Her eyes were blank—as though she was not there any longer.

On another night weeks after we arrived in Michigan, Mama was sweeping the floor of the small living room. Even though a seven-year-old can usually send troubles rolling off her like water, I found myself watching Mama and thinking about when I had climbed up onto her lap. She stopped sweeping at one point and looked out the small window in the door. She had been doing that most days, staring out that glass for what felt like hours without moving or saying anything.

Curious, I walked over and stood beside her. I rose up to my tiptoes and tried to look out the window.

"What are you looking at, Mama?" I asked.

She did not answer me. Instead, she continued to stare out the window as if I were not in the room. I did my best to follow her gaze, but I did not see anything all that interesting. When I looked up onto her face, there was no expression at all.

Before I could say anything else, the sound of car tires crunching up the driveway caught my attention. It was Daddy coming home. I moved, receding to the far corner of the room. The other children did the same. No one said anything; there was no acknowledgement of the tension that filled the room.

Her trance broken, Mama walked away from the door and stood at the kitchen. The car came to a stop and I heard the door slam shut. Footsteps approached the house. Brenda gathered us all together, trying to keep us quiet so he wouldn't have anything to get angry about.

"Once upon a time," she whispered. "A prince lived in a giant castle in a great kingdom. He was looking for a wife and . . ."

I listened to Brenda telling us the story of "The Princess and the Pea," but I watched my parents too. Daddy came into the house and fell heavily into one of the chairs in the kitchen. Mama rushed over to where he sat, got down on her knees by his feet, and pulled his boots off one after the other. When she was done, he handed her a package wrapped in brown butcher paper.

"Fix me this steak," he said as she knelt at his feet.

When she rose and spun toward the stove to do his bidding, he kicked her in the rear with his stocking feet. Mama stumbled but, thank God, did not fall on the baby in her belly. Daddy laughed and uncapped his mason jar of white lightning. He brought it to his lips and took a long drink, shuddering after from the taste.

Something boiled up inside me and I lost "The Princess and the Pea." In that moment, I wanted to run across the room and slap his face. The same realization that struck me among the redwoods returned. *I hate my daddy! But how could this be?*

The awareness came with a rush of pain and fear. I hated the way my mama had to cower. I hated the way he humiliated her under his feet. I hated that he took my mama away from me. Even more, though, I hated him for making me hate him.

I sat on that floor, barely pretending to listen to Brenda's whispers. I did not look at Daddy, because even at my age, I had enough sense to know if he saw my face he would know how I really felt. Instead, I stared off at that tiny window as the smell of searing steak filled the tiny trailer. Then came the sound of Daddy chewing that steak with his mouth wide open. My stomach growled, and I felt my insides turning.

I was frightened. A child could not hate her father. It was not right. No matter how I tried, though, the fact remained. From that moment until decades later, I hated him.

Mama remained distant for the month prior to giving birth. She did not tuck me in at night, nor did she tell us any stories. We children lived for those moments when Daddy was not at home, but there was a shadow cast over them. I hoped with everything inside me that the birth of my new sister would change Mama back. I dreamed of the days to come when she would make us bean patties again and dance her funny dances.

Then the day came. Mama followed Daddy out the door and they drove off together, leaving us with Brenda.

"Where is Mama going?" I asked.

"To the hospital. She has to pick up the baby."

"Oh, I hope it's a little girl."

Brenda didn't seem excited, but she pulled me to her and hugged me tightly. She gathered us up for the nightly washing before putting us to bed. I lay in the dark, listening to the other children breathing and moving around. I imagined dressing my new sister, feeding her, helping her to walk. I barely slept that night.

Mama and Daddy came back five days later. I thought the time would never come. I had been waiting for the sound of their car every minute since they left. When I finally did, I shouted out and rushed into the living room with the rest of my siblings. It was the happiest I had ever been. I could hear my parents speaking as they headed up the porch steps. I grabbed Susie's hand to keep from jumping up and down. She squeezed hard, and I knew she was as excited as I was.

Daddy walked in first. He saw us gathered there, and I half expected him to tell us to get out of the living room. He didn't, though. Instead, he stepped to the side and let Mama follow him inside. I did not notice how she looked, for I was staring at the pink bundle in her arms. My sister was wrapped in a fresh new blanket that the hospital had given Mama.

Suddenly, all of us circled Mama and welcomed our new baby to the family.

"Is it a girl?" I whispered.

Mama nodded, the hint of a smile at the corners of her mouth. "Her name is Katherine Yvonne."

The others asked Mama questions, but I didn't hear any of them. My full attention was on my new sister. She was beautiful! Her hair was jet-black and the thickest I'd ever seen. Her large violet eyes were open and looking right at me. Those eyes held me frozen for a moment, so wise and alert.

I finally broke free of her daze-inspiring beauty and reached out a finger. I touched her warm little cheek. Her skin felt like a feather that had floated down from heaven. I moved my finger down toward her tiny hand. It was pink and balled into a tight tiny fist. When I touched it, her hand opened and her fingers wrapped around mine.

I loved my sister even before that moment. When she held my finger, a bond even deeper than love spread through us both. It was the bond only sisters can feel.

"Can I hold her?" I asked.

"Not yet," Mama said, smiling. This was the first time she had smiled in so long! I wanted to believe that my mama was back and everything would be all right. I smiled back at her, holding back the urge to jump up and hug her around the neck.

Instead, I shadowed Mama as she took care of Katherine. Everyone piled upon the sofa to watch Mama feed the baby from a bottle. We heard Katherine's voice soon after. It was the sweetest sound I had ever heard, like the coo of a dove. Eventually, the others left to go outside and play, but I stayed close, sitting on the sofa beside Mama and my baby sister. At one point, Mama looked at me. Without saying a word, she gently placed Katherine, swaddled in the blanket from the hospital, in my lap. I nuzzled her, taking in her smell, so fresh and new.

I sat so still that Katherine did not fuss. Mama watched the entire time, smiling as she used to. After a while, my arms cramped up and my legs got uncomfortable, but I did not move at all. I knew that if

Katherine fussed Mama would take her from me, and I wanted to hold this soft bundle from heaven forever.

I fell asleep that night thinking about what I would do with Katherine the next day. I planned out the feedings and how I would find a more comfortable place to sit when I held her. I was smiling when sleep finally overtook me.

It felt as though I slept for only minutes when I awoke with a start. The trailer was filled with an awful sound, one I could not immediately place. Then, to my horror, I realized it was my baby sister crying. Even my inexperienced ears knew this was not the normal sound of a baby's cry. It was something far worse. She sounded as if she was in pain.

Above the screams, I heard Daddy's voice. I could not make out the words, but he was yelling at Mama. I tried to hear what was being said, hoping the words would tell me that Katherine was okay. Instead, the screaming and shouting continued.

The baby's pain-filled cries grew louder and louder. I had to know if Katherine was okay. I pushed the wool cover away and sat up. Brenda's hand immediately gripped my wrist, pulling me back to the floor.

"Kathy's crying," I whispered, trying to shake free of her grip.

"Hush!" Brenda whispered harshly. "Be quiet and lay back down! Don't make a sound!"

Her tone was like nothing I had heard from her before. She spoke harshly to me for the first time in our life together. I covered my ears with the blanket, pressing the rough fabric into my ears. Brenda held onto my wrist as the screaming and shouting resonated through the blanket in muffled waves. I lay there awake for hours.

When morning came, it brought tragedy.

Chapter 6

On the Run

That first Thanksgiving holiday after I was reunited with Brenda, finally being able to touch her and see her sweet face again started me thinking about my family even more than ever. It is sad how a shadow can fall over people, get in between them, and tear them apart. My family was scattered all over the United States. Worse, I believe there was a fear living in us all that somehow, getting back together might resurrect Daddy's darkness. Seeing Brenda again made me realize even more how much I longed for them all. The feeling was overwhelming. The intimacy between us returned with each story she told. I also felt something else stirring, as though a gaping hole deep inside my heart had slowly begun to mend. After only three days with my sister, I felt a peace, like what I hoped coming home would feel like.

On the last day of our visit, my husband, Wayne, was out front in the driveway of Brenda's house putting the suitcases in our van. I sought out my sister one last time. I found her in the kitchen taking care of everyone and everything. It was as though time shifted in that moment. She was fifteen again, the way she looked before Katherine was born and before we made that last trip all together to California.

One thing was very different, though. She was no longer that frightened, cowering girl. The shadow had left her, and she had found her place in this beautiful family of hers. She was deeply appreciated and loved by them all, and it warmed my heart. At the same time, it brought back the past. It was not long after Katherine's birth that Brenda left us.

"I missed you with all my heart when you left," I said to Brenda. "I felt like my soul was empty, and I didn't understand why."

"I missed you too, honey," Brenda said. "I thought you'd find a better life. I am so sorry."

I did not say anything right away. I could hear Wayne outside packing the car.

"I dream of Katherine sometimes," I said softly. "Her lovely angel eyes, mostly."

Brenda nodded. "She was a beautiful baby."

When I awoke the morning after Mama brought Katherine home, I knew something awful had happened. My sister was not making a sound, and Daddy looked like a wild man. He hadn't combed his thick black hair and his eyes were bloodshot. All of us children sat on the broken sofa, afraid to speak. There was a deathly quiet mood in the trailer, and Mama was not in sight. Daddy ordered us all into the back room. I heard him yelling at Mama through the closed door, and I heard her crying softly. Eventually, the front door opened and swung closed with a bang. The car engine sounded and the tires rolled up the drive. Then they were gone.

I did not see my parents leave with Katherine that next morning, but we knew Daddy had taken her somewhere because she was not in the trailer. We were alone for what seemed like hours. When the car returned, Katherine was not with them. Daddy walked into the trailer and ordered everyone to sit on the sofa. He glared down over us and his eyes had that fire behind them, the kind that seemed about to boil to the surface and erupt on us all. Mama walked through the room without a word or a glance in our direction. She closed the door to the back bedroom.

"Your baby sister is dead." The words burst out of Daddy without a touch of compassion. Instead, his eyes dared us to react. "Let's have it. What did you hear last night?"

He searched our faces, his searing glare landing on me, then Susie. He was searching all of our faces. He seemed anxious and angry at the same time. I almost answered him, but Brenda spoke first with enough authority to keep me quiet.

"We all slept right through the night, Daddy. None of us heard anything."

She squeezed my hand and I looked at her. Her face said one thing, *stay silent*. Daddy continued to stare at each of us.

"What about them? Ya'll hear anything?"

"No," Brenda quickly answered again. "We all slept sound."

"What about you, Nellie? I know you heard something."

Nellie shook her head and Brenda answered once more, saying she heard nothing. Daddy hammered us like a drill sergeant, but Brenda never wavered. Finally, he gave up. I could not understand at the time why he spent so much effort questioning us and didn't seem to be horrified that his baby daughter was dead. "All right," he barked.

"I don't want *any* of you mentioning Katherine's name—ever. Do you understand? She's dead, and I better never hear her name again."

I tried my best to hide my anger at Daddy and the fact that my heart was broken. We all quickly nodded our heads when he finished speaking. After he was satisfied that we had not heard the baby crying during the night, he started barking out orders.

"Brenda, go help your mama pack the stuff up. We're leaving."

Brenda moved like lightning, giving Daddy as wide a berth as she could, and rushed around gathering our belongings. Soon Mama joined her, and together they packed the few pots and pans, our handful of dishes, some flour and cooking oil, and the clothes and blankets we slept on. Daddy carried the small kerosene stove out to the car, and Mama and Brenda followed with their hands full. In no time at all, we were packed into the car. We left Michigan without my baby sister. Her death certificate read, "obstruction to the duodenum." But she didn't have an obstruction the five days she stayed in the hospital or they would not have released her. We weren't allowed to attend a funeral for Katherine. I sat in the backseat with tears streaming down my face as we drove away, leaving her alone. I silently whispered goodbye to her as we drove down the gravel road to the highway heading out of town. I knew that she was in heaven, in the arms of Jesus, and that I would see her again one day. I imagine her smiling face and large violet eyes will meet me one day, as she says, "Where have you been? I've been waiting for you."

At first, everyone was quiet. Daddy drove that old car as if the devil himself were chasing us. He did not stop when the sun set but kept driving into the night. We fell asleep leaning against each other as the car jostled and bumped on down the road. When I woke up the next morning, we were in another state.

As usual, Brenda did her best at keeping us silent and out of trouble. She played quiet games with us in the back, whispering fairy tales and reciting nursery rhymes. It was a long and boring drive, so the silence did not last.

"I miss little Katherine," I said. I looked around at the others. "Don't y'all miss her too?"

All of a sudden, the car veered off the road. The breaks shrieked and we were all jerked forward. A second later I saw Daddy's angry red face whirl around. His arm was raised, and his shoe was in his hand before I realized what was about to happen.

"I told you not to mention that name!" he bellowed at me.

He lashed out, striking any place he could reach with the hard sole of that shoe. The others scattered like rats fleeing a sinking ship as the heel struck me on the top of my head. I tried to protect myself, my hands in front of my face as I screamed, but the blows rained down on me. He hit me again and again until my right temple split open and blood rolled down the side of my face. Finally, the beating stopped and he turned back around, starting the engine. The car lurched forward, and we continued west.

Slowly, silently, the children returned to their spots. I was dazed and sobbing. Brenda eased closer to me and inspected the cut. She was careful to make sure he could not see her. That was the last time I mentioned my baby sister in Daddy's presence.

In time, our silent journey led to Phoenix, Arizona, and an unforgettable turning point for my family. There was no cotton or other crops to pick by the time we arrived. Instead, Daddy found a job at a large salvage yard called Johnson's Auto Wrecking.

Rusted and wrecked cars covered the yard like acres of dead bodies after a fierce battle. Piles of hubcaps and auto parts filled most of the space between and around the wrecks. We were met by a tall man with a beard, wearing dark coveralls. Daddy got out of our car and they talked. A minute later the man pointed to an old, rusting school bus parked in the corner of the lot. This bus would be our home.

Daddy went to work stripping the cars, and we moved into the old bus. All the seats had been removed, and a plywood shelf was installed along the side below one row of windows. Mama set up the kerosene cookstove on an orange crate by the front and placed our few belongings under the counter. In the back, she laid the old cardboard down and piled on our clothes and blankets, making two beds.

Although I did not know it then, the man my daddy spoke with was Mr. Johnson, the owner of the large salvage yard. He was a kind and, as I would soon learn, amazing man. He must have felt bad for us, allowing us as he did to live on the yard. Soon after we arrived, his wife came to visit, bringing food and friendship. She took an immediate liking to Mama and Brenda.

"I've spoken to your father," she said to Brenda one day. "And he's given me permission to offer you a job at my house. You can help clean house and take care of my children, if you think you'd like to do that?"

Brenda looked at Mama, but Daddy must have given his orders to Mama because she nodded right away. Brenda happily agreed. Mrs. Johnson smiled at her.

"I will pick you up in the morning and have you back after dinner, if that's agreeable." She looked from Brenda to Mama. "And I will pay her five dollars a day."

"Thank you, ma'am. We sure do appreciate it," Mama said.

"Okay, then. I'll be back in the morning early to pick her up."

That night, Daddy set down the rules. He gave Brenda instructions on what she could and could not say while at the Johnsons'. Brenda had never been away from him in her life, and I believe she would have agreed to anything for a few hours of freedom.

"You will say nothing to that woman, you understand?" he said, his fist full of the front of her dress. "And you will give me every cent she pays you. If I find out you talked about anything that goes on here, I will kill you."

Brenda assured him over and over again that she would do exactly as he ordered. Finally, he left for a night of drinking.

Brenda, it seemed to me, found peace while she was with Mrs. Johnson. After the first few weeks of working there, I noticed a change come over her. At first, it was her appearance. She came home with new, clean clothes that Mrs. Johnson gave her. I remember staring at them, thinking how pretty she looked. None of us had ever owned a new dress with the tag still on. She started to brush her hair every morning with a new hairbrush Mrs. Johnson gave her. Brenda always made sure she was shiny clean before Mrs. Johnson arrived to pick her up. In the past, her long dark hair had hung in her eyes as though she were hiding from the world. Now she clipped it back and showed her freshly scrubbed face every morning. She had always looked beautiful to me, but suddenly, she glowed.

At the same time, she changed the way she carried herself. At fifteen, her figure was already well developed. Before Mrs. Johnson's visit, Brenda did everything she could to hide her figure. She slouched over, caving her chest in, and she always cast her eyes down. After only a couple of weeks, she started standing up straighter. She seemed to be gaining confidence and a sense of pride.

Daddy, however, did not change. If anything, he grew meaner, and his meanness seemed more and more focused on Brenda. He would violently lash out at her without any warning or reason. He did worse, too, and many nights I would pet my sister's hair as she silently sobbed in the back of that bus. She continued to work with Mrs. Johnson each day, though, and handed over her wages to Daddy every Saturday.

On many occasions, his beatings left their mark. She would go to work with angry purple bruises on her face and arms. It was only a matter of time before Mrs. Johnson figured out what was going on in my family.

One night, Brenda failed to come back to the bus after work. The hour when Mrs. Johnson would normally drop her off came and went. Mama grew more nervous, pacing up and down the bus like a trapped animal. I remember hoping desperately that Brenda would return before Daddy got home, but that was not to be. When Daddy arrived, it was not yet dark. He came stomping up the steps with a whiskey bottle in his hand. He had an uncanny sense for trouble. One look around the bus and he found the heart of the problem.

"Where's Brenda?" he growled.

Mama did not say anything. None of us did. He knew without us saying a word. He roared like a grizzly bear and slammed his fist against the top of the metal ceiling. The windows rattled. I thought the bus would explode with his rage.

"I'm gonna kill her!"

The other children cowered in the back of the bus with me, trying to stay out of his way and be as quiet as possible. Mama stood by helpless, not speaking, not knowing what to do. His hand rose up and struck her in the face. She staggered back.

"You," he growled. "You set me up!"

Mama tried to regain composure, but she was dazed from the blow he'd given her.

"No, Broadus, I swear I don't know where she's at. Mrs. Johnson picked her up this morning like she always does."

I believe his anger was checked, at least for a time, because of how much in debt he was to the Johnsons. They let us live on their land and gave him a job. At least once a week, Mrs. Johnson brought us food from her kitchen. Instead, he ranted and cursed Brenda, calling her horrible names, threatening to go find her and kill her, but he stayed at the bus. As the sun set behind the mountains with no sign of Brenda, he could not contain himself any longer. He ordered us all into the car, and we drove off to the Johnsons' house.

It was a short drive, but he worked himself into a frenzy on the way. I held my breath and waited for the storm that I knew was coming. Nobody ever dared to cross Daddy. I knew that even if he found Brenda, it would not go well. He would never let Brenda get away with what he considered an act of rebellion.

I shook and felt sick to my stomach. I do not believe a single one of us breathed as we rode to the Johnsons' home. When we pulled up into their driveway, Mr. Johnson was standing on the back stoop. Whatever small bit of composure Daddy had earlier was gone. Mr. Johnson was no longer his boss. Instead, he was a man that crossed him, and Daddy was ready for war.

Amazingly, at least to me, Mr. Johnson had the courage to come right up to the door of the car before Daddy could even get out.

"Hello there, Broadus," he said, leaning against the driver's door. He put his hand over the open window. "You don't have to get out. What brings you here so late?"

Mr. Johnson's voice was calm, and he seemed completely at ease. I was able to breathe for the first time, and I thought maybe Brenda was not there after all.

"I am looking for my oldest daughter," Daddy said through clenched teeth. "You know why I'm here!"

Mr. Johnson's calm expression changed. He looked alarmed that Brenda had not come home.

"She left a few hours ago, saying she wanted to walk instead of having a ride. I hope she didn't run off."

Daddy's anger roared to life. He shoved open the door so hard that it pushed Mr. Johnson back. Daddy practically fell out of the car, he was so spitting mad.

"Brenda's here and I'm gonna find her! She ain't *run off*," he said, mocking Mr. Johnson. "If you're hiding her, I'll kill you both."

Daddy drove Mr. Johnson away from the car. Still cursing, he charged past the man toward his garage. He stormed through the Johnson's property like a bull, banging on the walls as if to scare Brenda out of hiding.

For his part, Mr. Johnson stayed calm. "I can understand your concern, Broadus, but she ain't here. I'll help you look for her in the morning, when it's light. She's probably just out being a teenager."

"She ain't no teenager," Daddy said.

He refused to give up. He opened Mr. Johnson's barn door and climbed up into the loft, kicking the walls and bellowing like a wild bull along the way. He cursed Brenda and ordered her out of hiding. He searched everyplace imaginable outside the Johnson home but could not find her. All the while, Mr. Johnson calmly followed him. This went on for what felt like an hour.

Finally, Daddy's anger ran its course and he stopped his search. He was left looking as if he did not know what to do next. He walked back toward our car.

"She had better be back by morning," he said.

Mr. Johnson nodded. "Yessir. Come back in the morning and we'll look for her together. We'll find her. I'll bet a nickel on that."

Later in life, I read a passage from the Bible: "A soft answer turneth away wrath" (Prov. 15:1 KJV). I believe that if Mr. Johnson had acted any differently that night, there would have been bloodshed. His soft answers kept Daddy from exploding and causing a worse scene. Daddy simply drove us all back to the bus. Little did I know at the time, Brenda came out from hiding as soon as our car was out of view. She had been inside an empty oil drum that sat not a foot away from where Daddy stood just moments before.

When I visited her for Thanksgiving, she told me about it.

"My entire body was shaking with fear while Mr. Johnson followed Daddy around the yard and right past the oil drum several times. I felt he could see through the metal and would find me. I was sobbing and stuck my whole fist in my mouth to keep him from hearing me. I thought I'd have a heart attack when he was standing right beside me. I was sure he'd find me and kill me. Worse, I thought he'd kill Mr. Johnson."

Chapter 7

Arrest

Wayne had already packed the van with our suitcases and was sitting down in Brenda's family room watching a movie, giving my sister and I all the time we needed. We couldn't stop talking. Time had turned back, and we were kids again. We talked about our lives, both the ones we shared together and after I lost her. Hearing her speak about the Johnsons made me want to know more about what happened when she went to their house. "Do you think Mama told Mrs. Johnson about . . . what was going on?" I asked.

Brenda shook her head. "I don't. Mama was so timid by that time. I think all she could do was try to stay alive." She paused. "*I* told Mrs. Johnson."

I stared at her in awe. "How did you ever find the courage?"

We were all so afraid of Daddy back then. He threatened our lives on a regular basis and made it clear that he *would* kill us if we dared tell a stranger about our life. Regardless, that is exactly what Brenda did.

"I told Mrs. Johnson what he was doing," Brenda said. It was still difficult for her to speak of Daddy, and I could see the pain on her face. I laid my hand over hers as she continued. "She then told her husband, who called the police. The sheriff and his deputies came out to the Johnsons' house and I had to tell the whole thing over again. It was so different back then."

"It *was* different back then," I agreed. "You didn't see these stories on TV like you do now."

"Nobody reported sexual abuse when we were little. That is part of why I waited so long. I was afraid nobody would believe me." She looked down. "The officer questioned me for a long time. They told Mr. Johnson that they needed *corroborating* reports. I didn't understand at first, until he said I would have to go back home until they got a warrant. The sheriff said that they'd have to go out and talk to Daddy, and the rest of you."

"He would have killed you," I whispered.

She nodded. "I begged Mrs. Johnson not to send me back"

"I remember when they came for him," I said, thinking back.

The sun had barely started to peek through the trees, and I lay in my pile of rags and listened to the birds chirping outside. The peace and quiet was soothing compared to the tension from the night before. Early mornings had always been a special time for me, even to this day. Back then, when Daddy was drinking as he did, he usually spent mornings recovering instead of cussing and beating us.

That morning, however, was different. The quiet turned to chaos when the door to the bus crashed open. Glass broke and metal slammed against metal as the police and sheriff stormed the bus. Everyone else was still asleep but were jarred awake by the crash and the pounding of heavy footsteps. I saw the sheriff and two other officers at the end of the aisle, their guns raised. I screamed in terror at the shock of it.

The officers rushed down the narrow aisle toward us. At that instant, Daddy sprung up, wide-awake. One of the officers was on him before he had time to escape. The officer wrestled Daddy to the floor of the bus, but Daddy fought hard. I watched in terror as the officer brought out his handcuffs.

Daddy thrust back his elbow, landing a hard blow to the man's midsection. The officer doubled over with the breath knocked from his lungs. Daddy used the narrow aisle and the clutter of bodies to his advantage; it kept the other officers from reaching him right away. He reared back and landed a vicious kick to the downed officer and was able to scramble free. He lunged for one of the open windows and jimmied his body through the tiny opening like a snake seeking cover.

Susie gathered up the children as far away from the fight as was possible. Robbie climbed over the top of my head in an effort to get out of the way. An officer reached my daddy just as the top of his legs were disappearing through the window. At the same time, the sheriff ran out of the bus. He confronted Daddy from the other side as he hung in midair, helpless. The sheriff cracked him over the head with his lead blackjack. Together, the two officers still inside grabbed Daddy's legs and roughly yanked him. Daddy came flying back into the bus, the fight knocked out of him by the blow he'd taken to his head.

By then, all three of those officers were on him. They threw him down, smashing his face against the metal flooring. Daddy struggled, but that just won him an even harsher beating. Billy clubs flashed in the dawn sunlight. I saw blows land on Daddy's head, and my hand went to the scar on my temple left from the last beating he'd given me.

None of us dared move when the beating continued. No one said a word. Mama did not jump up and try to stop the officers. Nor did we cheer the violence. It was as if time just stopped, and none of us knew exactly how to react to what we were seeing.

One officer got the cuffs on Daddy while the others held him down. They picked him up and dragged him off the bus by his arms and feet. Mama followed behind them with us in tow. I peeked around her back and watched.

I stared, unable to move. The sheriff pushed Daddy into the back of his patrol car, and I caught a glimpse of him as the door slammed shut. Blood oozed from his hair and covered the side of his face. One eye was already swollen closed. He looked small, almost harmless back there.

We all just watched as the patrol car rolled away, carrying Daddy out of our lives. Relief built up inside me as the sheriff's car disappeared. He was really gone. The police had taken him away, and he would not ever be able to hurt us again. We were free!

Chapter 8

One More Piece

Wayne came in to Brenda's kitchen when we finished talking and gave her a big hug. It warmed my heart to see how she had taken to Wayne. I was not surprised though. Wayne was a kind, gentle soul who attracted animals and the helpless to him like a magnet. Late one night in the middle of a horrific thunderstorm a few years before he found Brenda, the wind blew our barn door open and Wayne had to go out into the pitch-black night to get it closed. The electricity was out, the lightning was flashing all around us, and the rain gushed down in torrents. When he got out to the dark barn, something grabbed him around his legs and wouldn't turn loose! When he realized it was a stray dog, scared to death and drenching wet, his heart melted. This dog actually wrapped his front paws around Wayne and held on as if asking for help. I think Wayne was as scared as that stray mutt before he realized what had attached to him in the dark. But, needless to say, that dog had a home for life. That is the way Wayne was made; he always helps every living thing. I have never seen him kill a ladybug or moth; instead he returns them to the outdoors. He adopted Brenda as his sister the day we walked into her home. It was nice to know we felt the same way.

When I hugged Brenda good-bye, I held her close to me. I did not ever want to let her go. I was still afraid that I might lose my family again. When we finally got into the car and Wayne pulled away, I fought back tears and tried to stay strong.

"I don't ever want to lose her again," I said.

"We won't," he assured me. "She seems happy."

"Yes, she does." But I knew she had not forgiven our dad for the sixteen years of misery she lived through.

Wayne and I started the long drive home. I stared out the window, my mind walking back through the door and into Brenda's kitchen again. It was so hard to leave her after missing her for so many years.

At the same time, my heart felt different than it had prior to that visit. It was not fully healed, but a piece had returned to fill part of the hole inside me. I had finally found family. My prayers had been answered. Wayne seemed to read my mind. He glanced over at me as he drove the car down the highway.

"It's different this time." He smiled at me. "This time it's all going to work out."

I knew what he meant. This was not the first time Wayne had tried to reunite me with my broken family. Years before, he had tracked down Susie only to learn she had died of pneumonia at a hospital in California. On the phone, an attendant told Wayne that her ashes had been mixed with those of other bodies who had not been claimed and buried in a single, seven-inch space with no marker. I could not bring her home to rest. The man on the phone felt awful, but he told Wayne that they had held on to the ashes, on a shelf in a cardboard container, for someone to claim. No one had shown up.

Finding out Susie had died all alone with nobody to claim her remains broke my heart. Then Wayne located my little brother Robbie. I can remember it like it was yesterday; my husband walked into our kitchen with a large piece of typing paper in his hand and an even larger smile on his face.

"I think you might want to sit down, sweetie," he said, grinning from ear to ear.

Wayne could barely contain himself as he dangled the piece of paper in front of my face. On it was written my little brother's name and his address. My heart pounded and I started to hope, but I tried to stay calm. Slowly, I dried my hands on a dish towel and sat at the kitchen table beside Wayne, afraid to trust my eyes.

"Is it really him?"

Wayne nodded, still grinning. "It's really him!"

"Are you sure?"

He laughed. "Yes, honey. We've found your baby brother."

Tears ran down my face, one landing on the paper in my hand. I talked my next move through with Wayne, debating whether I should pick up the phone and call him. We decided it might be best to write him a letter so he could prepare for the news. I got right up from that table to do just that, but first I hugged Wayne around the neck with all my might. We were both laughing and smiling when I went to sit down to write that letter to my little brother, whom I had not seen since I was nine years old.

In the letter I told Robbie who I was and how much I would love to come and see him. I carefully enclosed two pictures of me, one current and the other from when I was nine, taken at Connie Maxwell Children's Home. I sealed the envelope, placed the stamp on perfectly, and took it directly to the post office. For the next week I felt as though I was pacing every second of the day. I could hardly wait to hear from Robbie. Time crawled, and I checked the mailbox dozens of times each day.

When I saw Robbie's return letter in our mail the next week, I was too excited to even open it. I ran into the house yelling and jumping up and down.

"It's here, it's here!" I was beside myself with excitement.

Wayne came racing into the kitchen to see what I was carrying on about. With trembling hands, I passed the letter to Wayne and asked him to read it aloud. He glanced over it, and it only took a few seconds for his face to fall.

I could barely get the words out. "What does it say? When can we go see him?"

"We can't," he sadly whispered. The hurt in Wayne's voice turned to anger. "He doesn't want to see us."

I took the letter, trying to convince myself that Wayne had read it wrong. He had not. My brother wrote that he had a new family and he had no interest in finding his original one. He asked me to lose his address and his phone number. He wrote, "Do not bother me or my family again."

When I finished reading, I reached inside the envelope and found he had returned my letter. Turning it upside down, I watched as the two photos I'd sent him slid out and floated to the tabletop.

I almost gave up hope. My dream of finding my family, my connection to this world, did not just fade. It crumbled. My hurt turned into anger in that moment, and I slapped his letter down on the table. I just about made up my mind that day that I would not hope again.

Wayne seemed to know that was what I was thinking about as we drove away from our wonderful reunion with Brenda.

"You know, I prayed real hard that night," he said.

"What night?"

"The night after we got your brother's letter."

"What did you pray about?" I asked.

"I asked God to not allow me to find any other family members unless they were alive and *wanting* to be found," he said.

I smiled at Wayne. "Your prayer was answered."

He reached up and pulled something from behind the sun visor. He passed me a small photograph that he had taken of Brenda and me holding hands and sitting at the dining table together on Thanksgiving Day, which he had printed for me sometime during our three-day stay. I keep that picture on my refrigerator to this day, where I can look at it any time I want. When I do, I never feel alone.

Wayne's prayer was answered with another miracle in the spring of 2005. Wayne and I were invited to appear on a local television station in Greenville, South Carolina, called Dove Broadcasting. I had been asked to share my story of survival and salvation with their audience and to sing a few songs as well.

We had a wonderful time, and hundreds of people from North Carolina, Georgia, and South Carolina called into the station wanting to talk to me. I was overwhelmed and humbled by the response! We arrived home in Greenwood, South Carolina, the next day, exhausted but content, knowing I would be leaving again to visit a small ministry at Mary Black Memorial Hospital in Spartanburg the next morning.

While Wayne was bringing in our bags, I rushed into the house to the kitchen phone to check the voice messages, hoping some of the listeners who had called the station the night before might have tried to contact me at home. To my amazement, the machine was full. I was thrilled to my toes, and I grabbed a pencil and paper to copy down the names and numbers so I could call each one of them back. I was concentrating, trying to keep up with the messages, when a voice on the tape stopped me in my tracks. I felt as though the world had stopped moving. I listened to a man's voice on my answering machine.

"I am not sure this is the right number, but I believe you are my aunt Frances," a deep male voice said. "My name is Tony. I think my dad is your older brother Jimmy. We live in Greenville."

When he said that, I felt my soul stir. Something wonderful happened inside me. I had just been in Greenville the day before. He had seen me on the television program. I was certain that God had ordained this miracle!

This time, I did not hesitate. I called my newfound nephew, Tony, and told him I was indeed his aunt. I talked with Tony long enough to learn that he was a preacher! Tony, in turn, gave me Jimmy's number. I hung up and tried to dial my brother. It took a good half hour to work up the courage, but I did it. When Jimmy answered, I knew right away that I had every reason to hope again. He had the deep Southern drawl that I remembered, but his voice had matured into a rich baritone. His voice was full of love and excitement. We talked for two hours! He told me he had five children and many grandchildren, and even a few great-grandchildren.

"I am raising two of my grandchildren," he told me. "My youngest daughter, Sharon, was killed by a hit-and-run driver when her two kids were still babies. When she died, my wife and I adopted her two children."

Jimmy went on to list nieces, nephews, and a sister-in-law who I never knew I had. With each family member he mentioned to me, I felt another little piece of me slipping back into place. Hearing the happiness in his voice and the matter-of-fact way he gave me their phone numbers, I knew for sure how glad he was to hear from me. I had never known the warmth of a large family before, and I was filled with gratitude that God had put my nephew in front of that television on that particular night at that exact minute.

"When can we set up a time to meet?" I blurted out.

I was incredibly excited by the thought of seeing him in person, but it was tempered when I heard the tone to his voice.

"Sure, but my work schedule is busy for the next month or two. Maybe we can get together after that."

I could not leave it at that, not after the reaction I had received from Robbie. I knew something was not right.

"Jimmy, do you not want to see me?" I asked, afraid of the answer.

"Sure I do, Frances," he said, and he sounded like he meant it. "But I want to look nice when I see you for the first time after all these years."

"What do you mean? I don't care what you look like, Jimmy."

I couldn't really understand. I thought he wanted to buy a new suit or something like that. He sounded so sheepish when he continued.

"I'd like to have some teeth in my mouth when I meet you."

"What happened to your teeth?"

"Well . . ." He chuckled. "I fell asleep in front of the TV one night after working all day. My dog was lying beside me, and my false teeth fell out of my mouth. My dog got hold of 'em and chewed 'em up before I could get 'em away from him. My dog ate my teeth!"

I laughed along with my brother as he described chasing the dog through the house, trying to recover his false teeth.

"Jimmy," I said, "I don't care what you look like. I just want to see you again. I won't even look at your mouth, I promise."

"Frances, I really want to wait for my teeth. It won't be long. Danny, my oldest son, has all the numbers for your nieces and nephews. I've already told him to give them to you." Jimmy gave me Danny's phone number and told me to call him. "You'll like Danny," he assured me.

I tried hard, but Jimmy would not budge. We ended our talk with no plans to meet until he got his new teeth. He promised to call me just as soon as he got them. I resolved to wait and see my brother. It had been so long already, I could handle a few more months. But God had other plans!

I called Danny right away. At the start of our conversation, my nephew mentioned that he and his dad worked together laying commercial tile. Casually, he told me where they were working that week.

"We'll be at Mary Black Memorial Hospital in Spartanburg all this week. That's where we'll be in the morning."

Wow! I was unable to speak. There was a long silence on the line. Danny thought I'd hung up.

"Are you there, Aunt Frances?"

Being called *Aunt Frances* jarred me back to reality.

"Yes, I am still here. You're not going to believe this—I can hardly believe it myself—but I am scheduled to visit Mary Black Hospital tomorrow. I am praying for a woman who is having surgery in the morning."

"What floor are you going to be on?" he asked.

"Fourth."

Danny whispered as if he was in awe. "We are working on the fourth floor tomorrow morning."

That's when I knew for certain this meeting was going to happen much sooner than Jimmy thought. My face burst into a smile of pure delight. I knew that this meeting was *meant* to happen. God wasn't going to let some chewed-up false teeth keep me away from my brother.

Chapter 9

A New Life

When I arrived the next morning at Mary Black Hospital, I did not hesitate. I walked through the beams of sunshine crossing the lobby and right to the front desk.

"Excuse me, can you please tell me where the workers might be?" I asked.

"Workers?" The receptionist raised her eyebrow.

"The men laying tile."

"Oh," she said. "They are on the fourth floor. Take the elevator down the hall."

"Thank you."

Wayne had already found the elevators. He waved me over, and I jumped on the first carriage with excitement. I could hardly contain myself the short ride up. When the door opened, I saw long strips of plastic hanging across both sides of the hallway. Most of the rooms near the elevator looked empty. The normal sounds of the hospital were muffled; an eerie but not unpleasant silence hung in the air. Even considering all the protective covering, dust floated in the air, flashing as it passed in and out of the light. A sign sat in front of the closest flap of plastic reading Construction: Do Not Enter.

I glanced once at Wayne, who shrugged. I pushed through the plastic.

"Jimmy!" I called out. "Jimmy!"

Wayne turned his head and tried to pretend he didn't know me. I kept yelling my brother's name anyway. I was sure it would be hard to recognize him after nearly forty years, so the only way I knew to find him was to make so much noise that he would have to come out. Either security would usher me out of the building, or my brother would appear to rescue me.

I walked down the hall, my head swiveling left and right. Several men poked their heads out to see what the commotion was about. When they saw me, they used their thumbs to point out that Jimmy was farther up the hallway. Then they ducked back in for cover, as though they thought I was crazy. Nobody wanted anything to do with a lady yelling up and down the hallways of a hospital.

I could not help myself. I felt deep inside that I was meant to see my brother that day. I kept shouting, and workers kept ducking back in for cover until finally I reached another area blocked off by plastic. Just as Jimmy's name left my lips, the plastic parted and a man walked out into the light. He was tall, about six feet two inches, with a thickly muscled frame and a strong handsome face. The shock of thick black hair atop his head was dappled by gray at the temples. Right away, I saw my mother in his face.

"I'm Jimmy," he said in a quiet, deep voice.

"I'm Frances!" I blurted out, the emotions inside of me erupting like lava. I ran the few feet between us and wrapped my arms around him. He hugged me back as though we had never been apart. All the lost years vanished, and we were kids again as we had been at Uncle Mose's house.

Both of us were crying. His returning hug was a long-awaited dream coming true. When we finally parted, and I looked at Wayne, he was crying and laughing at the same time. That's when I felt another piece of my heart snapping back into place. Another part of my family had returned.

At that point, a heavily built very tall young man stepped out into the hallway. He looked like Hoss Cartwright on the old *Bonanza* television show.

"This is Danny, your nephew."

I tried to wrap my arms around him, but they only got about halfway across. He was smiling from ear to ear.

"Hi, Aunt Frances." He had a rough, deep voice that sounded as though he was trying to keep from crying himself. He looked at his dad, then over at me. "I'm happy to meet you at last."

Those words were gold to me. I wrapped them around my heart, vowing never to let them go.

"We can't talk here," Jimmy said. "I'll find us a place to sit."

Like the perfect gentleman, he led us to a waiting room on one of the floors below. He offered me a seat on a small loveseat. My heart filled even more when he chose to sit down right beside me. We talked, the words coming as easily as breathing. My brother's mild manner told me he was more like Mama. Eventually, the conversation came around to Daddy.

"After he got arrested," I said, "we moved to Aunt Tessie's house."

"I didn't know her," he said.

I looked him in the eye. "You wouldn't have wanted to know her, Jimmy."

"Why's that?" he asked.

So I answered him.

After Daddy was taken away to prison, we lived in the bus with Mama. In my eyes, the salvage yard became a huge playground filled with wonderful places for hide-and-seek and cars that drove all the way to England in our imaginations. Daddy was gone, and even though we were living in an old bus and had no money to speak of and very little food, I was with Mama and I was happy.

Trouble was not far off, though. Soon a group of state workers arrived. Several men and women wearing suits and carrying clipboards came and looked around the bus, asking mama a lot of questions. After that, the newspaper reporters showed up. Flashbulbs burst all around me as they took pictures of the inside of the bus and our living conditions. They took pictures of the cardboard we slept on with the dirty clothes and the orange crate where Mama cooked. Every inch of our space filled with people I did not know. I flinched away as flashbulbs went off in my face. Whispered words carried on the air: *wretched* and *deplorable*. It struck me in that moment, watching strangers peering at our home, how truly different we were. I wished they would all just go away. I crawled up under the bus and hid in the dirt until they left. The pictures ended up plastered on the front page of the local newspaper.

After a day or two, the news media left us alone and we were allowed to play again and live in peace. Nellie, Robbie, and I raced through the junkyard. Mama gave us the leeway to roam free. In the evenings Mrs. Johnson came by with food: home-cooked biscuits and a chicken, maybe a stew or casserole. She also brought information for Mama. She was Mama's link to the outside world.

"He's being held until the trial, so don't worry. I did hear the state is close to finishing up their investigation. I think they may be coming soon," I heard her say.

I guess I did not understand what Mrs. Johnson meant. I sensed Mama was worried, but our nights were not filled with Daddy's bellowing rage and violence. In time, even Mama seemed to relax. I imagined this would be my life, and I did not mind the thought.

Everything changed early one morning. Police officers showed up at the bus and ushered me and the other children into the back of a cruiser. I thought we had done something really bad, that they were there to take us to prison just as they'd taken Daddy. When I saw one of the men holding Mama by the shoulder and speaking to her quietly, I knew she was not coming with us. Her mouth moved, and although she was too far away for me to hear, I knew she was begging the officers not to take her children. But the car door shut, and we were driven away. I lurched around in my seat and tried to see Mama through the cloud of dust left by the cruiser's wheels. All I could see, though, was Mama's shape, sobbing in front of a swatch of yellow.

I cried most of that trip. It was not until we reached our destination, the juvenile detention hall, and found Brenda waiting for us, that I finally let down my guard a little and realized that this new place was not the horror I imagined it to be. The five of us were housed together in one large room. There was a bed for each of us with a real mattress, though we spent most nights squeezed together on Brenda's bed. Having her back was like finding a warm, safe cave in a storm, and I clung to her for dear life. All I could think about was getting back to Mama. I was afraid of the loud noises and clanging steel doors that opened and closed, keeping everyone in.

I did not fully understand it at the time, but we were in the same facility where they kept runaways and other troubled teenagers. It was the Phoenix Detention Hall. We were segregated from the other children. We ate together as a family but sat at a table removed from the others. The room we shared during the day was isolated from the other inmates. It felt like a cage, but I am sure it kept us safe and out of reach of anyone who might want to hurt us. I learned later that they did not know what to do with us, so we were sent to the detention center; they were doing the best they could for us. But I was still afraid.

While we were there, Mama came to visit every day. She would sit down with us and tell us what was going on.

"They are holding on to you just until I can earn a little bit of money," she reassured us. "I got a job picking cotton. Shouldn't be long now until I can afford the bus tickets. We are going to South Carolina to stay with my sister. Your Aunt Tessie has already told me we can live with her, and we will have a nice life there. It won't be much longer that we'll be apart, I promise."

After she left, we sat huddled together at the long table and talked.

"She'll be back real soon," Brenda said, speaking to us all. "Things are going to be great once we get back to South Carolina. Just remember how good things were when we stayed at Uncle Mose's house."

"I'm going to Hollywood," Susie said. "I'll be an actress and travel all across the world and be famous."

I jumped up and hugged her around the neck. "I'm going with you."

Of all my siblings, Susie was my favorite. I adored Brenda, who was like a mother as well as a sister to me. But Susie was fun! Susie always found the bright star after a cloudy night, and she always knew there would be a rainbow after every storm. She taught me to look for those bright spots too. Susie gave me dreams and laughter in a world that was mostly dark. That is why I was sure she would be an actress, and I wanted to go along with her.

"I'm gonna join the circus!" Robbie jumped out of his seat. "I'm gonna be an apple eater, and I can eat two apples at once."

His large blue eyes twinkled as he danced on one foot and ate a pretend apple, chewing loudly with an open mouth. We all laughed and watched him until he tired. I looked at Brenda. I could see that she meant what she said. Things would be better for us. We would live with family, in a normal house.

"Do you think I'll be able to go to school?" I whispered.

Brenda brushed the long bangs from my eyes. "You will, Frances."

My heart soared.

While this was all going on, Daddy was sentenced to prison. By all intents, he was out of my life forever. The court originally told my mama that she needed to get a job and a home for us before we would be returned to her custody. She petitioned the court in return, telling them that she had family in South Carolina, and she would have a home there to offer her children.

Mama showed up at the detention hall a few weeks after we were first brought there with a huge smile on her face. I knew something great had happened.

"We have our tickets," she said. We cheered as she continued, almost to herself. "I earned most of it. They gave me some, those nice people at the courts. But I did earn most of it."

She sounded proud of herself for earning money. I had never heard that tone from her before, and I never heard it again after that day.

Mama held my hand as we left the hall. A car was waiting outside, and it took us to the bus depot. I saw the tickets in Mama's hand before we boarded. They looked so new and crisp, and the bus itself was a mansion compared to that old school bus we had been living in.

We boarded, and our long journey began. I was fascinated by the working bathroom in the back. I stared at it for some time, hearing the gush of water and wondering where the water went.

Mama saw me staring. She smiled down at me.

"Do you want to use the bathroom, Frances?"

"Yes, I do," I breathed.

"Well, go on," she said, smiling.

I sprang up out of my seat and nearly ran the first few steps. Then I slowed and started to inch down the aisle. I had not even imagined that a bus could have a bathroom in it. Pale circled faces watched me as I passed, like an endless lineup of moons.

I stood outside the door and listened. I was not sure if anyone was inside. A woman sitting nearby smiled at me.

"It is unoccupied," she said.

I said, "Thank you," but I was not sure exactly what that meant. She motioned toward the door, and I assumed no one was inside. So I cracked it open. The smell was like fresh pine needles. I slid through the door and locked it behind me.

The inside of that tiny bathroom surprised me. It looked so modern with a stainless-steel sink and toilet built right into the wall. I shut the door and just stood there for a moment, taking it in.

I did not use the bathroom that first time. Instead, I flushed the toilet several times, turned the sink on and off, and washed my hands. I returned to the bathroom time and again during our trip, but none of the visits rivaled that first one. I felt the world changing around me, and I liked it.

Later that first night, the bus rolled to a stop in the parking lot of a roadside café. It was hot, and bugs buzzed around the entrance, attracted by the light. Dust or sand covered most of the walkway inside. It puffed up in little clouds as I skipped along. Mama walked us right inside. At almost eight years old, I had never been inside a restaurant before. Mama led us to a large booth. We squeezed in.

"Are we gonna eat here?" I asked.

Mama nodded, smiling at me. She ordered for us—hamburgers. My mouth watered when she said that.

I remember almost eating a whole hamburger one time, I thought to myself.

It was before Daddy got arrested. He was out of work, and we had been without food for some time. We had been short on money, and even he was going hungry. One day he took us to an old country church so he could spread out the map and decide where we would go next. Robbie was whining because his tummy hurt. Daddy told Brenda and Susie to get out of the car and walk around so he could concentrate. Both back doors flew open, and we tripped over each other piling out of the car. I was so hungry. I leaned on Brenda's shoulder and whispered, "My stomach hurts."

She patted my head. "Drink some water, baby."

Drinking water meant I'd have to go back to the car where we kept a jug on the back floorboard. I didn't want to do that, not unless I absolutely had to. Trying to ignore my hunger, I walked around the churchyard. We found the door unlocked and went inside. We sang songs and sat in the pews. Soon, Robbie became restless, so Brenda took us back outside.

We got busy playing and barely noticed the pastor as he drove up the dirt drive. He looked surprised to see us at his church. Daddy got out of our car and walked over to the preacher's car. He spoke quietly to the man. He looked so humble and charming as he talked to that preacher. Once, Daddy glanced our way, kind of sad, like he felt sorry for us. I'd never seen that before. The preacher looked sad also.

As the preacher walked toward his car, Daddy called us all over and told us to get in the backseat of ours. He did not say another word, but we followed the preacher out of the driveway and to a nearby restaurant. Daddy got out of the car and walked inside the restaurant with the preacher. When Daddy came out, he was carrying a large white paper sack with grease stains on the bottom of the bag. Daddy shook that preacher's hand, thanking him for the food that he had purchased for his hungry family.

When Daddy opened the car door, the smell of hot, fresh-cooked hamburgers nearly overwhelmed me. It was like nothing I'd experienced before. I was so hungry, and that aroma was so overpowering, that I think I might have eaten even the sack they came in if given the chance. My mouth watered as I watched him remove one juicy hamburger after another from that bag, passing them around to us. My little hands could not get it unwrapped fast enough. I dove into the burger. I can close my eyes to this day and still feel my teeth sinking into that warm bun and the steaming juice of the burger filling my mouth.

Nobody said a word. I did my best to eat that scrumptious burger as fast as I could. At the same time, I could not help savoring every bite. I wanted this food to last forever, but it was not to be. Suddenly, Daddy's large hand shot back over the front seat. His fingers wrapped around my burger and tore it away.

"You don't want that, do you?" he said. He took a huge bite of my burger. "You're too slow, girl."

I sat in that restaurant with Mama and the others and tried to shake that memory out of my head. I convinced myself the bad times were over. I was going to live with a new family, and, best of all, I was going to school. Brenda had said so.

It was very different this time. Everyone at our table was laughing and talking. I knew I would not have to hurry or worry about my meal being taken away. I enjoyed every bite I took.

When dinner was over, we boarded the bus. Mama would get us something to eat every time we stopped along the way. Although the drive took forever, it was a fun time, and I cherished being with Mama. She let me lay my head on her lap when it was time to sleep. I cuddled up and listened to her sweet voice.

"Things are going to be real good for us once we get to your aunt's house," Mama said.

"Is she nice?" I asked.

"Of course," Mama said. She rubbed her hand across my back and my eyes grew heavy. "You'll see real soon. Things will be different for us from now on."

A soft hand woke me out of a deep sleep. I had been dreaming that I was on a large boat with a beautiful white sail. It was taking me to a fairyland far across the ocean. I did not want to wake up, but then I heard Brenda's voice.

"Wake up," she said. "We're here."

I was still in a dream fog, but I followed everyone off the bus. When I climbed down the steps, I saw my Aunt Tessie for the first time. She did not look at all like my mother. Instead, she was tall and stark. The dark dress she wore was starched and ironed so that it barely moved as she walked, and her dark hair was pulled back in a tight knot. There was nothing but harsh lines to her. When she looked at us through eyes too small for her face, we saw judgment, the kind that no child deserves.

I could not have been more excited. I wanted so much to hug my Aunt, hold on tight to this new chance for my family. I remember my feet prancing as she approached us on the platform. That stopped when she utterly ignored me.

Aunt Tessie scooped Mama into a big hug. They held each other for a long time as we children stood by the side and watched. As soon as they let go, Aunt Tessie whisked Mama away. We trailed behind as the two of them left the station and walked to Aunt Tessie's car. She opened the door for Mama but did not look at us. Instead, Brenda herded us into the backseat.

I watched Mama and Aunt Tessie speak softly in the front seat. I remember being happy for Mama, that she finally had someone in her life who would treat her kindly. By the time we arrived at the house, though, a darker feeling had crept into my stomach. We walked into a cool, large, immaculate house. The entire place had a cold feeling about it, like an icehouse. Not one thing was out of place. No books lay open on the tables; no toys or papers could be seen. It was like walking into a magazine ad for a doctor's office.

"Go into the living room and sit down," Aunt Tessie ordered in a cold, flat tone. "And don't touch anything!"

Chapter 10

Not What It Appears to Be

Considering everything that happened with Daddy in Arizona, it is hard to believe that first night with my aunt would begin one of the hardest, most difficult periods of my life. From the outside looking in, no one would have predicted the cruelty that waited for us in that cold house. My Aunt Tessie had a *beautiful* home. She had two young daughters whom she adored and spoiled. She treated Mama like the prodigal daughter. Tessie was Mama's protector, and she defended Mama as a bear might defend her cub. The problem was, Tessie protected Mama from us.

That first night, Mama and Tessie talked for a long time in the kitchen. We children stood in the living room, afraid to sit on her stiff sofa. She had warned us not to touch her perfectly kept furniture or the porcelain figurines that sat out on display in every room of the house. Instead, we stood around in a knot, one by one slipping down to sit on the floor. We were all so tired from the long journey. Eventually I could not take it any longer. I crept back to the kitchen, poking my head around the corner.

"Can we go to bed now?" I asked.

"No!" Tessie snapped. As she did, she put a hand on Mama's

shoulder and shook her head with disdain. "I haven't had time to make their sleeping arrangements yet. There are so many of them."

"I'm sorry to be such a bother, Tessie," Mama said humbly.

I walked back to the living room, tears of exhaustion and confusion staining my cheeks. Brenda seemed to sense the reality behind this perfect picture of a house. She took me in her arms and whispered in my ear, "It'll be okay, baby."

Brenda wrapped her arms around me as I sat down on the floor beside her. It might have been hours before Tessie walked out of the kitchen, supporting Mama with an arm around her waist. She led her to one of the back rooms.

"You sleep here in this room beside mine. I want to be close for you, angel," she said to Mama.

In a while, Tessie returned to us in a huff. She muttered and complained as she stomped angrily to the back of the house. We heard a bustle, but none of us moved until Aunt Tessie returned. I whispered to Susie, "Why is she so mad at us?"

Susie squeezed my hand and put her finger to her lips.

"Get in here," Aunt Tessie barked.

We followed her to the back porch. It was enclosed with clapboard and crammed full with the washer, dryer, a freezer, and a full-sized roll-away bed that she must have dragged back there. There were no windows.

"This is your bed. Now get to sleep," she said. "And don't you make a sound."

Aunt Tessie closed the door, leaving us to climb into bed and fall to complete exhaustion.

The next morning we got another taste of life with Aunt Tessie. Brenda and Susie had already left our makeshift bedroom. The rest of us dared not leave until she came for us. I could hear the murmur of soft conversation through the closed door. I had to use the bathroom but was afraid to open the door, so I did my best to sit still and wait.

The door opened, and the smell of breakfast washed into the porch. My stomach rumbled as I followed after Aunt Tessie with Nellie and Robbie close behind. She took us through the kitchen. Everything had been cleaned up, and there was no food in sight. Brenda and Susie were on their knees, side by side, bent over a pail filled with sudsy water. The floor looked freshly scrubbed. Aunt Tessie led us to three chairs spaced side by side in her living room. They were wooden with high backs and no padding. She pointed to them and told Robbie, Nellie, and I to each take one.

At that time, Robbie was five, I was nearing eight, and Nellie was almost ten. Aunt Tessie looked us over as Brenda and Susie slipped out the front door.

"You're a mess," she said. "Go to the bathroom and then get back in here. You sit in these chairs and don't speak or touch a thing. Do you understand?"

We filed into the bathroom. I took her words to heart and stared into the mirror. My hair was knotty, and my face had the grime of our journey still shadowing my features. I turned the water on and tried to wash it off. I did my best with my hair, but even clean it has always been unruly. In the end, I fussed so much that I forgot to use the bathroom. I went back out and took a seat next to Robbie. And the minutes of the day passed like a slug crossing the front walk.

As we sat there, I heard laughter. It came closer and closer before the front door swung open and Tessie's children came inside. They were flushed from running. When they saw us, they stopped and stared. One leaned over and whispered to the other. I heard the word *devil* but nothing else. Then they were off, back to their life of fun and music. The distant sounds of their jubilation made it almost impossible to sit still.

Most days were similar to that first. If we were given breakfast at all, we had five minutes to finish it before the table was cleared. We learned quickly to use the bathroom first thing in the morning because it would be our only chance during the day. We did not have much liquid going in and hardly any food, which made it easier to get through the day without a bathroom break. We marched to our chairs without being told to because we knew that breaking the rules meant no food.

We had to sit still. Even talking was not allowed. We learned to daydream and keep our minds active. All day, we would long for bedtime, when we could at least whisper to each other and stretch out our legs. It was also the only other time we were allowed to use the bathroom.

Our interactions with Tessie's children just got worse. They learned they had free reign to tease us as often and as badly as they wished. Often, one would skip by and stop long enough to pull our hair or pinch us. If we cried out, they would call us liars and we would get switched or worse. What they whispered that first day became open taunts and judgments. They repeated what their mother called us: "little devils."

The worst moments, though, were when we would hear Mama in the kitchen speaking with Aunt Tessie. The sound of her voice was like an escape for me, but it would make it all the harder to sit still in my chair. All I wanted to do was run to her, but I'd learned quickly not to do that. Instead, I sat and wished she would come to us. Sometimes I would hear her footsteps as she walked out into the family room. They would get closer and closer to our spot in the living room. Before I could see her, though, more footsteps would quickly follow.

Once, when Mama reached our doorway to look in on us, Tessie was right on her heels, saying, "Don't you fuss with them, angel." Mama flinched and Tessie put an arm around her, steering her back toward the family room.

"Why don't you go take a nap, angel? You need time to heal from what that man did to you. Remember, these are Broadus's kids and as evil as he is."

As they walked from the room, I could still hear Tessie's words. "They don't love you, and the devil is in them, like he was in their father. They steal food from me. I've seen them."

I could tell Mama wanted to come to us. I knew she loved us no matter what Aunt Tessie said. But Mama had traded one bully for another. Daddy had broken her. Aunt Tessie saw that and used it to control Mama. Abuse, as I have learned, comes in many different forms, each one leading to the same awful place.

Things were never good at Aunt Tessie's house, but they got much worse when Mama left. At first, she came in and said good night to us every night. When that stopped, we figured out a way to see her. Aunt Tessie would not let us drink water before bedtime. She told Mama we would wet the bed. We were all very thirsty, but we figured out that if we coughed long enough, Mama would come in and give us a spoonful of brown vinegar. She thought it was good for the cough. We children would all start coughing and coughing until she came in. The vinegar was bitter, but it at least helped wet our parched mouths. Seeing Mama was the real medicine.

One night, the coughing started. All of us joined in, but the door never opened. We coughed and coughed, but no one came. Eventually, we fell asleep without a visit from Mama.

The next day, I listened for her but heard nothing. It was not until the day after that I realized my mother was not in the house. I have no idea where she went, and Aunt Tessie never told us, but Mama was gone. Brenda and Susie had both left, too, and I never saw or heard from either while we lived with Tessie. I never asked where they went. Susie left one night and she never returned. Brenda told me later that Tessie threw her out of the house. Then Brenda moved out a few days after Susie. She found a job as a waitress and rented a tiny room in downtown Spartanburg. As time dragged on, things got far worse for those of us left in that house of horrors.

One of the first changes I noticed came the day after Mama left. Aunt Tessie had company over, and she moved our chairs into the dark hallway past the kitchen. A few days later more visitors came. This time she told us that "decent folk" didn't want to be near us. She told us we were devils because of who our father was, and she sent us to bed with no supper to make sure her friends did not have to bear the sight of us. It didn't make any sense to me that we could be devils if my mama was an angel, like she called her. But logic didn't seem to be one of Aunt Tessie's strong points.

As time passed, she grew more and more bizarre in her attitude and actions toward us. One Sunday evening our door creaked open. Aunt Tessie paraded a group of adults into our room. All were finely dressed and wearing hats and gloves, like they were on their way to church. They stood in the doorway, gawking at us.

"They are devious," Aunt Tessie said, patting her eyes with a handkerchief. "It is awful to have that devil's children in my Christian home."

They nodded their agreement, looking us up and down.

"I'm a churchgoing woman. I don't know what I did to deserve this burden," Tessie lied.

"You're a saint," one woman clucked.

"You deserve a medal," another soothed.

Aunt Tessie gravely nodded before leading her guests out of our room and leaving us alone for the night. I lay in bed and wondered, *Is that why I am still not allowed to go to school?*

It was about that time that Aunt Tessie decided to starve us. We never had much to eat there, but after Mama left, our allotted portions became even smaller. One evening, I smelled supper cooking. My mouth watered as I waited for Aunt Tessie to call us in to the table. Instead, she called in her children. I listened to the tinkle of their silver and the lilt of happy voices. Still, we were not summoned.

Eventually, Tessie's children appeared. When they saw us staring hungrily at them, they laughed. One rubbed her tummy.

"Mm–mm."

Giggling, they ran out. I could barely contain myself, I was so hungry. Finally, Aunt Tessie called out.

"Come on in here."

We rushed into the kitchen. I was the last to come through the doorway. As Nellie and Robbie took their seats, Tessie looked at me.

"Not you, Frances. You go out there and clean up my sewing. And fix that mess you all made in the bathroom this morning."

I froze, my stomach growling loudly.

"Get on with you," she snapped, staring at me with squinted eyes.

I rushed out to do as I was told. I finished up as quickly as I could and raced back to the kitchen. When I arrived, Nellie and Robbie had finished eating. The table was clean. Aunt Tessie smirked at me. It was truly a wicked sight.

"You should have finished your work faster. You missed your allotted time."

I believe that if Mama had been there, Tessie would not have dared starve me. The next morning, we sat down for breakfast. I was so hungry that I ate mine and licked the plate, without paying much attention to anyone else. Robbie was in one of his goofy moods. He started singing an Elvis Presley song that we'd heard coming from her young daughter's room.

"Won't you wear my ring around your neck?" he sang.

Had I not been so hungry, I might have hushed him. As it was, Aunt Tessie came in before I could say anything. She had a grim smile on her linear face.

"What were you singing, Robbie?" she asked.

Her tone was matter-of-fact, and little Robbie was so innocent he did not understand what was about to happen.

"*Wow* my wing wound *yoo* kneck," he said.

"Why don't you sing a little louder," she said.

Robbie, thinking he'd done something good, burst out even louder.

"Won't YOO WOW my wing, wound YOO neck?"

I did not see the coat hanger in her hand until she was bending it around Robbie's neck.

"Maybe this will remind you to keep silent with your devil's music," she said.

Robbie had to wear that wire around his neck all day. He never did know why. That was one of the last breakfasts we were served. We never got lunch, and after Mama left, supper became hit or miss until one day we got nothing. No food and no water; nothing for the entire day. It was like an experiment.

We sat in our chairs all the next day. Our stabbing hunger pains had been replaced by a dull ache. My lips cracked and my tongue felt twice the size it should. Each hour ticked by as slowly as molasses dripping from a spoon. When the sun set, we were sent to bed again; no water and no food.

The next day was the same until, in the afternoon, Aunt Tessie summoned us to the kitchen. She sat at the table as we stood with barely enough strength to stay upright. She looked us up and down. There was a strange glow behind her eyes.

"If you could have just one," she asked, "food or water, what would it be?"

"Water," we all said, our voices harsh.

Very slowly, she poured three cups. I stared so hard I thought she'd slap me, but she did not. Instead, she handed us each a cup and nodded. I drank like everything else in the world vanished. I gulped it down. It made me feel sick, but I could not stop.

I believe Aunt Tessie knew she had taken us dangerously close to complete dehydration. She let us drink as much as we wanted. I learned later in life that she was experimenting on us like lab rats. She wanted to know how long a person could go without food and water.

It was times like those that I wondered which had been worse, living with Tessie or with Daddy. My Daddy was far more violent, but Tessie watched everything we did. We could not flinch without her coming down on us, whereas Daddy spent hours paying us no attention at all while he was passed out or in a bar getting drunk. The only good that came of living with Tessie was that Mama never got hurt. I could suffer in silence for Mama, and I did.

Every night when the house was quiet, we prayed that Mama would come back and take us away from this misery. Kneeling together in the middle of the bed, the three of us prayed as Mama had taught us, with our hands folded together and our heads bowed.

"Dear Jesus, please bring our mama back and get us out of this house," we whispered. Then we said our nighttime prayer, "Now I lay me down to sleep."

I can still hear my little brother's soft voice whispering those words. He couldn't speak plainly yet, but his curly blond head bowed as he kept up with his sisters as best he could. Even though his speech was not clear, his little heart was filled with faith, and I was sure that God heard his prayers.

As suddenly as Mama disappeared, she returned to us. I was sitting in my chair one evening when I caught a glimpse of her walking down the hallway. Months before I would have jumped up and run to her, but Tessie had total control over us by then. Instead, I sat as still as usual, listening to a muffled voice rise and turn angry. Mama's footsteps approached once but stopped suddenly, and the voices grew louder still. Then it was bedtime. We did not try to cough, nor did she visit our room. Deep inside, despite the abuse Tessie had doled out, I hoped the cruelty would stop once Mama was home. It did not change.

Another few weeks passed and winter approached. The trees made stark shadows in the dark, long, freezing nights. One day, while we were sitting in our chairs, Tessie came into the living room.

"Come with me, children," she said. I wondered what cruel torture she had cooked up this time, a bit surprised that she'd even referred to us as children.

She led us into the family room and stood proudly, pointing to the giant Christmas tree she had displayed to the world through the picture window. It was painstakingly decorated with twinkling lights, ornaments, and tinsel. I could see the pride and pleasure in her face. She allowed us "monsters" to march around the tree, expecting us to compliment her hard work. Robbie enjoyed it, his little feet skipping as he walked. Nellie looked at it in awe and smiled sweetly at Tessie. She told Aunt Tessie how lovely her tree was and what a great job she had done on the decorations. Tessie glowed and waited for my praise. I refused to show any emotion. I acted as if the tree was not even present in the room. I stared at the beautiful lights reflecting off the perfectly arranged tinsel. It was a lovely sight, and a Christmas tree always gladdens a child's heart, but I had made my mind up. I would not love her or try to make her love me any longer. Instead, I made no comment and stared straight ahead. I refused to show any emotion. I knew it would hurt her, at least a little, and that was just fine with me.

My reaction infuriated Tessie. She shook with anger, and I didn't care. I would never let her hurt me again. I knew right then that there *was* a real monster in Tessie's house, and it sure wasn't me.

Aunt Tessie towered over me when I took my seat.

"If you had any vestige of goodness inside that wicked heart of yours, you would have found joy in seeing such a beautiful tree."

She turned her head and shouted for Mama to come into the room. Mama came quickly, and her eyes met mine. I think she could see what had happened to us while she was gone just in my face in that moment. I saw something inside her stir.

"That daughter of yours is consumed by the devil. There is nothing left of good inside her. She has to be punished until the evil inside her is gone. She has to be saved with fire, or she will take us down with her. There is nothing to love in that one, that's for sure."

Mama looked at me and then at Tessie. "You have a mighty nice tree, Tessie. I thank you for it."

That was it. Tessie seemed to want more. I am sure she wanted Mama to agree with her, but that is not what happened. Instead, Mama left the room. In my secret heart, I was amazed by the Christmas tree. It was the most beautiful sight I had ever seen. It may have been the only decorated tree I had ever seen at the time. We had never celebrated Christmas, and most of the time Brenda did not let us know when Christmas Day came around. I imagine that she didn't want us to feel sad or left out.

Later that night, I overheard the conversation between Mama and Aunt Tessie. Usually their words were not clear enough to understand, but I heard Mama say one thing loud and clear.

"Thank you for your kindness, Tessie, but we'll be moving out. I am looking for a place for us to stay."

Hope stirred in my heart when I heard those words. Mama had come back!

Chapter 11

First Day of School

My prayers were answered the morning a fat yellow cab pulled up out front of Aunt Tessie's house. Its horn sounded at the same time Mama called to us from the back room.

"Kids, ya'll come on back here and help me gather our things."

We bolted like lightning and found Mama in her room, stuffing a few dresses and blouses in cardboard boxes. We had never even seen her room before, nor had we been this close to Mama in months, but we did not hesitate. Instead, we jumped right into helping her. I couldn't get out of that cursed place soon enough.

I didn't see Tessie when Mama ushered us outside. We piled into the cab as the driver helped Mama place her things in the trunk. The cab drove off, and I never once looked back. I was happy to look forward, focusing on where we were going and what our new home might be like. Would it be an old school bus or a tent under a bridge? Either sounded great to me. As long as I could be with my mama, I was happy. When we pulled to a stop outside a big old house with a welcoming front porch, I was blown over with excitement.

"Mama, is this our house?" I asked. I couldn't believe it.

"Yes, this is all ours, and you can have your own room."

Robbie jumped up and down. He was out of the cab door before Mama.

"Robbie, wait for us!" she called out, laughing.

My brother was already halfway up the front steps of the porch. Mama hurriedly paid the driver, and Nellie and I helped lug her few boxes out of the trunk. Mama wore a huge smile and walked to catch up to him. She fished the key out of her pocket and took a deep breath.

"This is home," she whispered. "Nothing will ever hurt us again."

To me, our new house looked like a three-story Southern mansion. Robbie and I ran up and down the huge staircase, yelling out so we could hear our voices echo through the hall and stomping our feet up and down the wooden stairs. It was like exploring a museum! We ran through every room, our excitement growing. We discovered a small hidden door just under the stairs, about three feet tall and barely wide enough for us to squeeze through. After investigating that, we ran in and out of the vacant rooms, squealing with laughter.

Our mansion was actually a somewhat dilapidated antebellum home with paint made murky gray by years of accumulated dust. Dampness had overtaken the exterior, pushing itself between paint and rotting wood and leaving peeling scales here and there. Some windows were broken and others were cracked. Weeds threatened to swallow the entire place, particularly the oversized porch with its missing floorboards. To me, it was the most beautiful home anyone could dream of because we were all together.

One of the most delightful things about the house was that another answer to my prayers stood just eight blocks away. Mama enrolled Nellie and I in school the following Monday morning. My greatest dream was finally coming true; I was to attend school for the first time.

My first day of school was a moment in my life that can never be diminished. It was a great event in my life. I wanted to be good and learn everything the teacher could show me. We had clean clothes to wear, and Mama brushed the tangles out of my hair. I skipped to school with a smile on my face that wouldn't go away.

The school rose up in front of Nellie and me, the redbrick façade exactly as I had dreamed it would be. I sprinted up the stairs leading to the arched entrance as if it were the home of a long-lost grandmother. Mama had to rush to keep up with me. This was the day I had prayed for, and at last it was happening! I was inside a school building, going to school!

My feet danced as Mama spoke to the woman in the office. She wanted to know from what school we had transferred so they could request our past records. Mama talked to the principal, trying to convince him we had been to school in another state. There were no computers at that time, and records were sent by mail. It was not unusual to lose documents.

"It's the gosh-darnedest thing. With all the moving we done, I've misplaced her records."

She assured him that once she found the documents, she would bring them in. The principal accepted her story and gave Mama some papers to fill out. I could hardly stand the wait, but it was not long. I was quickly led to a third-grade class. The teacher was Mrs. Hayes. She stood up in front of the entire class and introduced me. I felt shy standing there with all of those new faces peering at me, but Mrs. Hayes found worth in my presence. This was a foreign concept to me, and one I ate up with relish. It felt wonderful to be a part of what I had only dreamed of until now.

Mrs. Hayes ushered me to a desk of my own. As the day went on, she showed real interest in me, and I soaked up everything she wanted to teach. When it was time for lunch, she made a point of sitting beside me.

"What is your favorite color, Frances?" she asked.

I felt uncomfortable with her questions at first. A part of me, the part created by my daddy and Aunt Tessie, thought it was a test. If I failed, I thought I would be spanked or told to sit in a chair alone, or worse, told to leave the school—a thought I could not bear. The teacher seemed to understand my hesitation because she changed the subject and told me about the school library.

"It has books you can borrow any time you want," she said.

"I can take them home with me?" I asked.

"Yes, you check them out and return them, and then you can check out more." Mama had taught each of us to read; it was a beloved pastime that we all enjoyed. Finding the library was one of the happiest moments I can remember.

I adored my new teacher and would do anything for her. Slowly, and with a gentle kindness, she helped me open up like a new flower and created a place of comfort and joy for me in her classroom.

As I flourished in the school, a new shadow threatened. At first, it was not out in the open, and I definitely did not understand it. What I did understand was that Mama started to have trouble caring for us. Sometimes she would forget to buy food. She would stay out late at night and not get up at all in the morning.

When the children at school started to point out that we did not smell very good, I realized she had stopped doing laundry. I showed up to school more and more dirty, my hygiene being left to my own doing. There was some name-calling, but it did not curb my excitement for school. I loved each and every day, and every day I learned something new.

Mrs. Hayes tried hard to help me with my appearance. Many times she tied the belt on the back of my dress or used safety pins to hold up the hem that had torn out and hung down to my ankles. She took the time to show me the correct way to button my dress when I came in half thrown together. Even though I didn't look like the others, she tried hard to show me I was the same as the clean children on the inside.

Mrs. Hayes quickly noticed my love of music. No one else had noticed it before. She encouraged me to sing. She had me sing a little song before class. I was embarrassed, but I did it for her. I think she was trying to build my confidence.

My reading and math progressed quickly. Socially, it was more difficult. It became clear that I was different than the other children. My shoes were three sizes too large, and I often wore the same dress for weeks at a time. I also had no undergarments or socks. Kids noticed these things and at times were very cruel.

One morning, I wanted badly to dress as the others did. I was embarrassed that I didn't have any underwear. Mama was sound asleep when I opened the door to her room. I purposely tried to make noise, but she did not stir. I worried for a time that she had died, she lay so still. I bent down low in front of her face to feel her breathing.

Finding no help from Mama, I decided to rummage through her dresser to see if I could find something that would fit me. I found a pair of her old baggy panties. But when I pulled them up, they fell right back to the floor. I tried again, this time cinching the elastic waistband and tying it into a loose knot around my small stomach. I used her hairbrush to try to remove some of the tangles from my long hair, but it hurt too much, so I let it be. At least I had some underwear.

Nellie called out from the front of the house.

"Come on, Frances. The others are passing us."

I heard the front door creak open and then slam shut again. I raced out of Mama's room, one hand holding up the panties through the thin fabric of my dress. As I passed, I tripped over the hem of my dress and fell to the floor. Mama's panties dropped to my ankles. I stood and pulled them up again, quickly tying another knot in the elastic waistband. I scooped up my books and burst through the door. Nellie was half a block ahead of me, walking with half a dozen of our classmates. I tried to catch up but I could not walk fast without losing Mama's underpants.

I gained a little ground as Nellie hollered at me.

"Hurry up, Frances! We'll be late."

I did my best, but every time I took a step, those underpants slid down just a little bit more. As they slipped past my tummy, I slowed to a snail's pace and held them up with my knees, waddling as fast as I could up the sidewalk.

That is when the knot I'd tied came undone. The panties slipped further down my legs with each step I took. When they bunched at my knees, I had to stop. Just then, Nellie and the other children turned around to see why I wasn't catching up to them. I tried to keep walking but those huge bloomers fell down around my ankles. I wanted the sidewalk to swallow me I was so embarrassed.

The children burst into laughter. Kids were jumping up and down, howling in the street at the sight. My cheeks burned, and tears rolled out of my eyes as I waddled into the shadows of the closest alleyway. Once there, I kicked the panties off and decided I was better off not wearing underwear at all than going through this humiliation. I left Mama's underwear on the concrete and followed behind the group of hysterical children.

Later that same day, I was sitting in Mrs. Hayes's classroom practicing my reading, when the woman from the school office came to the door. She spoke softly with Mrs. Hayes and pointed at me. I was called up to the front of the class and told that I had to see the principal. I thought I was in trouble. Maybe they knew I'd just left Mama's panties in that alley.

When I arrived at the office, I was prepared to explain myself. Nellie was sitting outside the office waiting for me. The door to the office opened and the principal stuck his head out.

"Girls, come in and take a seat, please," he said.

Nellie and I lowered our heads and did as he asked. Once settled, his questions began. They were in a nice tone and worded carefully, but I was very nervous.

"Where do you two live?"

"Who lives there with you?"

"Where is your father?"

"Where does your mother work?"

By the end of our meeting, I felt tired. The principal, for his part, was very nice to us, but I sensed danger in his probing questions. I realized that the meeting didn't have anything to do with the panties. We were sent back to class, and by the end of the day I had forgotten about the whole thing.

Regardless of some of the trying moments, I absolutely adored school. There were moments when the taunts of the other children hurt, but there were hours of time I spent absorbing everything Mrs. Hayes had to teach me. When the children called me "teacher's pet," I didn't even know it was an insult. I thought that they were telling me how much Mrs. Hayes liked me. I had never been someone's favorite, but even with my filthy clothes and wild, straggly hair, this teacher found something in me to love.

Class reading time was my favorite. We arranged our seats in a circle, and Mrs. Hayes read the first line of a new story. Each child took a turn reading the next line until everyone had read a sentence. My favorite stories were the ones with humor. If I found a story extremely funny, I would feel the laughter rising up through my bones. My mouth started to curl up at the sides, and the hilarity filled me inside until I could contain it no longer and it spilled out in peals of hysterical laughter. I laughed so hard that sometimes I fell out of my chair. At times, when it was my turn, I would have to stop reading my line and think of something very serious, just to find the composure to continue. Mrs. Hayes must have enjoyed my delight because she always treated me with patience. She made a lasting impression on me that I carry to this day.

At night, when Mama had company, I entertained Robbie by reading the books I borrowed from the school library. We sat under the stairs by the small door so we would go unnoticed. Robbie loved the stories as much as I did and would sit still the entire time.

"What is that wud?" he asked, pointing to the book.

I followed along with my finger as I read very slowly, allowing him to see what each word was. He was entranced, cuddling close to me and putting his head on my shoulder.

As the story unfolded, it seemed to come alive around us. Robbie and I entered the world of *The Princess and the Frog.* I was the Princess. We were so engrossed that I did not notice the man until he tapped me on the shoulder.

"Hey kid, why don't you go with your sister and get some ice cream?"

I had never seen this man before. Mama had many male friends over, and I tried to stay out of their reach. This one wore blue coveralls and smelled of automobile oil. He reached out a hand with fingernails stained black. I could hear the tinkle of spare change. Tentatively, I reached out my hand, and he dropped the coins onto my palm.

I wanted ice cream, but it was already getting dark outside. Without making eye contact with the man, I already knew that I could not call out to Mama and ask her to come along. That was not the point. The man wanted us out of the house.

I called to Nellie, who spent most of her time alone on the second floor. She came down, and the three of us walked into downtown Spartanburg, South Carolina. This was not the first time we'd been sent out of the house. We found the ice cream shop right away. It was not busy, so we got our cones in no time at all. I knew we had to find something to do to occupy more time, so we started to wander the streets. It is amazing that the police did not pick us up for runaways, especially considering the dirty torn-up rags we wore for clothing.

From down the block, I heard voices floating around the corner. Normally, I would avoid people, especially when we were alone at dusk, but the sound was like a strange beacon. It drew me toward it until I rounded onto the next street. That is when I saw the church.

The building was enormous and sat on a wide-open lot behind a paved parking lot. A spotlight illuminated the white steeple, and other lights blazed under the overhang as the crowd spilled out between the two white support columns.

I stood as still as a tree as I watched the people and stared at the church. Robbie tugged at my arm, wanting to keep walking, but I didn't want to move. Nellie stood watching beside me. By the time we got home, the strange man was gone.

In the days following that night, I returned to that spot by the church. Each time, I got closer and closer until I finally went inside. The sight took my breath away. The building was huge but warm, with tall stained-glass windows and red-cushioned pews that were soft and clean. A balcony hung over the aisle, and I could see the pipes of an organ rising from the shadows above.

From that day on, I went to church every Sunday. I brought Robbie with me, and I worked real hard to clean us up before leaving the house. I loved being surrounded by the pretty dressed-up ladies and the men in suits. Wearing the cleanest dirty dress I owned, I guided Robbie down the aisle, and we slipped into the end of a pew. I could not wait for the time when the choir director asked us to pick up our hymnbooks and sing. I stood straight and tall between all the adults, holding my hymnbook open. When the music started, I sang my heart out and soared above the world.

At first, I sang line after line, like reading a book. I quickly realized that I was not singing the same words as everyone else. I was confused and wondered why everyone else was singing the wrong song. Then the Lord sent a kind woman standing beside me to show me how to sing the right way from a hymnbook.

"You read each top line first, until we get to the second verse."

She patiently showed me the way. Soon, I was singing along in perfect unison with everyone else, with a huge smile on my face.

The adults were kind to me, and I listened to everything the preacher had to say. Even though I was too young to understand it all, I bowed my head for the prayer and sat quietly through each service. Robbie squirmed and wiggled and wanted to play, but he stayed in his seat. My faith grew during each service, and I wanted to know more.

I loved the feeling of the church—how clean it was and the wonderful words of the preacher. Singing, however, was what kept me coming back Sunday after Sunday. Many times I went alone. I walked those blocks in every kind of weather. Once I picked up the songbook and sang, happiness flooded my soul. The words floated out, echoing off the floors and walls and resonating in my heart. It was alive, and I felt it deep inside me. Singing became an expression of everything I had ever felt in my soul but could not express.

Unfortunately, our condition at home did not improve. Even I began to understand what was wrong with Mama. She was drinking. As time passed, new signs of her illness appeared. Men kept on calling at the house late at night, and she woke up hungover and sick most mornings. We ran out of food some days, and Nellie and I never did have a lunch to bring to school or money to spend. Instead, we would go hide behind the janitors building while the other children ate lunch in the cafeteria.

One day, Nellie had a brilliant idea. As we crouched behind the squat shed filled with mops and brooms, she turned to me.

"Why don't we just start recess a little early?"

My eyes brightened and she laughed. When she ran out to the

back of the school, I followed close behind. We found the swings and the slides empty of children. It was our own private playtime, and for a while I forgot how hungry I was.

It was great! We had our choice of swings or slide. I had never had such freedom before. I found the perfect tree in the far corner of the playground and pulled myself up, branch by branch, as if reaching for the heavens. My dress caught and my hem tore, but I paid it no mind. When I climbed, I could fly. When I reached as I high as I could go, I looked down. I felt alive and free up in the top of that tree and was sure I could fly like the birds as they soared through the air.

As I sat on a branch near the top, my stomach growled. I hovered there, in between two worlds. I did not think ahead to what the next day might bring, nor was I thinking back to what had happened with Daddy or Aunt Tessie. I was just there, enjoying the trees.

From down the block, I heard the sound of my brother's laughter. It carried on the wind like a phantom. I moved a branch away from in front of my face and searched in that direction. The joyous sound came closer.

"Robbie?" I called out.

From where she sat on the swings, Nellie called back. "What are you yelling about?"

Before I could answer, Mama appeared. Somehow she knew we were on that playground. She stood outside the fence and didn't try to come in. She held a large brown paper bag from the grocery store in one arm. Robbie was with her, holding her hand.

Even from atop the tree, I could see the melted chocolate on his cheeks and chin. A half-eaten candy bar dangled from his other hand. He was laughing and dancing about, the sugar doing wonders for his already active constitution.

"Frances! Nellie!" Mama called out.

I scurried down the tree like a squirrel, almost beating Nellie over to where Mama leaned on the fence. She was smiling cheerfully.

"I got you some lunch," she said.

She opened the brown grocery bag and showed us its contents. It was filled almost to the top with huge bunches of bananas and all sorts of candy bars. I giggled at Robbie, who was smiling from ear to ear. He took a huge bite of that chocolate as Mama handed the bag over the fence to Nellie.

"Where did you get the candy and bananas?"

I was surprised that she was awake this time of day.

"I wanted you to have some lunch, honey. I stopped at the store up the street."

I was beyond happy. The fact Mama had taken the time to walk all the way to the store, buy lunch, and bring it to us meant everything to me. Regardless of what it was she brought us, she had brought us lunch. Mama left us on the playground. I watched her walk down the sidewalk, Robbie in tow. His little feet skipped beside her.

"Bye, Mama," I called, waving.

She turned and blew me a kiss. The recess bell rang and children poured out onto the school grounds. They gathered around me and Nellie. Instantly, Mama's lunch made us popular. All the children wanted to be our friends that day. There was plenty to share, and Nellie opened the large sack to everyone.

The bananas and chocolate were the perfect lunch from a third grader's perspective. Most parents, though, would not imagine that as a healthy meal for growing children. None of that mattered to me. That moment stuck with me forever. It was the confirmation of what I knew all along: no matter what had happened to us, Mama loved me! And I would carry that truth through the doubt and darkest hours of my life and hold it in triumph when I found the light. My mama loved me!

Chapter 12

The Orphanage

I was sitting in the living room reading a book when I glanced up.

"What is that?" I asked, looking out the window.

The sun had set, but the sky glowed soft gray. Laying the book down, I went to the window to get a better look. My heart beat faster when I saw it again—tiny white specks falling from the sky. One touched the glass and disappeared, leaving behind its small wet fingerprint.

"That's snow," Mama said from behind me.

With that word, Nellie and Robbie came running. They crowded around me to stare out the little window. The house was drafty, but their warmth filled me as I stood amazed by the sight. We could hardly contain ourselves.

"I'm gonna make a snowman!"

"I want to go sledding!"

Only one thing dimmed my excitement. I turned back and looked into Mama's face.

"Does this mean we won't have school tomorrow?"

Mama smiled at us. Her eyes looked clear and beautiful. I hugged her around the waist and she patted my head.

"We don't know if it will be snowing in the morning," she said. "Let's all get to bed and you'll find out when you get up."

"Aww," Nellie and Robbie moaned.

Mama ushered us to our shared bedroom. Although the house was large and had many rooms, we slept together for warmth. She sat down on the edge of the bed while we piled in and snuggled under the thin blanket.

"Anyone want to hear a bedtime story?" she asked.

All three of us yelled out in unison.

"Yeah!"

"I want 'Thwee Pigs,'" Robbie shouted.

"No," Nellie said. "Mama, tell us 'Little Match Girl.'"

As she told us the story, I kept watching the window. More and more flakes touched the glass and melted away.

After the story, Mama spread a moth-eaten quilt over our blanket.

"Go to sleep now," she whispered. "I'll see you in the morning."

She leaned over the bed and kissed each of us on the cheek. I fell asleep wondering if we would have snow on the ground when we awoke.

The next morning I thought we were having an earthquake! I woke up to the bed shaking. When I opened my eyes, though, I saw Robbie jumping up and down on the mattress.

"It's snow! It's snow!" he yelled at the top of his lungs.

I sat up in bed, rubbing my eyes. From the bedroom window I could see a blanket of pure white covering everything in sight. It was still falling in large, soft flakes. It was probably about six inches, but to me it was the most amazing blizzard in the history of the planet. When Nellie saw it, she nearly did a backflip. Robbie, on the other hand, just ran out the door with no shoes on.

Mama was there to shoo him back inside. It was the earliest I'd seen Mama up and about in a long time. When I looked up at her pretty face, her eyes still looked clear. At the same time, there seemed to be a sadness hanging over her.

"Are you okay, Mama?"

"Of course I'm all right, worrywart," she laughed it off.

I was still suspicious. I didn't have a word for what I felt, but I thought about the meetings we'd had with the principal.

"Come on," Mama said, her voice sounding excited now. "Snow like this is as rare as hounds' teeth."

We danced around the windows, pressing our noses to the glass as Mama bustled about the house. We put on our shoes and Mama returned with what seemed half of the clothes we owned. She bundled us up as best she could and then handed us each a pair of socks. Nellie and I just looked at them. Robbie tried to pull them on over his shoes.

"For your hands." Mama laughed.

We used those socks for mittens and ran on out into the snow. The world was totally silent. Snow was so rare in South Carolina that nobody got out to drive unless they absolutely had to. It was early in the morning, and we seemed to be the only ones stirring. All the dirt and debris around the house was covered in white. The front yard was a winter wonderland. Even Nellie's and Robbie's laughter sounded different, clear, like a melody. We had one little part of the world all to ourselves.

We played for hours. I had so much fun I forgot all about school being canceled. From time to time, I'd take a break from throwing snowballs at Robbie or making snow angels and take a look at the window by the front door. There I saw Mama watching us, a smile on her face. It warmed me, even as chunks of ice and snow snuck down my neck and melted against the skin of my back. I wore canvas tennis shoes, and they quickly soaked through with melting snow. My feet were numb, but I continued to roll a ball of snow until we had a giant, round lump to start our first snowman.

When we couldn't take the cold any longer, the three of us trudged inside. Mama was there waiting for us. She guided us into the kitchen; we were all talking at once, telling her everything we'd done in the snow. We dripped on the linoleum as she turned on the gas oven and opened its door. She sat us down in front of the heat and put our feet up on a chair, stripping our wet socks off and hanging them on the back of another chair. The warmth felt wonderful to my freezing toes.

"You shoulda seen it," Nellie said. "We slid all the way down the hill out front. Robbie almost rolled right out onto the street."

Nellie kept on chattering. Mama, listening to every word, knelt down and rubbed our bare feet between both her hands, trying to get the blood flowing. I kept my mouth shut tight. I was afraid that if I said anything, if I moved even a muscle of my body, the magic would break and the moment would be lost.

That next Monday, reality struck. The principal called Nellie and me into the office again. It was the third time, and I knew it was a far bigger issue than my leaving Mama's bloomers in the alley. The questions were getting deeper and closer to the mark.

"What did you have for dinner?"

"How often do you bring a lunch to school?"

"Are you ever left alone in the house?"

"Does your mother have visitors often?"

Nellie and I did not lie to the principal, nor did we offer any more in our answers than we had to. Again we went back to class, but we did not soon forget that meeting. When I got home that afternoon, I knew something was very wrong. The house was quiet, and Mama was sitting in a chair waiting for us. I could tell she was sober, but this time it was not a happy feeling. I suddenly understood why the house was silent.

Looking around the room, I asked, "Where's Robbie?"

"Social Services took him away. They are gonna find him a nice home to live in."

I didn't understand. *Who took my brother?* "What is Social Services? Why did they take Robbie?"

Mama reached her arms out toward Nellie and me.

"He's going to be happier now. We have to leave him alone."

"They can't do that!" I shouted.

"Calm down and sit, Frances. You, too, Nellie. I have something to tell you."

Nellie and I looked at each other. Neither of us understood. I felt as though some alien had taken over Mama's body and was making her say these things. She couldn't be sitting calmly and talking while my little brother had been kidnapped!

Mama went on to explain what had happened. The school board had a meeting and contacted Social Services. They told Mama that she had to find safer arrangements for the two of us as well. What I could not totally understand, and what was left unsaid, was that Social Services had deemed Mama unfit to care for us any longer.

"What about us?" Nellie asked.

Mama sounded excited when she answered. "I found a great place for you two. It's in Greenwood, not too far from here. It is called Connie Maxwell Children's Home. It's a beautiful place, and they'll take good care of you. They have lots of toys for you to play with, and hundreds of other kids live there. You'll both have bedrooms all your own. And Frances, guess what! There is a school right there at the home."

I barely heard the words she said. Instead, I heard that we were to be shipped off and abandoned. I could not understand why she sounded so cheerful. I hid my feelings and forced a smile on my face. I didn't want Mama to be sad or know how upset I was. Nellie questioned her.

"Will I have a doll of my own?" I looked at Nellie, not believing what she was saying. *Who wants a doll? Let's try and get Robbie back home!*

Mama went on building up a beautiful story about toys, food, and children. Nellie listened with wide-eyed interest. I just wanted to be alone. Robbie was my best friend. I went up to the third floor of the old house. We never used the top floor because it was so hard to heat the whole house, and some of the windows were broken, but I knew no one would look for me up there. I sat for a long time with an open book in my lap, staring thin-lipped at a page that would normally make me laugh. I couldn't find any joy at that moment.

The next day started what felt like a month of doctor's appointments. We had shots and examinations. We were pricked, prodded, and poked. When I got tired of it, I asked Mama why we had to go through all this.

"They just want to be sure you are healthy. You need your shots before you live with all those nice children."

It was not just physical health they were testing, though. Toward the end of the week, Mama made an announcement.

"We have to visit the psychiatrist today."

What? "I don't want to talk to a kyatrist," I said.

Mama shrugged. "Well, you can't get in the Children's Home until you do."

"No!" I said, folding my arms across my boney chest. "I'm not goin'!"

My response took her by surprise. I had acted so stoically since she let us know we would be leaving.

"Frances, don't you act up now. It isn't gonna hurt or nothing."

"I'm *not GOIN'*."

I rarely disobeyed Mama, but this was the line. I wasn't worried about pain. At that time in my life, I knew I was very different from the other children. I didn't look like them and I didn't act the same. I didn't know if I was crazy or not, but I didn't want to find out. I had also heard that psychiatrists put crazy people in cages like animals. I had visions of being stuck in a Frankensteinlike movie with a wild-eyed, mad doctor coming at me, cackling and wringing his hands.

"Mama, what if he says I'm crazy?"

She laughed. "Frances, you're not crazy."

"What if I am, though, and you just don't know it?"

Mama looked down at me. "Stop worrying. I would know."

"But suppose that he says I *am* crazy," I persisted. "What if they want to take me away?"

"Frances, you're not any crazier than I am."

That didn't help me a whole lot.

"Will you promise that I won't get locked away if he decides I'm a little nuts?"

"I promise no one is going to lock you away. He's just gonna ask you a few questions. Then you'll be able to go to that wonderful home."

After getting Mama to promise me a few more times that I would not be locked away, I finally let her take me to the appointment. I crept into the office, afraid to look up.

"Hello Frances," a man said.

I peeked through my blond, stringy bangs to find a normal-looking man sitting in a leather chair. He did not have a white lab coat or wild hair standing up straight. Nor was he laughing like an evil villain. It was the most painless appointment of my life to that date.

Mama didn't have any visitors over that week, and she didn't go out at night. I knew that life was changing. Robbie was already gone. Nellie and I would be next. But Mama spent her days telling us how happy we would be.

"You should see it," Mama said. "Oaks bigger around than you can reach. And big houses—mansions. The people are so kind there. You'll never want for anything."

The day finally came. That morning, Mama led us around the house. I gathered my meager belongings into a small sack, and Nellie did the same. Neither of us spoke to each other, but Mama filled our silence with more stories.

"The Connie Maxwell home is so beautiful. You will love it there."

I cringed inside as she spoke. It sounded to me as though she wanted us to be happy, so I tried to put on a smiling face to spare her feelings. Secretly, I started to believe that Connie Maxwell was an evil place, full of danger. My biggest worry was that I would never see my mother again.

As Mama walked us out the front door, all I could think about was missing her. I noticed a car parked on the street. Mama led us to it and opened the back door. Nellie and I climbed inside, clutching our belongings. The door shut, and I watched Mama get in the front seat. That is when I first saw the driver. It was Aunt Tessie. Suddenly, I was starving for food. I felt like I hadn't eaten for days! I was absolutely famished.

I was very surprised and disappointed to see Tessie. I had hoped that we could spend this time alone with Mama. The car pulled away from the curb, and Tessie never spoke a word to either of us. I was still very afraid of Aunt Tessie, so I didn't speak for the entire ride to the children's home. After a few minutes on the road, Tessie reached back from the front seat, a loaf of bread in her hand. Nellie, more composed than I was, took it. A full jar of mayonnaise followed, along with a butter knife. Aunt Tessie didn't protest when we opened the jar and made mayonnaise sandwiches. I nearly swallowed mine whole, expecting her to whirl around and take it from me. She never did, and Nellie ate until she was full while Mama and Aunt Tessie talked in the front seat.

When Nellie was finished, I continued to eat. I ate all the bread that was left. When that was gone, I dipped the knife in the jar and ate the mayonnaise by itself. An hour or so later, when we arrived at Connie Maxwell Children's Home, I was still starving for food.

"We're here," Mama said.

I had been leaning my head against the window. When I raised up and looked out, what I saw amazed me. Just as Mama had said, the street was lined with hundred-year-old oak trees. Mansion-type houses sat scattered across acres of well manicured green lawns. The car rolled slowly by a concrete statue of three children running and playing with a huge cross shadowing them. We passed several two-story brick buildings with giant white columns; they looked like the mansions Mama had promised us.

The car came to a stop outside the largest of the buildings. Mama unloaded us, and I was relieved to see that Aunt Tessie stayed behind. We walked up to the front door, and Mama opened it. I clutched her hand, afraid to walk inside. Nellie just stepped right in as if she was happy to be there.

Mama took us into a large, spotless office with a huge window that opened up to the grounds. A woman with dark hair sat behind an oversized desk. She smiled at us and spoke in a friendly voice.

"Can I help you?"

Mama introduced us. Nellie said hi while I hid behind Mama's dress. Another person arrived and led us on a tour of the grounds. Under different circumstances, it would have seemed an amazing place. It had its own church, post office, grocery store, swimming pool, school, and even a cemetery. Mama asked a lot of questions and prompted me often, but I hung back. I knew what was coming, and she had to push or pull me along.

We arrived at one of the two-story buildings, and our guide announced that this would be our new home. I was slow to grasp what she meant until Mama took a step away from me. I reached out for her, but she pushed me back. Mama knelt down on the front porch and looked me in the eye.

"Frances, this is your home now. They will take better care of you than I can. You'll have a great life here. The one you shoulda had before."

"No," I moaned. "I don't want to stay here! I'll be good and I won't eat much. I promise I'll be good! Mommy, don't leave me here!"

Mama looked away and wiped at her eyes. "I want you to be strong for me and take care of Nellie."

"I don't want to be strong. I wanna go home!"

"You can't come with me this time," Mama said. "I love you. I'll be by to visit all the time. You'll see. I promise you will love it here."

I knew it was going to happen. No amount of crying would change things. I forced myself to stand up straight and wiped my eyes with the hem of my dress.

"Mama, will you *promise*, cross your heart and hope to die, that you'll come back?"

Mama made a cross mark on her chest and put her index finger to her lips and then to mine.

"Frances," a new voice said from behind me.

I turned away from Mama to see who it was. There was something about the voice that touched me. It was gentle but firm, lilting with a Southern drawl.

"I'm Mrs. McDonald," the woman said. "I'm your house mother."

She had soft white hair, matching her voice. It fell to her neckline and was combed back from her face. Curls reached around her perfect cheeks, and there was not a single wrinkle, even though I would later learn that she was already seventy-two years old. She was thin and petite, with merry blue eyes that seemed even larger through her round rimless glasses.

"Welcome to Eason House. Come inside with me, Frances, I will show you your new room."

As I looked from Mrs. McDonald to Mama, I forced myself to stay calm and not make a scene. I silently said a prayer that Mama would remember her promise and one day come back to get us. Nellie waved good-bye and walked into the house and up the stairs ahead of me without any urging. I tried to copy her attitude on the outside, but inside I was screaming, *Mama, come back!* I let Mrs. McDonald take my small hand in hers. We stood together on the porch and watched quietly until Mama disappeared out of sight.

I repeated Mama's words in my head, *Be strong; be strong.*

"Come with me, Frances," Mrs. McDonald softly urged.

The entry was brightly lit by a chandelier hanging from the high ceiling. A wooden staircase wound up to the second floor, its polished banister reflecting the sparkling lights above. Through the foyer, I caught sight of the visitors' room with its comfortable seating and baby grand piano standing by a bay window.

I followed Mrs. McDonald up the stairs. She pointed to a bathroom on the left.

"This is the bathroom for your room."

It was clean and large with two stand-alone porcelain sinks. Black and white tiles covered the floor. I followed Mrs. McDonald down to the end of the hall, where she stopped at an open door.

"And this is your room, Frances."

I walked through the door, settling into the only real home I would ever know during my childhood. I had no idea I would enjoy it for less than a year.

Chapter 13

A Safe Harbor in the Storm

I slept fitfully that first night at Connie Maxwell. Lying in my twin bed with its own wooden headboard, I listened to the other four girls in the room breathing. It was dark, but the bright December moon caused the sheer white curtains at the end of the room to glow. Moonlight danced on the chest of drawers across from my bed, where Mrs. McDonald had told me to put my clothes and other belongings. It was to be all my own, but I didn't have enough at that time to fill one drawer. Even in the dark, it seemed a warm, cozy, safe place, but I had never felt so alone. I missed Mama and my little brother so bad that I ached inside. I put my face down into the pillow and cried myself to sleep.

The sun slowly rose, and the sky outside our window slid from black to purple to pink. The morning light poured into the room. The other girls stirred, and I tried to remember their names as they each woke to the new day. For them, it was just like the day before. For me, it was the first of a whole new life, one that frightened me.

The girl beside me got up and immediately began to make her

bed. I had never before slept in a bed with a new mattress, nor had there been any bedding to remake. I watched her with a mix of interest and amusement, wondering why someone would put so much effort into something they would just mess up again the next night.

The bustle in the room grew, and I did not want to be the last to rise, so I got up. The girl beside me smiled and said good morning. I did the same. She watched me for a moment. When I just stood there, she spoke.

"Mrs. McDonald wants us to make our beds before breakfast."

"Breakfast?"

The girl tilted her head. She looked bemused. I just stood there staring at her.

"You should make your bed," she said.

"Okay."

I had no idea what to do. The other girls went about it as if they'd done it a million mornings before. I tried do what they did, but I struggled with the two flat sheets and the bedspread. Before I knew it, everyone was finished. The door to our room opened and Mrs. McDonald walked in. The girls lined up in front of her, and I followed.

"Go downstairs, girls. Breakfast will be ready soon," she said. "Frances, would you please stay with me for a few minutes?" I stopped at the door. She put her arm around my shoulder, drawing me into the room.

"We make our beds each morning before breakfast," Mrs. McDonald said.

Her words were kind, but I was embarrassed. "I did already."

"I'll show you this morning."

Mrs. McDonald had me watch as she made my bed. She did it quickly but explained each step.

"Tomorrow, you'll be able to do it better," she said. "Now let's go have our breakfast." She smiled at me.

"Yes, ma'am."

She led me down the stairs to the dining room. Even before we entered, the smell reached me and I quickened my step. When I walked in, I saw all the girls sitting at a long table. Bowls of scrambled eggs, fluffy golden biscuits, gravy, sausage, fruit, syrup, butter, and large pitchers of milk covered the space between them. There was Nellie, right in the middle, beside the girl who would eventually become her best friend. No one was eating, and everyone was watching me walk in. Nellie gave me a look that said, *hurry up*.

I sat down, and Mrs. McDonald took the seat at the end of the table. Her head bowed, as did everyone else's. It took me a second, but I followed their lead.

"Lord, thank you for our food. We ask you to bless this meal and all who partake of it," Mrs. McDonald prayed. "And thank you, Lord, for bringing Nellie and Frances into our family."

Mrs. McDonald continued her prayer, thanking God for every girl at our table. I listened and felt a warmness filling me up from the inside. I felt welcome, as though they wanted me with them.

After the prayer, Mrs. McDonald started passing the food to her left. I watched as the girls sitting closer to her took their portions and passed the bowls along. I had never eaten at a table like this, among people who knew proper etiquette. I felt confused and a little ashamed. I didn't want to make a mistake. When the first bowl reached me, I stammered.

"Can I have some gravy?"

Some of the younger girls giggled. Mrs. McDonald immediately called their names.

"You can have as much as you like, dear. Until you are full."

She probably should have used a different choice of words for me. She had no idea that I never felt full, not since I almost starved at Aunt Tessie's. It was a condition that was new to me at the time, but it followed me through more than half of my life. I learned, when I was much older, that the emptiness inside of me was not a hunger for nourishment. There was not enough food on the planet to fill the gap that losing my mama had left inside. But that's a whole other book.

On that morning, when the bowls full of hot, rich food were offered, I couldn't control myself. I could see I had taken twice as much as the others, but everything looked better than the bowl that came before it. When the last bowl reached me, my plate looked like I was bringing dinner home for a family of four. Some of the girls stared in disbelief, but Mrs. McDonald did not seem to notice. I barely noticed either. Instead, I dug in with relish, savoring every bite. The girls may have found it strange, but I paid them no mind. It was the first time in my life that food had been unlimited.

I ate my way through three biscuits drowned in syrup and cleaned my plate. I forced myself not to lick it clean. I had already figured out that licking one's plate clean was not considered proper. Most of the other new rules didn't make any sense to me. As long as I was fed, though, I was willing to try and learn.

"May I be excused?" one girl asked.

Mrs. McDonald nodded. I continued to eat as I watched her rise from the table. She carried her plate into the kitchen. Soon other girls were following her out. I watched in disbelief, my mouth full.

"We got more to eat," I said with a mouthful. "We better eat it while it's here."

No one seemed as concerned about that as I was. So I tried to eat enough for all of us. Finally, I realized I was the only child at the table. I believe that had been the case for some time, judging by the way Mrs. McDonald was fidgeting. I took one final bite of the big biscuit that was left on my plate and looked at her.

"May I be excused?"

I said it as courteously as I could, trying to emulate the other girls. Mrs. McDonald smiled at me.

"Carry your plate into the kitchen and put it in the sink. Then come back in and I'll give you your chores for the week."

I looked around to make sure no one was watching me. Then I stuffed the rest of my biscuit in my dress pocket. I thought I might put it under my pillow for later.

After breakfast, Mrs. McDonald approached me with a short list.

"Frances, I've explained to Nellie already that each girl is assigned a chore for the week. This week, I would like you to sweep up the dining room after meals. Help me carry the serving bowls into the kitchen and I will show you how."

We went to the pantry in the kitchen, and she showed me where the broom and dustpan were stored and how she wanted the work done. She expected the table to be wiped clean, all the crumbs brushed into the dustpan, the floor swept, and the chairs pulled away from the tables. She left me to my work.

I had never swept a floor the right way before and didn't understand the significance of the chore. The sound of the girls outside playing was intoxicating. I rushed along with the broom, wanting more than anything to get outside and join in the fun. When I had the floor done, I looked at the chairs. My attention span had reached its limit, so I swept the refuse under the table. Running to return the broom and dustpan, I was outside in no time at all.

I met many of the girls I would be living with. They were open and friendly, and it took no time at all for us to feel like sisters. I was so happy jumping into the games of hopscotch and jump rope that I barely noticed Mrs. McDonald until she was right next to me.

"Frances, can you come with me please?"

"Yes, ma'am."

I followed her inside and back toward the dining room. I knew she'd found the mess under the table. I expected to be yelled at. I even feared a spanking, but that is not what happened.

"Frances," she said, her voice as kindly as ever, "Please go and get the broom and dustpan."

I did as she asked and was amazed as she patiently showed me how I should perform the task again. This time, she stood with me as I completed the work.

"A job is not worth doing if it is not well done," she said. She continued on by reciting a poem while I swept the floor again.

> *"Once a task has first begun,*
> *never leave it till it's done.*
> *Be the labor great or small.*
> *Do it well or not at all."*

Although I wanted more than anything to get outside, I heard those words, and they stuck with me forever.

The next day I was sent to the dentist. This may sound like a small thing, but I was nearing ten, and it was the first time I'd ever had my teeth looked at. I was frightened when the hygienist walked me back. I had never seen such a place. Everything was so clean and sparkling. I thought it was going to be awful, but he made me feel at ease as he scraped and prodded my teeth. I had my first fillings and left with my mouth feeling wonderful and strange.

Back at Eason House, Mrs. McDonald took the time to teach me how to brush my teeth. At the same time, she showed me how to take care of my hair. I was given my own hairbrush, and I brushed my hair every morning. If I hurt myself playing outside, she cleaned the scrape and gave me a Band-Aid. It was my first of those too.

As the days passed, I became friendlier with my new sisters. Instead of staring at me, they'd ask me about my peculiarities.

"Why does it take you so long to eat?"

Between mouthfuls, I'd explain. "You should eat more too. You might not have any food tomorrow."

I could tell they didn't understand, but I could not stop myself. I ate and ate until I felt near bursting. Mrs. McDonald showed nothing but patience. At the same time, she was teaching me what was normal for the other children.

"You don't want to be late for school, Frances," she said as I continued eating long past the time everyone else left.

After a while, her urgings worked, and I left a biscuit uneaten. It was hard, but I learned to trust that the food would be there at the next meal. I left the table behind and rushed to meet up with my dorm sisters. We walked together down the long sidewalk leading to school. On the way, we laughed, talked, and exchanged secrets. I barely noticed the fact that I wore new shoes and clean clothes anymore. My hair was washed and my teeth brushed. I was taken care of. I still missed my mother—we had only seen her once since she left us there—but I loved life at Connie Maxwell. I knew I was accepted.

I grew in the safe and loving arms of the Connie Maxwell Children's Home for about half a year. I loved school as I always did, and I also embraced every part of life at the home. Mrs. McDonald taught me with patience and care. I found a new family in my many sisters, and we were treated as equals.

Each morning my housemates and I walked to the school building a few blocks from Eason House, the home we lived in. We filed into the classroom along with both girls and boys our age. Everyone, including the teacher, stood up and we all held our hands over our hearts and faced the American flag. We recited the Pledge of Allegiance and then the Lord's Prayer. We were taught to pray before we ate lunch at school. I thrived during the short time I lived at this home. If I had not spent time at Connie Maxwell, I would never have learned the simple things in life that people take for granted, such as making a bed, sweeping a floor, or brushing my hair and teeth properly. I didn't realize it at the time, but my time spent with Mrs. McDonald would be my only opportunity to learn them. I certainly wouldn't have learned had I not been there.

The school on the grounds was in perfect order. Our teacher, who was kind with a colorful sense of humor, taught us from behind her large desk or at the huge chalkboard behind it. We sat in our little desks, and occasionally I would look out the window at the lightly swaying branches of the surrounding oaks.

As the weather got warmer, school let out and the swimming pool opened. We had structured visits there twice a week. The girls and boys of my age would go at the same time. The pool was large, surrounded by cement decking. There were two small buildings: one a changing room for the girls and the other for the boys. A play area sat in the grass beside the decking. One day I was sitting there with some girls from my house when a small boy came over to us. He handed me a note and a stubby, chewed-up pencil.

"This is from Mark."

Mark, I thought. I looked across the pool and saw him on the other side. He was tall and skinny with dark hair, and he sat in a group with his friends. He looked away, and his friends laughed. I unfolded the paper. The message inside was short and to the point: "I like you. Do you like me?" Under that were two boxes, one labeled yes and the other no. I checked the yes box and sent it back with the messenger.

From that day on, Mark and I sat at the pool together and talked about school and the other kids. He was my first little boyfriend. It was innocent puppy love. Sometimes his friends and mine would play chase. We'd scream, and the boys would have no idea what to do if they caught us. I imagine this is what childhood was supposed to be. For me, it was perfectly wonderful!

One morning in the spring, the teacher came into class and announced that it was a special day. A local ladies' group, called the Goldenrod Garden Club, had brought hundreds of flowers for a flower-arranging contest at the school. We were led out onto the grounds, and there I saw more fresh cut flowers than I ever thought existed. There were roses, lilies, tulips, and gardenias, along with gladiolus and Queen Anne's lace.

Beside the flowers, vases of all shapes and sizes were aligned on a long table. The teacher told me I was allowed to pick any vase I wanted and that I should try and make the prettiest arrangement I could. I did not have to be asked twice. I enjoyed anything artistic, so I relished the opportunity.

I found a quiet spot at the end of one of the long tables that were set up for us. I mixed colors and shapes to make the most vibrant arrangement I could imagine. The local newspaper was there, and the judges had ribbons for each first, second, third, and fourth place winner. When all the entries were laid out and judged, I never even considered that mine might win. I had never been in any sort of contest, and making that arrangement was just pure pleasure.

After looking over all of the entries, the judges announced the ones that they felt were the most artistic.

"Second place in the flower arrangement contest goes to . . . Frances Horton."

I couldn't believe it. All the Garden Club members and the other children applauded. I was called up to the platform. As I walked up, I felt a mixture of excitement and embarrassment. I was amazed that someone felt I deserved a ribbon. There was a photographer there who took my picture as I accepted my prize. I noticed later that Mark won an award for making the best birdhouse. I ended the day with a huge smile on my face, holding tight to my ribbon. It was a burning ray of sunshine in my life, and I wanted to hold on to it forever.

Unfortunately, that was not to be. It was summer and we had lots of time to play as school was out. We still had our chores to do, but that morning Nellie and I were assigned our favorite one. All the children loved taking a turn to walk to the community store and bring the groceries back to the house. It got us out in the fresh air where we could run and push the cart for several blocks.

Nellie and I pushed the cart to the community grocery store on the grounds—we called it the commissary—to pick up supplies. We set off together, arguing as children do over who got to push it. While it was Nellie's turn, I shoved her.

"Can't catch me," I yelled.

Laughing, I raced ahead. We reached the commissary and settled down somewhat. Together we wheeled the cart up to the long counter. Behind it, rows and rows of supplies were neatly organized. An older girl was in front of us, so we got in line behind her. Once her cart was full, she left. Nellie stepped forward and gave the man behind the counter our list.

Nellie and I argued quietly over the cart again as the man filled our order. It took no time at all to fill our cart with sugar, flour, lard, syrup, and other necessities. When he told us we were ready, we both pushed the cart out the door, laughing and bumping each other with our shoulders.

We did not get far. My attention was on the cart, making sure nothing spilled out, when we eased it onto the sidewalk. Suddenly, Nellie stopped. Confused, I looked up and saw a stout, dark-haired man with steel blue eyes barring our way.

At first, I did not know what was happening. I glanced up at the man and thought he was a stranger. A woman appeared beside him; I did not recognize her either. I did notice a car parked very close, right up against the curb. That was the first thing that lifted my suspicions. Then I saw Nellie's face.

Pure terror reflected from her eyes as she stared at the man. I knew then that something was not right, but I did not know what it was or how to fix it. I looked at the man again, and a glimmer of recognition crossed my mind. I knew him.

At the same instant, I was nearly yanked out of my shoes. At first, I thought the man had grabbed me, but as I stumbled past him, I realized Nellie was dragging me down the sidewalk. She broke into a full sprint and had my hand in an iron grip.

"What are you doing!?" I screamed.

Nellie could barely talk. Her face was rigid with fear. Her mouth cracked open but she only shouted one word.

"Run!"

Nellie kept running, dragging me behind her.

"What's wrong?" I shouted.

"That was *Gracie*!"

Nellie's voice was frantic, so I ran along with her. I had no idea who she meant or why we were running. All I knew was that she was terrified.

Nellie could be dramatic. I knew that, but there was something more real about that moment. I let her yank me along until we burst into the front door of Eason House.

I expected we'd go to Mrs. McDonald's room but was surprised when Nellie pulled me into the kitchen. She threw open the door of the pantry and pushed me inside. She followed and slammed the door shut. I watched as she scurried under the bottom shelf, pushing aside a bag of potatoes to make room. She waved at me to sit beside her and I did.

"What is going on?" I asked.

"Shh," she hissed. "Don't you know who that was?"

"No."

"You didn't recognize Gracie?"

I shook my head. "Who's Gracie?"

"Our aunt! Uncle Mose's wife!"

When Nellie said that, an icy feeling dripped into my stomach. That was the first time I had an idea of who that man was. I had no idea how I could have forgotten him. I must have blocked him deep into my mind, a nightmare never to visit again. Suddenly, I realized the nightmare had returned.

"Is it him?" I whispered.

Nellie held my face in her hands. She looked into my eyes and nodded.

"How did he find us here?" I whispered, my body starting to tremble.

Nellie didn't answer.

"Why did he come here?"

Nellie looked at the tiles on the floor. She said in a chillingly low voice, void of emotion, "Daddy's come to take us away."

Chapter 14

A Changed Man

My grown brother and I sat in the hospital waiting room and talked. Jimmy listened to every word of my story. Afterward, he gave me a hug. "I wish I could have been there for you. Well, you are here now, and I don't ever want to lose contact with you again." I cried when I had to leave him that day, having just found him, but somehow I already knew that we would be fast friends. A piece of my heart had returned, and I thanked God for that on the drive home with Wayne.

From that day on, Wayne and I visited Jimmy and his family almost every week. We would have dinner at each other's houses, and I would sing gospel songs with him and play the guitar. When his voice mixed with mine, I could see how much he looked like Mama and hear how much he sounded just like her. In those moments I felt as though she was back with us—back to being a part of my life.

I loved his wife and two teenage grandchildren with all my heart. Jimmy and Wayne got along very well and teased each other like brothers. Wayne loved Jimmy. One night, after dinner, Jimmy turned to Wayne.

"You know, you better watch out when you're passing by Kentucky Fried Chicken."

Wayne lifted an eyebrow. He knew a joke was coming, but he played right along.

"Why's that?"

"It's sheer, blind, lottery-winning luck that you can pass by a fried-chicken restaurant alive with those skinny chicken legs of yours."

Wayne laughed with everyone. I looked at Jimmy, seeing the physical similarities to Mama in his smile. He also had her humor. When the laughter faded, Jimmy reached into his pocket.

"I brought something to show you," he said.

He pulled out a legal-looking piece of paper and handed it to me. It was a notarized bill of sale showing that he had been sold to Daddy's brother for five dollars. I examined it and looked back up at my brother. He seemed so hurt by it. He tried to joke, but I could feel the pain behind his words.

"You'd think they would have sold me for more than *five dollars*," he joked.

Jimmy is a wonderful husband and father. He works hard and provides for his family well. At the same time, I learned that he was an alcoholic and he had little control over his addiction. He told me that he drank himself to sleep every night. He also said that he wanted more than anything to quit, but he had no control over his addiction.

When we were not together, Jimmy and I spoke on the phone often. Most of the time we talked about the time we missed, the years we were apart.

One warm summer evening, with the rain lightly misting outside, I sat on the covered front porch talking with him on the phone.

"I don't want to drink, Frances. I *want* to be free," he said.

I thought about my own journey. Not just surviving my childhood, but about fighting to be free of Daddy's ghost and overcoming alcoholism and an eating disorder. I understood Jimmy so well in that moment that it felt as if we were the same person. I answered him. "Jimmy, do you want to be saved and give the alcohol to God?"

"I do want to, Frances," he said. "But I've drank for so long, I know I can't quit."

"With God, all things are possible," I said, quoting my favorite scripture.

I asked my brother if he was in a place where nobody could overhear our conversation. I sensed that he was bashful about revealing his inner turmoil in front of his grandchildren. Jimmy walked out of his house, phone in hand, and sat at a picnic table on their back patio in the misting rain. Over the line, I spoke to him about trusting Jesus. He listened quietly, the rain soaking through his clothing and touching his skin.

Jimmy was a new man after that night. God made an amazing change in his life. He never touched alcohol again, and he started going to church. I wrote a poem about that night.

My Brother

Only the Lord and Jimmy know
what happened that Saturday night.
When God reached out and touched his heart
and the devil lost the fight.
My brother said, "Frances I can't!
But Jesus said, "You can!
"Because I died and made a way,
reach out and take My hand."
I held my breath as I waited,
afraid to say too much.
I knew that Jesus was pleading,
and all he needed was one touch.

We prayed and asked for Jesus
to give him the strength and His power
and the angels rejoiced in heaven
as Jimmy was saved in that hour!
Jesus is coming back sooner
than many may understand,
And now I can rest in peace knowing
my brother will be holding His hand.

Not long after that, I spoke to Jimmy about how much he had changed.

"Sometimes change isn't for real," he said.

I could tell he was frightened that his addiction might return.

"I know the difference," I said.

"How do you mean?"

"Daddy acted like he was a changed man once. But I could tell it was not real."

"How do you mean that?" he asked, so I told him what happened after my father arrived at Connie Maxwell.

Nellie and I hid in that pantry for what felt like an hour. I am sure it was not that long, but by the time Mrs. McDonald came in and called for us, I was as panicked as Nellie.

"Girls," our housemother said. "Your father is here and he wants to talk to you."

I wouldn't come out. Nellie cowered deeper into the shadows. I could hear Mrs. McDonald's footsteps on the tile. She paced back and forth before leaving the room. A few minutes later one of the school's counselors came in.

"Girls, your father is here to visit with you. Don't you know how special you are? Not many of your dorm sisters have a father who cares enough to come see them. Don't you want to come out and say hello?

He's not going to take you anywhere. You should come out and see him. I'll stay with you, and so will Mrs. McDonald."

The counselor kept on talking to us, but the seed was planted. I knew she was telling the truth. Not many of my friends at Connie Maxwell had fathers. We should be thankful. Maybe things hadn't been as bad as I remembered. Maybe it would be okay.

Nellie bought in as well. Hand-in-hand we came out of the pantry, and the counselor led us to the visitors' room. Just past the beautiful grand piano, I saw Daddy sitting in one of the burgundy leather chairs. Aunt Gracie sat beside him. She smiled ear to ear when she saw Nellie and me.

"Come here and sit down, children," she said. "Let me have a look at you."

I did as bidden and took a seat in front of her. At first I tried not to look at Daddy. As Aunt Gracie continued to speak, gushing about how nice we looked, I shot a glance or two toward him. He sat leaning forward, smiling as well. That may have been the first time I'd seen him do that.

"You have done such an excellent job," my daddy said to Mrs. McDonald. "The Lord's work."

I saw Mrs. McDonald smile. Daddy turned his attention to the counselor.

"Beautiful place here," he said. "And the children look so happy. I want to thank you for taking care of my young ones."

He was charming the pants off the adults, but he never said anything to me or Nellie. Aunt Gracie did all the talking to us.

"Susie's been staying with us," she said.

My eyes shot wide open. Brenda had always been a second mother to me, but Susie, with her dreams of stardom and greatness, was my idol.

"Is Susie okay?" I asked, inching to the edge of my seat.

I noticed Daddy looking at me with interest as Gracie told me that Susie was doing well. I thought nothing of it, though, because I was intent on hearing anything I could about my sister. When Gracie passed to a different subject, though, I glanced back at him. He was talking to one of the adults. His voice sounded velvety. My head tilted as I listened; I saw him almost as a stranger but also remembered that smooth way of talking. Hadn't he spoken to Mama that way after he hurt her?

At one point, Aunt Gracie looked at Daddy, and I knew the visit was coming to an end. I was not sad about that. Although I liked hearing about my sister, I wanted to go back to my life at Connie Maxwell. I had no interest in sitting there and listening to my daddy talk to the adults. I squirmed, and Mrs. McDonald noticed.

"Frances, Nellie, why don't you go on up to your room? It is almost time for dinner."

Aunt Gracie asked for a hug. I reluctantly agreed. Daddy just smiled. Nellie and I left the room. On the way out, I could hear Daddy talking again.

"I would like to come visit again soon. It is so nice to see my children. You've done such an excellent job."

The next week I was busy sweeping the dining room floor when Mrs. McDonald came in to find me.

"I swept under the chairs," I proudly said.

She smiled. "You have visitors."

My stomach turned when she said that. "My daddy?"

"Yes, and your sister."

"My sister? Is Susie here?"

She nodded again. I bolted out of the dining room, letting the broom fall to the floor. When I got to the visitors' room, Nellie was not there yet. I rushed over to Susie and gave her a great big hug. She looked wonderful, like a movie star. Her long blond hair curled around her beautiful face. I plopped down on the arm of her chair, close enough that I could hug her whenever I wanted.

Nellie came in soon after, and she was ecstatic to see Susie too. That's when I noticed something different about Susie. She did not seem as bubbly as usual. Instead, she sat there in silence. Daddy did the talking this time.

"Hi, girls," he said. "Look what I brought you."

Daddy reached out his hand. In it, he held two identical dolls. They had smooth porcelain faces with cherub cheeks and long black eyelashes. Their hair was curly and blond and combed perfectly. Each wore a long, white satin wedding dress with a veil.

"Bride dolls!" Nellie said in awe.

Nellie had wanted a bride doll forever. She was lost now. I was afraid he'd won her over. She oohed and ahhed and even smiled at him.

"It's just what I wanted," she gushed. "It's what me and Frances always wanted. Isn't it, Frances?"

"No, it's not! I wanted a guitar," I said.

Nellie gave me an angry look. She snatched her doll up and gave it a hug. I took mine, holding it limply by the arm, letting the dress drag on the floor. I didn't even like bride dolls. They were too fancy and frilly.

"Do you girls want to come visit? I can bring you to our house. You can see Susie and Jimmy. It'll be fun. I can pick you up right after the Fourth of July. What do you think?"

I did not want to go. In spite of the idea of seeing Susie, my instincts told me to stay away.

"What a great idea," the counselor said. "Don't you think, Frances? Think of how much one of your sisters here at Eason would give to be able to visit with her father. What a blessing."

Nellie agreed, all smiles now that she had her doll. I said nothing, hoping my silence would speak loud enough, but the decision was made for me. All of a sudden Daddy was making arrangements with the counselor, planning to pick us up on July 5, 1959. Before he left, he leaned in close.

"Don't forget to bring those dolls with you."

On the morning of July 5, I packed a small bag. I almost left that doll behind, but a part of me that had survived living with Daddy before kicked in. I picked it up, feeling that if I didn't, I'd be in trouble.

Aunt Gracie's car pulled up outside. Nellie and I were ushered out, and we climbed into the backseat. Daddy was on the passenger side. He turned around and smiled.

"You remembered your dolls," he said.

We nodded.

Aunt Gracie drove us to her house. Jimmy was there waiting for us. He was older now, about sixteen. Susie, however, was not there; nobody told us where she had gone. Aunt Gracie put us up in a spare room, and Daddy showed us the room he was staying in. It looked clean, and I saw a pair of grey striped coveralls hanging from the door.

"I'm working up at the station as a mechanic," he said.

Sure enough, the next morning he was off to work. Nellie and I were left to playing outside. Aunt Gracie fed us lunch. That night, when Daddy came home, he was still smiling and friendly. He washed up and changed his clothes. "How would y'all like to go out with your Daddy for the evening?" he asked. Nellie and I agreed.

"Let's go into town," he said.

He borrowed my uncle's car and drove us to a diner. We had hamburgers and milk shakes. Afterward, he walked us to the theater. *Sleeping Beauty* was showing. To my surprise, he bought us tickets and even let us get candy. The three of us settled in seats toward the front. The movie took me away. I felt as though I'd entered one of the beautiful stories Mama used to tell me.

I remember being sad when the movie was over. It was one of the most beautiful things I'd ever seen. Daddy was all smiles when he walked us back to the car. Once we got on the road, he talked to us.

"You know that your Mama left me," he said. "I've been trying to find you ever since. She was mad at me and told lies about what happened. She got me in some trouble with those stories, but the police figured out they weren't true. I'm so happy I found you, but you can't trust a word she told you about me."

We didn't say anything, but later that night after we were put to bed, I moved closer to Nellie.

"I was young when he was taken away," I whispered.

"Me too," she said.

"You remember how mean he was?"

Nellie paused. "Sometimes."

"You think he's changed any?"

"I don't know. Maybe." I felt Nellie shrug her shoulders. I did the same and then curled up and fell asleep. Oftentimes, children believe what they are told. It had been nearly three years since he had been sent to prison. The memory of the man he used to be had been suppressed. I wasn't sure what to believe now. He bribed us with gifts and candy. He didn't seem like the same man at all.

As our vacation with Daddy continued, my doubts increased. Daddy treated me and Nellie like princesses. At the same time, I never did see Susie. When I asked Aunt Gracie where she'd gone, she just told me that Susie came and went as she wished.

I knew our visit was coming to an end soon. I'd heard the adults at Connie Maxwell say it was to last two weeks. So when July 18 came around, I figured we had one more day. I was excited to return home. I missed my dorm sisters, Mrs. McDonald, and everyone else there.

July 18 was a Saturday, but Daddy left for work early in the morning. Nellie and I were playing outside when an old gray 1952 Studebaker rattled up to the curb.

"What do you think?" Daddy asked as he got out of the driver's seat.

I took a look at the car. "What is it?"

I spoke without thinking. Nellie peeked inside and told me to come have a look. When I did, she put her head near mine.

"Tell him it's nice," she whispered.

"Let's go for a drive," he said. "Go get those dolls I gave you."

I looked at Nellie. She hesitated on the sidewalk beside the car.

"Hurry on up," he said.

Although his tone was not one of anger, it carried something that startled us and made us rush into the house. I came out carrying my doll. Daddy had the backseat door open. We jumped in and he hurried into the front. The engine roared to life, and the car rolled away from Uncle Mose's house. No one was there to see us off.

Chapter 15

Taken

Minutes turned to endless hours, and Daddy drove on in silence. I knew that we would never be returning to Connie Maxwell, the only real home I'd ever known. At the time, I did not understand the word *kidnap*. Even if I had, I never would have dreamed that a father could kidnap his own children. It never occurred to me to run away or call the police. He was our dad, and we were his property.

As the day passed, we never stopped for food or turned back. The car moved ever westward, away from South Carolina and Connie Maxwell. At one point, I dozed off in the backseat. When I came to, the car was shaking and rattling over a dirt road. When I looked outside, I could barely make out the access road we were on in the growing darkness. Soon we slipped into a copse of trees, and the car came to a stop.

Daddy told us to stay in the backseat and lay down. He had to sleep, he said. We obeyed, and I fell back asleep. It seemed as though a heavy blanket weighed me down.

The next day passed in somewhat the same way. Several hours down the road, Daddy decided to stop at a service station that had a small grocery attached. He offered us food, but I could not eat. All

I could do was shake my head in response. I got out and shuffled to a water fountain. I drank and visited the bathroom but returned straight to the car. Once in the backseat, I curled up in a ball and went back to sleep.

When Daddy returned to the car I woke up for a second. He turned to look at me over the back of his seat.

"They didn't want you in that home anymore. That old woman begged me to take you off her hands. You two can't do anything right, can you? They wanted to pay me to get you out of their hair. Your lying, no-good Mama didn't want you either. Looks like I'm all you got, so you better be real good or I may leave you in the woods." I tried to push the terror I felt at his words out of my head, but I could not.

I managed to drift to sleep again, and my mind filled with images from Connie Maxwell and pictures of Mrs. McDonald's sweet, gentle face. I slept the entire trip. As long as I could sleep, I could dream about the life that had been torn from me. I never wanted to wake up again.

I was asleep more often than I was awake during Daddy's flight from South Carolina. The farther we got, the more the shiny veneer he'd shown the adults at Connie Maxwell peeled away like the skin of a rotten onion. He had put on a good show, but it was all an illusion. Late one night, as I slept in the back, the car came to a stop. Nellie woke me up, and I looked out the window. I knew for sure that we had returned to my nightmare.

Outside sat a cabin. It was much like those we'd lived in before Daddy was arrested. This one, though, sat alone on a small rise with a patch of woods blocking it from its nearest neighbor. Inside, there was only one room. Cobwebs and dust covered the place, and without Mama there to do her cleaning, they would remain long after we moved in.

Daddy threw a quilt on the floor in the corner. He told us that was to be our bed, and then he walked out, leaving Nellie and me alone in the dark cabin. I could barely find the strength to walk over to the quilt. Once there, I collapsed again. I had no idea that I was suffering from a deep depression born of being ripped away from my one chance at a normal childhood. Nellie and I did not even say a word to each other that night. Instead, we slept.

The next morning our old life began again. Daddy woke us early. There was no breakfast. We did not have clean clothes or toothbrushes, and there were no electric lights to turn off when he led us outside.

"Get in the car. Both of you," he ordered.

Daddy drove about a mile to a cotton field. When he parked, we got out of the car without saying a word and walked through a patch of scraggly pines. The trees parted, and a sprawling cotton field opened before us.

"Welcome to Texas," Nellie whispered. That was the first hint I had of where he had taken us. Like zombies, we filed in and received our cotton sacks. Soon our bloody fingers were picking balls of white out of their sharp nests. It was as if everything in between this and the last cotton field we'd worked had been a dream.

The hours passed in a haze of backbreaking work and numbing silence. If I slowed my pace, Daddy needed only to give me a look to speed me up. There were other children there, but I spoke to no one. I just pulled cotton and stuffed it into my bag.

At the end of the first day, Daddy collected our pay and told us to get back in the car. Off we drove to the town's only food store, the general market down the road. Inside, Daddy pointed at a red-wrapped torpedo of bologna, and the man behind the counter sliced it for us. He also grabbed a loaf of bread from the rack.

As Daddy got ready to pay, the old man behind the counter looked me and Nellie over. Daddy started to get uneasy, especially when the man reached down behind the counter. He came up with a stack of magazines and comic books.

"Your girls like to read?" he asked.

Daddy nodded, looking none too friendly. The old man ignored him and stuck the stack of books out to us.

"Go on, take 'um. They're old, and I'm ready to toss 'um anyway."

"Thanks, sir," I muttered.

Although I did not show it, I knew this man had just handed us treasure. I hid my excitement because I was afraid that if Daddy knew how much the magazines and comic books meant to me, he'd snatch them away. So I stayed silent, acting as though they weren't worth anything.

After paying for our food, Daddy had plenty of money left. He shoved that into the pocket of his pants, and we walked outside.

When we arrived at the cabin, Daddy handed us the food but did not get out of the car. Instead, he rolled down the window of that old gray Studebaker.

"Make your dinner. And you better not leave the cabin," he said.

He drove off, and we went inside. There was still an hour or so before sunset, so I made a sandwich and curled up under a window to read a comic book. Nellie did the same. As the shadows crept across the small cabin, she lit a kerosene lamp. We lay on our stomachs on the cold plank floor with the light between us. I read until I could not keep my eyes open any longer.

"I'm going to sleep," I said.

"Me too."

I walked over to the quilt Daddy had thrown on the floor. I had gotten accustomed to a bed and pillow, so it was hard to get comfortable. Nellie shuffled about beside me.

"You think they're looking for us?" I whispered.

Nellie did not say anything right away. I rolled over and could smell Daddy on the ragged quilt. I twisted onto my back, startled by a vivid flashback of a night long ago—me petting Brenda's hair as she sobbed herself to sleep. A chill ran up my spine as I stared into the shadows.

"They are *not* looking for us. They didn't want us any longer," Nellie stated flatly.

"Why did they make him take us away?" I asked Nellie. "What did we do?"

"They didn't want us there no more," she said. "That's what he told us. That's it."

"Maybe they *are* looking for us," I said. "I wonder if Mama knows we're gone."

"Hush up and go to sleep," Nellie grumbled. "I don't want to talk about it anymore."

I hushed but did not fall asleep right away. I listened as her breathing evened out and was replaced by the sound of insects in the woods. A fox cried out in the distance, sounding like an injured child. I shivered again and thought about everything and everyone we'd left behind.

The crash of the door hitting the wall woke me with a start. The moon was full, and by its light I could see the silhouette of a man I assumed was Daddy. A jug hung from one of his fingers as he staggered into the cabin. The stringent stench of pure alcohol burned the inside of my nose.

"I'll show that mongrel witch," he grunted. "Left me in prison to rot."

I knew from his words that somebody was going to get a beating. I tensed up and tried to stay silent. That didn't work. He stumbled over our legs and cursed like a madman. He started kicking my legs and back. I don't even think he knew what he was kicking. Nellie and I scrambled out of his way and prayed silent prayers that he would pass out. The past washed over me like a typhoon. I knew the nightmare was back, and we were right in the middle of it. Only this time, I was wide-awake. I did not want the pain. I was afraid of it. What I did not realize was that this night would be far worse than any pain he had inflicted on me before.

Before morning, I awoke to Daddy sleeping between me and Nellie. When he stirred, his rough, dirty hand found my body. I lay next to him, unable to cry out for help and wishing I could die. I *wanted* to die. I wanted to forget forever the horrid quilt I was forced to lay on beside him, the abomination of a father violating innocent trust, the stench of mildew, whiskey, and my daddy that made me physically sick to my stomach. I was unable to stop him, and I felt like a trapped rabbit in a fox's den. I cried silent tears and stifled the noise by holding my hand tight over my mouth. And at the same time I knew if I made a sound, he would kill me.

I cried out in my mind, *Daddy don't!* My body felt dirty, and I was ashamed. I thought it was my fault, that I had done something to cause this abomination. For some unknown reason, he didn't consummate the sexual acts he forced on me and Nellie, not like he did Brenda, but the humiliation, disgust, and loathing was the same. He violated my body, soul, and mind and made me wish I could die and never be touched again.

I didn't understand how a father, even a bad father, could ruin his child's life. I still don't understand it. I said nothing to Nellie. She looked at me, and I guessed she knew. What she may also have known, which I did not that first morning, was that this was to be our lot. She must have known she was part of it now. We were alone together with him, without Brenda or Mama as a buffer. There were no limits to his repulsive acts, and nobody to stop him. We were his prisoners now, and we could never predict what his twisted mind might cause him to do. If we did not lay beside him on that filthy quilt, we would be beaten without mercy, and after the beating, the abuse would happen anyway. I suspected that he enjoyed our resistance so he would have an excuse to beat us.

Every night, I prayed. I asked for Daddy to not come back home. Often, he came back too drunk to touch us. One morning, he awoke and grumbled about how ungrateful we were and how no one else wanted us. Then he ushered us out to the fields as if nothing was amiss. When we got there, the foreman was late. Daddy stood a little removed from the other workers. One man came over and introduced himself. Daddy grunted a response, but the man did not get the hint.

"These your kids?" the man asked.

Daddy nodded.

"Their mother about?"

"She's dead," Daddy said, a wicked smirk on his face.

"That's a darn shame."

"What business is it of yours?" Daddy hissed.

The man shook his head and walked away. It was the last time that anyone there bothered to speak to us. Instead, we did our work and trudged back to the cabin. We went to the market and bought bologna and bread most days. Some nights Daddy sat on the one chair in our cabin and ate. All the while, he'd have a jar of white lightning or a quart of whiskey nearby. Once he started drinking, he just got meaner and meaner.

"That nurse in the infirmary was a pig," he slurred. "Stupid cow. She bought everything I fed her. She's the one that helped me break out of the rat hole your Mama and sisters put me in!"

I tried to ignore his words. Instead, I cleaned the cabin top to bottom, watching him swig from the bottle and mutter incoherently. I suddenly understood why Mama cleaned all the time. I did it in the hopes that I could stay out of Daddy's way until he passed out.

Although Nellie and I never spoke about it, I knew he abused her as he did me. She endured the dirty quilt much as I did, in utter silence. I noticed, though, she tried to stay out of his way as well. As I swept away cobwebs, she read in the corner, eyeing Daddy just as warily as I did.

"Frances," Daddy suddenly barked.

"Yes, sir," I said, my eyes on the floor, my heart missing a beat.

"What are we picking again?"

I blinked, confused and panicked. I thought it was a trick question.

"Cotton, sir," I said.

"That's right."

Daddy took another swig and his head bobbed forward. I realized he was poisoning his brain, killing his brain cells with the moonshine he was drinking. All I cared about, though, was that he fell fast asleep where he sat, sparing me and Nellie for the evening.

Life stagnated for a time. Both Nellie and I dreaded being the one that had to go to sleep beside Daddy on the quilt. Nellie, always the brasher of us two, would blurt out her hatred for him and didn't seem to notice if he heard or not. To silence her, fearing the wrath that would be lashed on her if he heard, I would take her place those nights. On other nights, I would pass my dinner to her, knowing what would befall her once the sun set.

One night, Nellie sat petting me. It was to be my turn to endure, and Daddy was in a fouler mood than normal.

"Where is this doctor?" he barked.

I knew what he meant. He had heard that Mama let a doctor and his family adopt my baby brother, Robbie. Daddy had made his intentions clear before we left South Carolina. He wanted his son back.

"I don't know, Daddy," I whispered.

"You do, and I'll kill you for lying to me."

I pleaded with him. "Mama never told us. One day we came home from school and he was just gone."

He slapped me hard enough to knock me off my feet.

"Liar."

"Mama was never honest with us," Nellie blurted out.

It was not true, not really. I knew that Nellie was using another tactic, one I never learned. She was using Daddy's utter hatred for Mama to distract him.

"She was a lousy mother," he spat.

I knew he had switched to talking about Mama, so I inched away, not making a sound. A splinter lodged into my bare foot as I shimmied across the floor.

"I don't want to hear that name again, understand. She is a lying, backstabbing Jezebel."

Daddy went on like that for hours. The entire time I just wished and wished that he'd pass out. But that night it was not to be. When he ordered me to the quilt on the floor, I could barely breathe for the bile rising up in my throat. He took away everything, and reveled in the degradation. I knew in my soul how evil he really was. I suddenly understood how Brenda and Mama had been pushed so far as to consider murder.

I started making up poems and songs in my head to help relieve the tension of life. This is one I wrote after I escaped.

Cotton Fields and Faith

Picking cotton for the farmer,
feeling dirty, sad, and low.
Blistering sun high in the heavens,
cannot let my feelings show.
Drag the cotton sack behind me,
feels so heavy on my back.

I dream of better days and freedom
as I pick and fill the sack.
My swollen hands are cracked and bleeding
from the sharpness of the boles.
Blood stains white cotton as I pick it
with each handful that I hold.
From dawn to dusk out here we labor,
until too dark for me to see.
The farmer waits up at the trailer
to weigh my cotton sack for me.
As I leave field and sack behind me,
slowly now I walk alone
To a sad and shabby dwelling,
the farmer's shack that we call home.
Not to a bed or clean white linen,
a frayed dirty quilt lays on the floor.
And a meager meal to share with
the little sister I adore.
My sister's cowering in the corner
as I walk inside the door.
Horror once again assaults me.
Mama's bleeding, daddy roars.
Whiskey breath and heavy footfalls
make me turn about to see.
The face of terror, that's my daddy,
screaming angry words at me.
When at last the whiskey takes him
to the sleep for which we pray.
Holding onto one another,
we two sisters kneel to pray.
Whispering quietly in the darkness,
to the Lord above we say,

Please, God, give us strength and courage
just to face another day.
God gave us strength to face each peril,
with His love He lit our day.
We could not have faced the horror
without His light to guide our way.
We knew He'd free us from our prison.
He always lights our darkest roads.
God kept us safe and gave us courage.
Jesus carried our heavy load.
So the cotton sack, though heavy,
and the terror of each night,
Did not ever break our spirit;
we kept Jesus in our sight.

Chapter 16

Attempted Murder

"*Brenda, Susie, where* you at?!"

The shout woke me from a sound sleep. For a moment I was disoriented, thinking my sisters had returned. As my eyes adjusted to the darkness around me, I began to understand Daddy's words. More and more he was mistaking us for our older sisters, whom he blamed vehemently for sending him to prison.

Even in the partial darkness, I could see the blood. It stood out, a dark, black path down his face.

"Wake up!" he shouted. "I know what you told them cops. Only an evil daughter would testify against her own father. I'm gonna show you what happens to liars. Then I'm gonna beat you and that good-for-nothing sister of yours to death. I'll crush your skull with a rock and bury you at the back of this cabin. Do you hear me?" He punctuated every word, bellowing like a crazed bear. I used to wonder to myself, *Do you think we're deaf?* How could everyone in the state not hear him?

He kicked toward the quilt, and we huddled together in the dark, trying to dodge his blows. There was nowhere left to hide but inside myself. I withdrew; each punch landed on a husk of a human. When he beat me really bad, or when I had to watch him hurt my sister, I tried to pull myself out of the scene. I asked God to give me strength and to take me away from this place. I tried to remember what Mama had told me before leaving me at Connie Maxwell.

"Be strong; take care of Nellie." I felt guilty that I was unable to protect her. Even though Nellie was twenty months older than me, Mama had always treated her as the youngest.

Some nights, if he was in the house drinking, I would sneak out the door. There was a tree out front that had low-hanging branches. I climbed up and went as high as I could. There was a crook in the branches near enough to the top that I could nestle in and see the stars. I curled up there in the cool night air, the crickets drowning out the slurring cusses filtering through the open cabin door.

Those rare moments, I was free of him. He could never climb up a tree even when sober, let alone ripping drunk. Some nights he'd come out looking for me and would stand at the base of the tree and strike the trunk with his fists.

"Get down here, Susie! I'm gonna pay you back for sending me to prison."

"I'm Frances," I told him for the hundredth time, but he didn't seem to notice.

I stayed up there until he got tired or he went back in the cabin and passed out. He'd stumble inside, and I would go back to looking at the stars. Soon enough, though, I realized this was not real freedom. One night when he went back in, I heard his roaring curses and the sound of slapping and a thick thud. I tried to drown out Nellie's screams. I did not get out of my tree that night, but I knew I could never be free. If I broke free, then all his rage would fall on my sister. I never forgot the last words Mama spoke to me. Sometimes the guilt could be worse than just enduring his abuse. I tried to take Nellie's place to keep her from being beaten to death.

One night, after eating a sandwich, Daddy got up and went to the door. We thought he'd leave and we'd have some peace, but this night was different. He seemed to have a plan.

"Get on out here," he said.

We followed him out to the car, wondering what new hell he had thought up for us tonight.

"Get in the backseat."

Daddy drove us into town. He stopped at a beer joint on the side of the highway, and we all got out. Leading us inside, he told us to sit at a table near the door. He proceeded to take a seat at the bar. I watched as he spent the money we'd earned picking cotton on drink after drink. He swallowed down shots of whiskey. It seemed to me he was drinking a lot faster than usual.

A woman tended bar. After a while, she noticed us. When she came over to our table, she had two comic books and two Cokes.

"Here you go, kids, look at these," she said in a kind voice. I hoped that she would talk to Daddy and keep him here until he passed out. He was so drunk already that I doubted he could drive us back to the cabin without killing us.

We thanked her, and I watched her walk away. I started to read, hoping the story would take me away. After I finished the first book, we switched. I heard the lady talking to Daddy.

"Those your girls?"

"Yup."

"What's their names?"

"Brenda," he slurred. "And that blonde one over there is Susie."

"Pretty names," she said.

"Not as pretty as you."

Not long after that, Daddy slammed a shot glass on the bar.

"One more for the road!"

The lady filled him up with whiskey, and he knocked it right back. The stool fell over when he stood up, and he had to steady himself on the tables as he headed for the door.

"Get on out there," he growled at us.

Nellie and I followed him right out the door. Neither of us made a noise as we climbed into the backseat. The car engine roared to life, and I could see Daddy shaking his head like he was confused.

"You think I'm gonna let you get away with what you did to me?" he muttered.

Something in the way he said that told me we were in real trouble. He had called us Brenda and Susie so many times that we knew it meant his mind was blacking out. Usually, this turned into a beating or some other abuse. That night, however, there was an intent in his drunken voice. He had threatened to murder us in the car so many times, but tonight was different. He had made up his mind. This was the night.

When he pulled out onto the road, it didn't take long for my fears to be confirmed.

"Let's see how brave you are when we're all dead," he said.

Lights approached us from up ahead. I could see it was a massive semi. Daddy laughed like a wild man.

"It's all your fault. You drove me to this. I'm tired of putting up with you. You're gonna die tonight!"

He drove head-on right at that truck. The semi's horn blasted, and I heard breaks squealing, but they were not ours. Daddy swerved just in the nick of time to keep from crashing head-on into the truck.

"Stop, Daddy! Oh, please stop," I begged.

Nellie shrieked like death itself. I continued to plead with him.

"Not this time, Susie," he yelled back at me. "You're gonna die for the years I spent in prison. You and that lying Brenda. I'm gonna run this car into the next phone pole I see and kill you both. Right now!"

Screaming and laughing, he swerved off the highway toward a light pole. At the last possible second, he jerked the steering wheel, and the car narrowly missed the pole. Dust billowed in front of the car like a tornado crossing in front of us. Then he was back on the highway.

He seemed to be feeding on our terror. The car barreled out of town on a dark two-lane road. The farther we traveled, the fewer cars we saw. Eventually it was just us and the darkness, and Daddy started in once again.

"You think it was nice in prison, you lying heathens? Wait until your bloody brains are splattered all across the pavement. I'm gonna wrap this car around a light pole. See how smart you are then!"

The car swerved, and we popped into the air when it crossed the median. Daddy raced down the wrong side of the road, spouting more hatred and venom. I was near hysteria as I cried and pleaded. Suddenly, he pounded his fist on the dashboard. He whipped the wheel back and forth in an effort to flip the car over. The tires screeched, and we teetered on two wheels.

Giving the dashboard another pound, Daddy switched off the lights. Since there were no streetlights, we were thrust into total darkness. His driving calmed for a moment, and he went silent. I felt we had entered the eye of a hurricane, the calmness hinting at what was to come. I huddled close to Nellie, and we wrapped our arms around each other in the backseat. She was shaking; or I was. Neither of us was begging for our lives anymore. Instead, I whispered a prayer.

Just as suddenly as they'd vanished, the car lights burst on again. We entered a small town. It was after midnight, and everyone seemed to be asleep, but the streetlights gave me hope. I felt as though we had returned from the twilight zone and were back among the living. Then the lights from a service station appeared in front of us. When the car slowed and he turned in, I thought we were saved.

"Fill it up," Daddy said to the man working the pump.

He got out and went to the bathroom. Nellie was still shaking.

"I wished we had run outta gas," she said. "I gotta use the bathroom."

To my shock and horror, she got out of the car just as Daddy disappeared around the corner. Nellie ran up to the service attendant.

"My Daddy's drunk," she told him. "Keep him here talking 'til he sobers up."

I could not believe it. My fear kept me planted in that seat. I felt sure he was going to kill us eventually, but if he saw Nellie out there talking to that man, we'd be dead for certain!

Nellie did not say anything about Daddy trying to kill us. She seemed to rethink what she'd done.

"Don't tell him I said anything about drinking."

She hurried back to the car and got in before he reappeared. A drizzle started to fall just as he came back around and neared the attendant.

"Hey, buddy, how's it going?" the man asked.

"Not bad," Daddy answered.

"Slow night."

Daddy nodded. "Yeah, well, I gotta get goin'."

The attendant seemed to be trying to come up with something else to say, but the words failed him. Daddy nodded once more and got into the car. In no time, we were back out on the deserted highway. The sprinkling rain turned into a drizzle. I saw a flash of lightning in the distance. The faint glow was enough for me to see that Daddy wasn't looking at the road at all. He was staring down as if lost in his own thoughts.

Daddy drove faster and faster, and the tires found less and less purchase on the slick roads. I lay down in the backseat so I would not see what was coming. Nellie did the same. We clung to each other, crying but not making a sound. Daddy started to cuss at us again, calling us Brenda and Susie. The car must have been going ninety miles per hour just as Daddy veered off the road. It catapulted across a deep embankment and plowed through a fence. Barbed wire whipped against the window just before it shattered into a million pieces. Clods of dirt flew into the car and seemed to swirl around as if caught in a tornado. My body left the seat and hovered in the air for just an instant before hitting the side of the door. The door gave way, and I flew through the air, losing consciousness when I struck the ground.

Chapter 17

In the Arms of Angels

I woke, choking and coughing up dirt. Mud was in my throat, and I couldn't breathe. My body screamed out in pain each time I coughed. I opened my eyes, but there was dirt blocking my sight. Blinking again and again, I could see the front of our car. It must have struck a wall of earth and was sticking up in the air with the headlights glowing upward. The entire back bumper had been buried in the wet dirt. The back half of the car had been swallowed, and only the front door and headlights were visible. The inside of the car was filled up as if a bulldozer had pushed the earth right inside.

I tried to lift my head, but each move was like a hot poker searing my flesh. My body was caught between the remains of the barbed-wire fence and the muddy ground. The barbs wrapped around my body, cutting into my legs, hips, and back.

"Frances."

It was Nellie, sounding as if she was calling to me from a great distance. Then I saw her stumbling up the hill toward me in the light of the headlights.

"Oh, Frances!" She put her small hand up to her face.

That's when I saw that her cheek had been nearly torn in half. It was split open from her cheek bone down to her mouth.

Her hand passed over the open flap of skin on her face. The darkness fell over me as I passed out again.

When I came to the second time, I could feel every place where the barbs had gouged my flesh. I moved an inch, and it was as if a knife pierced me in a thousand places at once. I remember hearing my voice screaming in agony. I kept blacking out from the pain. When I opened my eyes again, I found myself in a man's arms, cradled liked a baby. The rain had stopped, and the air smelled fresh and new.

At first, I thought the man was Daddy. But there was such a kindness to the way the man held me, as if he wanted to be sure not to hurt me in the least. It couldn't be Daddy. This man was much larger and very gentle. He carefully stepped down the muddy slope with me in his arms. He carried me to a car parked beside the road. The inside lights were on. The light was golden; it looked like no light I had ever seen before or since.

A young woman appeared as well. She was helping Nellie climb down the muddy embankment.

"Nellie, are you okay?" I tried to shout, but it only came out a rough whisper.

She did not say anything. I noticed that the woman held a bright-white handkerchief to Nellie's face. My mind flashed back to the barbed wire. The man must have carefully cut me free. I tried to look up and see his face, but it always seemed to be turned just enough that I could not make out his features.

The man gently placed me down on the backseat of his car. I expected Daddy to come raging up and tell this man to get away from me, but he never did. I am sure Daddy must have been somewhere in the man's car, but I did not see him. Nellie was helped in beside me, and we drove off to get medical treatment.

This was a lonely stretch of highway, with no lighting except the moon and stars. It was about three in the morning, and the chances of someone passing our wrecked car must have been near zero. I will always believe that God sent his angels in the form of that young man and his wife.

Amazingly, I do not remember being in any more pain after I was placed in the car. The barbed wire had torn away a good portion of my dress, so the lady covered me with a beautiful, soft, pale-blue blanket. This kind couple, who just happened to be driving along on a deserted road at the exact time we needed help, also happened to have everything they needed to free me from the barbed wire and give us comfort.

I tried hard not to get their nice, clean car dirty. I lay very still and tried to push the soft blue blanket away from my bloody, mud-caked body, but I was too weak. Each time I made an effort, the woman gently covered me back up again. I looked into her warm eyes.

"I don't want to get it dirty."

"It's all right," she whispered, touching my hand. "It *belongs* to *you*."

I drifted in and out of consciousness. I sensed the woman fussing over me, rearranging the blanket or patting my hand. The soft golden light remained on in the car all the way to the hospital. It was that light, more than anything else, that offered me peace and comfort on the long ride to the emergency room. It was strange that I never did see my daddy or feel his terrifying presence, but I know he must have been in the car with us. After arriving at the hospital, the man and woman vanished. I never did see them again. The golden light went with them, along with the peace I'd felt. The pain returned. I asked the nurse later if I could have my blue blanket, but she didn't know what I was talking about.

The nurses took me and Nellie to separate rooms. A doctor came in and gave me a shot for the pain and went to work stitching up what seemed like every inch of my small body. Later, I learned I received over a hundred and fifty stitches that night! I was terrified at the thought of leaving the hospital and getting back into an automobile.

After I was stitched up, the doctor stepped out of the room and left me alone sitting on a gurney. A minute later, a nurse brought Nellie in to join me. I broke into tears when I saw Nellie's face bandaged from her chin all the way up to her swollen eye. Once the nurse stepped out, Nellie turned to me.

"Don't you say anything about Daddy drinking," she warned.

I was a little confused. Her face was stitched up and her eyes looked tired and unfocused. Her words, however, were sharp and sure. When the door opened again, the doctor came in leading two police officers. I understood. Being the younger, I decided to let Nellie do all the talking. I still felt as though I was caught in some horrible dream.

One officer took the lead. He was a heavy man and very tall. His face looked as hard as concrete. I was scared of men, so seeing him made Nellie's instructions to stay quiet all the easier to follow.

"What are your names?" he asked.

"Nellie, and this is Frances."

The officer narrowed his eyes. "Who are Brenda and Susie?"

"That's our older sisters. They are grown." Nellie seemed to have an answer for everything. I didn't understand how she could be so unemotional. But she was just being Nellie.

"Hmm. Has your father been drinking alcohol tonight?"

Nellie did not say anything. I glanced at her when the officer looked at me.

"Listen, we can help you. All you have to say is yes, and we'll take care of you. You don't have to go back with him if he's hurting you."

Nellie sat up straighter. For a second I thought it was all over. I thought she'd tell them everything, just as Brenda had years before. We'd be taken right back to Connie Maxwell. Everything would be okay. But then I saw the fear behind Nellie's eyes. I knew that fear. It coursed through me at the same time. It was as if Daddy stood right there before us, his eyes screaming murder if we said anything at all.

"No, he ain't been drinking," Nellie said.

I looked down at the floor.

"You know, you almost died out there," the officer said, losing patience with us. "That accident should have killed you. Not to mention you should still be out there on the road." He turned to look at the doctor. "How *did* those people come by them, anyway? Did you speak with the couple when they brought the girls in? Be sure and keep them both here. We need to talk to the witnesses before they leave."

The doctor shook his head. "They're gone."

"I think they were angels," I whispered.

The officer paid me no mind. He went back to drilling us about Daddy. It was a lost cause though. Daddy's murderous grip was stronger than it had ever been before. That officer had no chance of breaking our silence. Had he been kinder, like the man who cut me from the barbed wire, maybe we would have opened up. But his harsh manner and rough voice silenced any secret we might have told him. I relived that night so often that I wrote a poem about it, hoping that if I put my feelings on paper, the nightmares would go away.

The Crash

Speeding down a dark black road,
father drinking as he drives,
Two frightened little children,
softly praying for their lives.
He yells and screams in anger,
the whiskey has him in its hold,
He does not see or think or feel,
the anger drowns his soul.

Arms wound around each other,
the children cower in the car,
The lines upon the highway,
flying by like shooting stars.
He doesn't see the light pole,
nor does he really care,
Off the road at ninety,
children flying through the air.
But saving little children
is what Jesus likes to do,
He caught us safely in His arms
and protected me and you.

Chapter 18

On the Run Again

The police questioned me and Nellie for hours. At one point they said that Daddy's car had been towed, and they found beer bottles inside. I knew that wasn't true because he only drank cheap home-brew stored in quart-sized mason jars, or whiskey if he could get it.

The police gave up on gaining information and left us alone. When we thought they were not coming back, we whispered to each other.

"Do you think they believed you?" I asked Nellie.

She shook her head. "No, they knew he was drunk, but they can't get him. Nobody can touch him. And we can't ever tell. Not ever."

When Daddy came into the recovery room to take us back to the cabin with him, he seemed so penitent that the doctors and nurses believed him. He was so convincing with the hospital staff that even I thought he might be sorry for the whole thing. Surprisingly, the old car was still drivable. Since there were no charges filed, it was returned to him.

Before leaving, the doctor pulled him aside.

"Your children need rest while they recover. This was a traumatic experience, and they need special care. In two weeks, bring them back to get their stitches out."

"Of course," Daddy said. "I'll take good care of them."

I wanted so much to go to sleep and not wake up. Sleep was wonderfully peaceful, and I was so tired. When Daddy got me to the car, though, my body started to shake uncontrollably. I did not want to get inside that thing, especially not with him driving.

Daddy pushed me in, and I shivered in the backseat as he drove home. Dawn was just breaking when we pulled up in front of the little shack. Neither Nellie nor I could work. Her face was swollen to twice its size, and I had dozens of bandages over the many deep gash wounds caused by the barbed wire. I had lost a good deal of blood and was still so weak that I could barely walk. The doctor had prescribed medication for us both, but Daddy did not get the prescriptions filled.

Amazingly, Daddy did not have a scratch on him after the accident. Luckily for us, he knew just how close he'd come to going back to prison. So he didn't bother us and allowed us to sleep alone and heal.

The days passed in a blur. I remained in shock after the accident. The wreck alone was a horrible experience, but on top of that I knew Daddy had done it on purpose. Daddy had tried to kill me, and he made no attempt to apologize. I knew it would not take much for him to try again. Along with the abuse that soon continued, I survived a constant threat of death at Daddy's hands. Every noise made me jump two feet off the ground, and I was plagued with paralyzing nightmares.

Night and day mingled as I slept on the floor of the cabin. We were allowed to lie on the pallet until he thought we had recovered. His drinking never stopped, though, and he still liked to fight. He fought everybody.

A few nights after we were out of the hospital, I awoke to curses and loud, raging male voices. When I opened my eyes, I stared up over my head in wonder and amazement at a strange man sailing like a bird through the air right above my face. It was a surreal sight to wake up to, and I remember thinking, *I hope he doesn't land on me or my sister because we're hurt enough already and it would tear our stitches out.*

I could not move, and I gazed without emotion as he struck the wall a few feet away and crashed to the cabin floor. Daddy was right on top of him in an instant. He reached down and grabbed a handful of the other man's shirt and hair, dragging him around Nellie and me and out the front door of the shack.

Angry shouts filtered in from outside for another few minutes until they were replaced by silence. I still did not move, but I listened as footsteps approached the door. I half expected the other man, who had seemed much larger than Daddy, to come walking into the cabin. Who knows what he might have done to us, but it probably could not be worse than what we were living with daily.

But it was Daddy. He walked back in as if nothing had happened. He sat down in his chair and tipped back a quart jug of white lightning. It was all like something from a film moving in slow motion in front of my eyes. But we knew this was real, and the blood, the murderous grappling, and the sounds of fists smashing flesh were just more examples of the chaos and madness that made up our lives.

Several weeks after that night, we were on the move again. Daddy was uneasy since the night in the hospital and wanted to get away from the local authorities. So he drove us out of Texas. After we settled at a farm in Stilwell, Oklahoma, he decided we were healed enough to get back to work. I knew we had lived in Stilwell when Mama was with us, but I could not remember if it was the same farm. I asked Nellie, but she never wanted to discuss the past.

It was here that I first met the Willoughbys. Their family was working the same farm we were, and their two daughters, Faye and

Judy, were about our ages. We found each other in the fields and became instant friends. Although they were free to come and go as they liked after work, they understood the migrant life and felt a kinship with me and Nellie. Our new friends did not attend school either and worked in the fields to help make a living for their large family. They didn't seem to mind though. The big difference between us was that their parents showed them much care and love.

After we lived at this new camp for a week or two, Daddy loosened his iron grip to a degree. He met Mr. Willoughby in the field, and I believe this was the first man I had ever seen Daddy sit and talk to without getting into a fight. To my surprise, Mr. Willoughby and my dad became good friends. Saturday rolled around, and Faye and Judy told Nellie and me about the big camp dance that was to be held after dark. All the farmworkers attended it every Saturday night. All that day, Nellie and I whispered about it, trying to figure out how we could get Daddy to let us attend.

That afternoon, Mr. Willoughby stopped by our cabin. I heard him tell Daddy that he would be playing the guitar and singing that night.

"There will be banjos, mandolins, and other strings," he said. "Even a set of tin-tub drums. A bunch of the men bring along whiskey."

That was the magic word. Once Daddy knew there would be free alcohol, he would not be able to stay away, and he'd want us along so he could keep an eye on us. We were going to the party!

It was scorching hot that workday in the dusty cotton fields, without a hint of shade. The rows were so long you couldn't see the ends of them. The sun blazed down without mercy, and many women wore bonnets as protection from the sun. As was common, the workers took off from the fields early on Saturdays. Nellie and I ran back to the cabin and grabbed the cleanest dresses we had and left before

Daddy could change his mind. I ran along behind Nellie toward Caney Creek, a babbling brook around the bend from the camp that was hidden by an outcrop of underbrush and trees. Faye, Judy, and the other girls from the camp waited there. The oldest of the bunch assigned one of the young girls to keep a lookout for any boys while the rest of us bathed in the creek. We stripped down to our underwear and jumped into the water, letting the cooling current wash away the dirt and grime of the fields.

We laughed and talked in the creek far longer than it took us to get clean. Once done, we dressed and helped each other fix our hair. We all wanted to look pretty for the evening's entertainment. I brushed my hair over and over, trying to get the unruly tangles out so it would feel as thick and silky as it had when I was at Connie Maxwell. In that moment, I could almost forget our secret life of lies and feel some bit of normalcy returning.

"I like to bathe," Faye said. She had a wistfulness about her and she looked up at the sky while she spoke. "I hear some folk bathe every day of the week, not just on Saturdays."

"We took a bath every night when I was in the orphanage," I said. "In a real tub."

Faye's eyes widened. I realized it was not the idea of a tub that caused her reaction.

"You was in an orphanage?"

Nellie glared at me. I wished I could take back those words. I looked around, half expecting Daddy to be there listening.

"Course not, silly. Hey, you forgot to wash your face."

I splashed water at Faye and she dunked me back in the creek.

"You need help brushing your hair?" I asked, trying to keep everyone distracted from what I had accidently let slip. I climbed out of the water again, onto the bank, letting the sun dry my clothes. It was so hot and dry that it did not take long. "Come on up!" I yelled to Faye. "I'll brush your hair."

"Sure," she said.

Before she could say anything else, I asked her about what would happen that night. She loved explaining everything to me, and soon my words were forgotten—at least I hoped they were.

Not long after, the sun neared the horizon, and rays of light cut through the trees, splashing on the gnarled old trunks that surrounded the creek. The older girls led the way back to camp. As we neared, I could already hear music floating through the air.

The cabins in camp ran along an old dust road. The Willoughbys' cabin was near the center. They had a big truck to which Mr. Willoughby had added high wooden sideboards. Tattered canvas covered the top, and Mr. Willoughby sat on the open tailgate. He was a tall man with rough dark skin from working so many years in the sun-baked fields. He was as gentle as he was thin. Most of the times I saw him, he was quiet, but on Saturday night he transformed. Mr. Willoughby never drank anything stronger than a coke, but he strummed on the beautiful homemade guitar resting on his lap and sang out from his soul.

When Mr. Willoughby sang and played, the entire camp went quiet. I stood on the fringe of the crowd watching the respect and admiration in everyone's eyes as they watched his expert fingers move up and down the neck of his guitar, transfixed by his soft baritone voice. I watched Daddy make his way over to where the crowd of musicians had started to gather. He found a group of men sharing a bottle of something and sat on the ground beside them, making quick friends. Even he seemed in a festive mood, although he never showed his true self in front of outsiders.

The song Mr. Willoughby sang was a love song he'd written for his wife, Mable. She stood beside him, her tiny smiling face overlooking the crowd like a queen. Mable Willoughby did not work the fields with us. Instead, she stayed back and cooked her family's dinner and cleaned up their camp area.

"Lookie here," a boy said from behind me. "A bunch of hens all dolled up for the party. How about a little peck for me?"

Even without turning, I knew the voice. It was Dallas Willoughby, the second oldest boy in the family. I cringed. At fifteen, Dallas was wild and mean. He loved taunting the girls, and he had an ugly habit of grabbing our chests if we weren't on guard. He was loud and rough.

"Go off and don't bother us," Faye said.

"Shut your mouth, girl," Dallas said. "Before I shut it for you."

"Make me," Faye said.

I took a step away, frightened. I never knew what Dallas might do. When he took a step toward Faye, I got nervous.

"You back off, Dallas," another boy's voice called out.

I turned to see Bobby, Dallas's older brother, approaching. He was tall like his dad and had the same mannerisms. Everyone liked him except Dallas, who was scared of his older brother.

"This ain't your business," Dallas muttered.

Bobby stood in front of Faye. "Go find something to do and leave these girls alone."

Dallas pointed threateningly at Faye but backed off. Soon he was lost in the crowd. Nellie and I gathered around, thanking Bobby for his help. His dark brown eyes did not leave my face.

"If he ever bothers you, Frances, you just call me," he said softly.

I nodded my head and left to join the other girls. Together, we raced off to the dance. I glanced back once, and Bobby was standing in the same spot, watching me as I walked away.

The dance was starting to kick up. Several men picked up their instruments and struck an upbeat melody after Mr. Willoughby's touching song. They did not match his talent, but they played with so much energy that many of the folks around the circle got up on their feet and started to dance. An old man played the banjo and stomped his feet to the music as everyone clapped or danced. A few of the older boys stood close by, admiring the scene. Another man played an old empty moonshine jug, providing the base. The man we all knew only as Duck played the fiddle and jumped from one foot to the other along with the beat. The women clogged, and many children danced around the campfire.

Faye, Judy, Nellie, and I sat on the sidelines, listening and watching the boys watch us. I was finally able to release some of the stress that wore me down the rest of the week. I lifted my face up to the sky and gazed at the millions of brilliant stars scattered across the heavens. They seemed to shine so much brighter in the country with no streetlights. Stars always made me think of my sister Susie. She used to recite a verse every night there was even one single star in the sky: "Starlight, star bright, first star I see tonight. Wish I may, wish I might, have the wish I wish tonight."

She never told me her wish. She was certain that if she told, it would not come true. I missed her terribly that night. I knew she would have loved the dance, and my wish would have been to share the time with her. I wondered where she and Brenda were. I felt their absence deeply.

By the end of the night, as the fireflies hung high up in the branches and a small campfire gave off the only light, I sat as still and silently as possible on a patch of grass so I would not be sent off to bed. I listened to the hauntingly beautiful music and memorized every song I could. Nellie, Faye, and Judy had already gone to bed, and I was alone. I just could not pull myself away from the music. I watched as a young couple slipped into the woods while old men hung their heads, heavy from too much drink.

Daddy stood across the way, chatting with a woman I'd never seen before. She took a step toward him. He kept on talking. Then an older man, probably the woman's father, called her away. Daddy watched her go, and I saw the darkness come over his face. He saw me and beckoned. I knew I had to follow, but I wished more than anything I could just stay close to the music and watch the stars. As I headed out of camp, I caught snatches of muffled conversation, tales from folks remembering better days and times long past.

Chapter 19

Choices

We left the farm in Stilwell one rainy day, piling in the car and following a caravan of other rickety old vehicles to the next farm that had posted a Pickers Wanted sign. Nellie and I were excited to see the Willoughbys' truck up ahead. We all arrived at the new place at the same time. This farm didn't offer cabins to live in, so we made a campsite near our vehicles and slept in the car. The others did the same. The campsite was filled with the noise of the men chopping wood, women making fires to cook dinner, babies crying, and couples squabbling. A spring ran nearby where the children filled jugs and buckets with water for cooking and washing.

In the morning, before the sun came up, we went to work like locusts, picking the field clean. Every day we spent with the Willoughbys, we grew closer and got to know them better. Mable Willoughby insisted that we eat our meals with them, which was a welcome treat.

It usually took several weeks to pick a farmer's field clean, and then we moved on to the next one. The farmer paid the workers every day at quitting time, so they could have money for a little food and gas for their old cars.

Days turned to weeks, and eventually we broke off from the others. Nellie and I hugged our only friends good-bye, and Mable gave us some fried cornbread to eat on the road. Bobby came up to me just before I got into the car while Daddy shook hands with Mr. Willoughby.

"I'll miss you, Frances." He seemed shy and looked at his feet, which was not usual for Bobby.

Daddy drove us northeast. Each mile was torture to me. I had constant flashbacks of the wreck. Something strange had happened in my mind after that horrible accident; whenever we were driving, I saw things that were not there. From out of nowhere, I would see a car coming straight at us. I would hear the sounds of the wreck and feel the damp earth around my body. Involuntarily, I would scream, "Watch out!"

More often than not, I earned myself a curse or a slap for opening my mouth. Sometimes Daddy would shoot his big fist out behind him, hitting anything that moved.

I was thankful when our journey finally came to an end. We arrived at an apple orchard in Michigan. It was fall, and the leaves were blowing across the dirt trail as Daddy stopped the car and we unloaded our few belongings into another drafty old one-room cabin.

The next day, we went out picking apples. It was a large orchard, so I figured we'd be around for a while. I missed Faye, Judy, and especially Mrs. Willoughby, who had treated me as one of her own daughters. Mrs. Willoughby had talked to me when we were alone, often seeking me out and inviting me into her cabin.

"Tell me about your Daddy," she would say.

It made me uncomfortable, as if she could see right through me to the secrets I kept. But when we were separated, I missed them all very much, as though they were a part of my family. I often found myself singing the songs I'd heard Mr. Willoughby play. If Daddy caught me, he would give me a smack in the head. That would quiet me down, but the tunes never left my heart and mind.

Early one morning, while the dew was still on the grass, I was picking under a large tree so full of apples the branches touched the ground. I had been humming softly, and suddenly realized Daddy had not yelled at me for singing. I looked around but he was not in sight.

"Where is Daddy?" I asked Nellie

She had an apple-picking bucket strapped around her neck and shoulders. Daddy felt picking apples was the quickest way to make money. Of all the farm jobs, this was my favorite. It was cool under the large trees, and it was clean work. The smell was delicious, and we could eat apples when Daddy wasn't watching.

Nellie shrugged in response to my question. "I saw him off talking to some woman."

This was not odd or unexpected, but for some reason I felt curious to see who it was. I crossed the lines of apple trees, looking down each row until I found him. He was indeed talking to a woman. He was all smiles, and he had changed his voice to a soft purr.

The first thing I noticed was her face. She was very pretty with long, flowing blond hair and big blue eyes. Her features were strong but feminine, and she smiled as she spoke with Daddy. She was a little taller than him and built much heavier. As I watched, a little girl about four years old, as dark as her mother was light, appeared from behind her, playing under the fruit-laden branches.

I was shocked when I saw Daddy pick the small child up in his arms. He patted her long, shiny black hair and did a little magic trick, making a quarter appear behind her ear. I heard the little girl laugh. It was a bubbly and infectious sound, and despite myself, I smiled.

I thought little of that scene until the next night, when Daddy brought us home from working the orchard. He was excited and agitated. Daddy told me and Nellie to clean up the cabin, and he left in the car. There was not much to clean, considering we had so little of our own, but I worked at getting a layer of the ever-present dirt off the floor and the cobwebs from the ceiling. Daddy came rushing back in with a sack full of fried chicken and some fixings.

My mouth watered at the smell of it, but I was wary. Daddy didn't bring home food like that for us. I figured it was some kind of trap, and that if I ate it, he'd hurt me. So I hovered around, my stomach rumbling and my mind fighting the almost uncontrollable urge to snatch up a chicken leg and race out of the cabin.

Things became clearer when a soft knock sounded at the cabin door. I started. Visitors were usually unwelcome, but Daddy hurried to the door and opened it. There stood the tall, heavyset blond woman and her young, dark-haired daughter. I would come to know them too well: Millie and Mary Anne. Unbeknownst to them, they were walking right into my nightmare.

I saw Daddy flirting with Millie in the fields many times over the next few days. She and Mary Anne came by the cabin every night. Mary Anne played with me and Nellie. She was an adorable little girl and I loved her. In spite of my mind warning me not to get too close, my heart melted inside my chest when she called me "Fances." Millie told me that Mary Anne's father, who was not around any longer, was a full-blooded Native American.

Mary Anne loved to play, and I would sit for hours tearing out paper dolls for her. She was a happy child, filled with curiosity and a desire to learn anything. I read comic books to her, and if we had nothing else, I recited stories that Mama had taught me.

We started picking apples alongside Millie. Mary Anne, however, was too little to work. She just played in the apple orchard beside her mother, sometimes trying to get me and Nellie to join in.

"Why'd you gotta wuk so hard?" she asked, her little brow wrinkled.

Any other child saying that to me would have made me laugh. Her big, dark eyes were so serious that I could tell she just didn't understand why I couldn't play with her. So I answered her with gentleness.

"I'm older than you, honey," I said. "I need to work to get money."

She stared up at me with wide, dark eyes that made me think of a baby deer.

"I'm four years old."

"You are? You're getting so big."

"I am a big girl. Pappa says so."

I lifted an eyebrow. "You got a daddy?"

"Pappa's my granddaddy. My daddy is gone off. I think he's building a bridge someplace far-off." She looked out over the tops of the apple trees. "Far, far-off."

"What makes you think he's building a bridge?"

She shrugged. "Mommy says he'll be gone for a long time."

I nodded, but I was not sure what she was talking about. She just stared at me as if waiting.

"Frances!" Daddy called out.

I jumped and quickly started filling my sack. Mary Anne danced around me.

"Here, I'll help," she said.

She'd pick an apple off the ground and shove it into my sack. Her little hand could barely grip the ripe fruit. It made me smile to watch her try to help so earnestly, but then I caught sight of Daddy giving a warning look.

"I gotta get back to work, baby," I said, taking a step away from Mary Anne.

"I'm helping."

"You are a big help." I put my hand up as if to stop her following me. "But I'll see you tonight, okay?"

"Can we play hide-and-seek?"

"We sure will, Mary Anne. Tonight, after work."

"Okay," she said with a big grin.

I watched Mary Anne skip off, and even with Daddy's threats, I could not help but smile after her.

One day while working in the field, I stopped to get a cup of water from the large tank the farmer had left out. I had found a shady spot under one of the tall apple trees and sat down for a short break. I heard rustling down the row and thought it might be Mary Anne. She always seemed to know what area I was at in the apple orchard. When she'd find me we would wrestle in the soft grass for a minute or two, or I would give her a piggyback ride. She climbed all over me like a monkey whenever she caught me sitting down.

I braced myself, only to find it was Millie instead. She saw me, and her broad-featured face broke into a smile.

"I was looking for you, Frances," she said.

"Here I am."

I was not being sassy. I liked Millie well enough, but I felt reserved. A thought had crept into my mind one day while I was babysitting Mary Anne. Mama had no choice in the matter, but Millie seemed to be seeking out Daddy's attention. Couldn't she see him for what he was? It gave me the creeps to watch her hand Mary Anne over to Daddy. He would play and cut up with the little girl, but I knew it was an act. I thought poorly of Millie when she brought Mary Anne around.

Millie did not seem to notice any of my reservations. She sat down next to me as if she were a girlfriend come to talk about boys. In a way, that is exactly what she was doing.

"You know, I might be coming with you when you pack up and leave next week," she said.

I felt every muscle in my body tense up. Was she crazy? I wanted to scream at her, tell her to run away and flee for her life before she and her daughter got hurt. As the words formed in my mind, however, they were quickly replaced by an image of Daddy, his fist pounding on the dashboard, his eyes filled with madness and hatred. My tongue tied up, and I had to look away.

"Tell me, Frances, what does he like?"

"Huh?"

"What does your daddy like? I want to make him happy."

I could not believe what she was saying. Could she really be that blind? Not knowing what else to do, I just shrugged.

"I don't know."

"Don't be shy," Millie said. "It's about time you had someone to care for you and Nellie."

I could not stand it any longer. I was scared to death, but between clenched teeth I forced out the only words I could think to say.

"My mama is not dead," I said.

"What? Oh, Frances! I know it must be hard."

"She ain't dead," I said. "She's in South Carolina."

Millie shook her head as if to say I was a silly child.

"Your daddy said that Mary Anne can come along. I know you like her, and she loves you."

I tried once more.

"I don't think you really know him," I said.

I could not believe the words left my mouth. I knew how dangerous it was for me to talk this way. I had no doubt Daddy would kill me if he knew, but the thought of Mary Anne gave me the courage to at least hint at the dangerous road Millie was choosing.

Millie tilted her head and squinted at me. She had made up her mind already. I could see it as clear as the sun. She paid my warning no mind. Instead, she patted my shoulder and walked away.

Millie and Mary Anne lived with her elderly parents in a small house near the orchard. That night, Daddy went to visit her. When he came back to our little cabin, he had fire in his eyes.

"What'd you tell Millie 'bout me?" he growled.

My mind raced. He grabbed a fist full of my dress, tearing the fabric and almost lifting me off the ground.

"I didn't say nothing bad," I stammered. "She asked me what you liked and I said I didn't know what you like. I didn't want to say the wrong thing to her and mess things up for you."

I saw something register behind his eyes. It was as if the character he was playing in front of Millie and Mary Ann came back out. His grip loosened.

"I like her a lot," I said. "And Mary Anne too."

"I don't care if you like 'em or not. You just better keep your trap shut if you don't want some of this!" He pushed his hard fist against my mouth.

I did not say anything else. I knew I was on shaky ground. His anger could flare at any moment, and I knew I'd provoked him by saying what I did to Millie.

"If you say anything to her again, I will kill you."

He said it like someone might say, "I will take a breath."

When Mary Anne came over the next night, Daddy bought her a sucker and bounced her on his knee. Millie looked at me once. I half expected that she had told him to get me in trouble, but her expression hinted otherwise. She looked sad on my account. When she came over to me, I understood why.

"I am not replacing your mama," she said. "Don't worry about that, okay?"

I nodded. I knew at that moment she had utterly misunderstood my hinted warning. I had tried, God knew I had, but I didn't think there was anything I could do to save little Mary Anne.

Chapter 20

Another Child Lost

The orchard was picked clean by the next day. Back at the cabin, Daddy told us to load up the car. We did as bidden and climbed into the backseat when done. I looked out the window but didn't see Mary Anne or Millie approaching from the road. When Daddy started up the engine, I felt total relief and happiness for Mary Anne. Maybe Millie had understood my warning after all.

Daddy drove the car toward the highway, but my heart sank when he turned off toward the small house sitting up on the hill overlooking the orchard. As we rolled to a stop, I saw an elderly couple who had to be Millie's parents. They were much older than Daddy. Her mother was a soft-looking, kind-faced woman. She was hanging laundry on the line at the side of the house. Her father sat on the porch, a cool expression on his face as he eyed the car.

Daddy jumped out and walked quickly toward the house.

"Hullo there, Harley. How you doin' today?" Daddy said in a cheerful tone.

Millie's father nodded but said nothing. I could see the open suspicion on her mother's face. Then I heard Mary Anne laughing as she pushed open the screen door and ran to the car. I did not open the door for her so she stopped outside.

"Let me in," she yelled.

She held a rag doll tightly in her arms. Nellie, rolling her eyes as though to say I was stupid, leaned across me and opened the door. Mary Anne scurried inside and snuggled up beside me. She was so excited.

I could barely look at her. Instead, I watched as Millie came out of the house carrying a large leather bag. She leaned over and kissed the top of her father's head, but he did not move. He stared off into space as if he did not see her. Millie went to her mother, and I saw the woman fighting back tears. She hugged Millie but looked suspiciously at the car. It was as if she wanted to pull Mary Anne out and hold onto her forever.

Daddy took the bag from Millie's hand and loaded it in the trunk. He called out to her parents, saying he'd care for their daughter. They said nothing. He opened the passenger door and held it as Millie got inside the car. I was so afraid, knowing what they were in for but not able to warn them for fear of my own life. It made me sick to my stomach. When Daddy got in, Mary Anne leaned forward.

"Hi, Daddy," she said.

My heart ached for her.

Millie never saw it coming. I am sure of that. We were in the car for only a day when Mary Anne started to cry. She had lived an easy life with three caring adults to fawn over her. When she had to use the bathroom and Daddy refused to stop, she lost control.

"I gotta go pee pee!" she shrieked.

"Hush, sweetheart," Millie said over her shoulder.

She looked at Daddy as if wondering why he would not stop. I could see his grip on the steering wheel tighten, and I felt a deep panic coming over me. I looked away and tried to close my eyes. But closing my eyes in the car filled my head with visions of barbed wire and the sound of crashing metal and breaking glass. I opened my eyes again quickly.

Mary Anne screamed again. Suddenly, Daddy spun around so fast I barely saw him. I dodged as his hand came crashing back at us. This time, I was not the target. It was Mary Anne. His hard slap crashed across her face, and her small body went flying back against the seat as if she weighed no more than her rag doll.

I could not believe what I saw next. Millie smacked Daddy hard across the face with her open hand. I had never seen Mama raise a hand to him. She survived his abuse by not fighting back. Millie, I knew then, was very different. She lashed out at him like a mother bear protecting her young. Mary Anne was wailing in the backseat in pain and shock. Daddy pulled off the road in a hurry, slamming his foot on the brake and screeching to a stop.

Daddy grabbed a handful of Millie's hair and tried to drag her across the car and out his door. I had seen him do the same thing to Mama before, but Millie did not budge. She was bigger than him and outweighed him by at least fifty pounds. Instead, she tore away from him and jumped out her door. He raced after her, and they came together like two rams crashing horns on a hilltop.

Millie was no match for Daddy. She never stopped fighting, though, and she took his punches, but he was used to fighting grown men. She didn't have a chance. He beat her until she could not lift a fist in retaliation and then beat her some more.

Mary Anne cowered in the backseat, sobbing.

"Hush now," I whispered, petting her with shaking hands. "You must be quiet, or it'll make him worse. Please, don't cry, baby." I tried to soothe and warn her at the same time. "You must be quiet, honey. Please sit down," I pleaded.

It was too late. Daddy heard her and swung open the back door.

He tore Mary Anne out of my grasp, lifting her out of the car by her hair. She hung, her feet suspended above the ground, and she cried out in fear. Daddy punched her square in the face.

Mary Anne had never endured or witnessed any violence before. Her bowels let lose as she gurgled and sputtered to breathe. Blood dripped out of her nose, and Daddy threw her to the ground. He walked back to Millie.

"Get your no-account brat cleaned up and back in the car before I kill her," he said.

Millie had lost her fight for the moment. She looked pale and shaken; bright red blood spouted from Millie's ear, and her eye was swollen, but she concentrated on her daughter. Mary Anne's body shook as if she was crying, but no sound came out. Millie took off the soiled dress and left it on the side of the road. She wiped Mary Anne's face with the end of the dress and put a clean dress and fresh underwear on her while Daddy growled and threatened to run off and leave them. When Millie laid her in the backseat, both Nellie and I shied away, keeping one eye on Daddy. We knew if we dared misstep, Daddy's rage would fall on us next.

Once Millie was back in the car and Daddy started the engine, I inched closer to Mary Anne. I carefully placed her small head in my lap. A tear slid down my cheek as I caressed her silky black hair.

Chapter 21

A Trap Set

We traveled from small town to small town that winter, and Daddy eked out a living by working in gas stations or mechanic shops. If we could not work alongside of him, he worked only long enough to get gas money and move on. Daddy would often drive at night, as if he thought the police were hunting for him everywhere we went. During the day, he would park the car off of a dirt road and kick us out so he could sleep. Since I could no longer sleep in a moving car, I spent weeks living on little more than catnaps. Days started melting together. I had a hard time even telling where we were when we stopped for a week or two of work.

Often, we did not find a place to stay when we stopped over in a town. We lived out of the car instead. At least it was not moving at night, so I could sleep. In many ways our lives were better with Millie there. Daddy never bothered Nellie or me when we went to bed. But still, it was horrible when Mary Anne got beat up or when he would yell at her. She was so small and innocent, and she did not understand how to stay out of his way.

As winter's icy hand pressed harder down on us, work turned scarce. Daddy's anger flared more often when he couldn't get his alcohol. He beat us all and constantly got in knockdown, bloody fights with Millie. When they would start, I tried to get Mary Anne out of his sight as quickly as possible. Often we walked off into the woods. Sometimes I would look for a good climbing tree and pass the time teaching her how to climb up beside me. She was a natural, and soon we were able to scurry up a tree together and weather out the worst of Daddy's maniacal moods.

Sometimes, though, I could not save her. Once, while we were stopped for the day next to a reservoir, Daddy and Millie were trying to sleep in the car. Nellie, Mary Anne, and I were outside playing on the gravel road. I was trying to skip rocks off the sparkling surface of the water. Ice laced the edges of the man-made lake, and Mary Anne kept herself busy pulling up pieces of ice and pretending to make dinner for us all.

I walked away from her, looking for the perfect stone to skip. Nellie's nose was in a book we'd found in a church a few stops back. Mary Anne must have slipped because I heard a splash followed by the loudest shriek I'd heard her make. I raced over, but was too late. Daddy exploded from the car and was on her as fast as lightning.

"What is wrong with you?" he screamed.

I could not see Mary Anne due to the dipping bank around the reservoir, but I did see Daddy reach down. He yanked her out of the water and threw her behind him. Water cascaded from her clothing as she flipped in the air and skidded to a stop on the gravel road. Her screaming grew louder. I took a step toward her but saw the murder in Daddy's eyes. It froze me. I watched as he walked toward her.

"That lowlife father of yours ruined you. Are you a dummy or what?"

Daddy's foot reared back. I couldn't watch anymore. I bolted for the woods, tears running off my cheeks as I heard Mary Anne's screams grow louder.

That evening, Daddy decided we would stay in that place for a while. He left us to go out drinking. I sat on the ground by the campfire, watching Millie clean the blood off of Mary Anne's face with water she had drawn from the reservoir. I had no idea where Nellie was, nor did I care. I just stared at Millie.

As the sun set, reflecting a rainbow of pink, orange, and purple over the surface of the water, Mary Anne fell asleep on Millie's lap. I inched closer.

"How can you let him beat her like that?" I asked.

Millie looked at me. I think I expected anger. Maybe I wanted to make her mad because I was so upset by seeing Mary Anne hurt with nobody to protect her. But Millie only looked confused.

"'Cause it only makes him worse if I fight."

They were simple words, but they somehow forged a bond between me and Millie. It was not that I loved her, or even trusted her to protect Mary Anne. But I did understand her. She knew the reason I had run off during Mary Anne's beating. There was no stopping Daddy. If there had been, I would have done it long, long before.

I sat there looking into the fire, feeling the cold wind cutting into my back and thinking about a night long ago. Brenda had meant it when she planned to kill him. I was sure of it now, and I understood it completely.

Spring crept over the land and left the dull ache of winter behind. I was twelve that year, and Nellie was fourteen. One day in April, Daddy came home from the gas station he had been working at and told us to load up. We took off and headed southwest. It was time for another cycle of farms: peas, strawberries, cotton, and apples.

We hadn't been working the farm circuit long when we met up with some familiar faces. The one family I looked forward to seeing that year was the Willoughbys, and when we reached Arkansas, there they were.

Nellie, Judy, Faye, and I rekindled our sisterhood without hesitation. We tried to work close together during the day, although there was no time for horseplay. Sometimes in the evenings, especially when Daddy went out drinking, we went to their cabin. Their mother fed us, and we girls sat outside and talked about what each of us had been doing in the time we were separated.

One evening not long after arriving, Millie sent me over to the Willoughbys to borrow some flour so she could make water gravy for our dinner. When I got to their cabin, I found Mrs. Willoughby's six-year-old son by himself. He was standing up on a chair beside their wooden table with a knife in his hand.

"What are you doing?" I asked, afraid he was going to hurt himself.

The little boy had a serious expression on his face. His big brown eyes looked at me from under a wrinkled, dirty brow.

"I'm cuttin' this dirt offa my arms."

I raised an eyebrow. Then I looked down at my own arms. They, too, were caked with dirt and grime, as they always were.

"Don't do that," I said. "You're going to cut yourself. Come on with me."

I took the little boy by the hand and led him down to the creek. I dunked the hem of my dress in the water and scrubbed at his arm. It took awhile, but I got most of the dirt off him.

"I hate being dirty," he said.

"I do too. But you can't go cutting it off with a knife."

"But it'll just come back."

"And you can wash it clean again," I said.

"I hate it though," he muttered as I walked him back to camp.

When I arrived at the cabin, little boy in tow, Mrs. Willoughby was there. She looked at me with curiosity on her face.

"Frances, come on in. What are you doing?" she asked.

"I just helped your youngest son wash his face and arms."

Her son ran back out to play as Mrs. Willoughby sat down at the table. She started to peel potatoes as she spoke to me.

"How's your daddy?" she asked without looking up.

"He's okay."

"How long has he been traveling with that girl Millie, now?"

"About a year," I answered.

"I seen her little girl this morning." Mrs. Willoughby looked at me over the half-glasses she wore. Wisps of her black hair covered one eye, but from the other I could see that she was turning something over in her mind. "Is there anything wrong with that little girl?"

I shook my head. "No, she's okay."

"She seemed mighty quiet to me."

I didn't know what to say. I, too, had noticed a change in Mary Anne. Unlike Mrs. Willoughby, though, I had no question about the source of that change. My friends' mother just watched me with that one eye, searching for an answer. Even though I said nothing, I think I gave it to her.

"You better head on out before your daddy gets mad and comes lookin' for you," she said. "Do you want a piece-a tater to take with you?"

"No, thank you. Millie asked me to borrow some flour so she could make gravy for dinner."

I left her cabin with a cup of flour and rushed back to ours. Millie was outside watching me.

"What took you so long?" she asked.

"Mrs. Willoughby got to talking."

"To you?"

I nodded.

"What about?"

I paused. "Nothin'."

Her eyes narrowed.

"I better go gather up some wood," I said, passing the cup of flour to her.

I rushed out before she had a chance to ask anything else. The conversation with Mrs. Willoughby stuck with me for a while, but I was soon distracted by the burning in my muscles that came from dragging long limbs up to the cabin to be cut into firewood.

Mrs. Willoughby often drove into town in the evening to pick up supplies. On most occasions, she would take one of the camp children along with her. Sometimes it would be one of her own, sometimes someone else's child. She liked the company, and even more, she appeared to love the fuss we made over her.

"I'm heading to the store if anyone wants to come!" she announced in the center of camp.

A number of us children were out playing a game. I rushed over with everyone else, jumping up and down with my hand in the air. I hoped she would pick me, but I was way in the back.

"Frances, come on, get in the car," she called out.

I barely heard her over the din of the other children, so I was sure I was mistaken. I stood there for a moment.

"Come on, if you want to go with me," Mrs. Willoughby called out, looking right at me.

The other children groaned and muttered as I pushed my way through the crowd. I was smiling, basking in the attention. Their envy did not bother me one bit. I climbed into the Willoughbys' truck and we drove away.

Mrs. Willoughby did not say anything to me during the drive. We headed out of camp, but I was surprised when we pulled off the road far before the highway. She drove her big old truck down a dirt path toward the creek.

"Where we going?" I asked.

"Just making a stop first, that's all," she said.

Mrs. Willoughby had a strangely determined look on her face.

I sensed something was out of the ordinary, but I had no idea what. When we rounded a bend and I saw Bobby, her oldest son, standing in the clearing before us, I got a touch of fear in my stomach that I could not explain.

Mrs. Willoughby slowed the truck to a stop.

"Come on, Frances," she said as she got out.

I followed her, and she led me right up to Bobby. His cheeks looked flushed, and he would not look at me. I couldn't understand his attitude.

Mrs. Willoughby put a hand on my back as if to guide me forward.

"Why don't you and Bobby take a walk down by the creek," she said. "You can get better acquainted."

I was totally clueless about what was meant to happen. Although part of me was so unsure, I trusted Mrs. Willoughby and liked Bobby as my friend and protector from his brother Dallas. The way he stared at the ground made it seem as if he knew exactly what his mother wanted. Mrs. Willoughby cleared her throat. As if that was a signal, Bobby reached out his hand. I took it and we started to walk down a narrow path leading to the creek.

"Hey, down there!"

The shout came from the road, up behind us. My blood froze. I knew the voice all too well. It was Daddy, and he sounded spitting mad.

Chapter 22

Bobby Willoughby

Daddy stormed into the clearing like a raging bull. He reached out to grab Bobby just as Mrs. Willoughby stepped in between them. Daddy's eyes were bulging and his face was red.

"Get to the car before I kill you!" he ordered me. "How dare you try this stunt with my daughter!"

Mrs. Willoughby did not budge. She stood firm in front of my daddy as if she had no fear.

"Calm yourself, Broadus. Nothing's happened."

"Nothings *gonna* happen, either. Do you know how old she is?"

Daddy's voice was louder and meaner than I'd ever heard it before in public. I climbed up the hill to the car, afraid to look back but having no idea why he was so angry. When Daddy was upset, I knew enough not to ask questions. I was worried for Bobby and Mrs. Willoughby, but I was also relieved that his fury wasn't directed at me for the time being.

Millie and Mary Anne were waiting in the car. I could see fear in their eyes. I still didn't know what I had done to make him so angry. I climbed into the backseat of the car and closed the door.

"Why is he so mad?" I whispered to Millie.

"Just be quiet," she said, shaking her head.

Daddy's angry curses and threats floated up the hill and into the car. He was consumed with rage over something, but I hadn't figured it out yet. Confused and afraid, I hoped Millie would explain, but she wasn't talking.

I heard Daddy shouting outside, but Mrs. Willoughby never raised her voice. I was worried for her. At the same time, she was a titan like Daddy, a force of nature that seemed unstoppable. Finally, he looked back toward the car. I heard his warning to Mrs. Willoughby as he pointed his finger in her face.

"You better keep this skunk and them other heathens away from my camp. If I see this skinny kid jackass near Frances, I'll tear him apart with my teeth."

He cursed her once more and turned, storming up the hill toward the car.

"Jesus, help me," I prayed.

Daddy opened the door and got inside. He turned toward the backseat, and little Mary Anne dove for the floor. He slapped me across the face with the back of his hand. I tasted blood in my mouth and felt it running from my nose. Still, I didn't speak. Hot tears spilled from my eyes. *Why!?* I screamed in silent anger. *What did I do?*

We arrived back at the cabin, and Millie looked shaken. Mary Anne ran in ahead of us to hide in her favorite corner by the bed. Daddy didn't get out of the car right away. Millie and I hustled into the cabin as fast as we could. She paced around the shack, picking things up. I watched her for a moment, my head tilted. It reminded me of something, but I was not sure what it was.

A few minutes later, Daddy charged through the door.

"You tramp," he spat at me.

I was still confused. I had no idea what he was talking about, but it was not an uncommon thing for him to call me, so I thought little of it. Then he started to scream at Millie.

"She was going to prostitute her out to that son of hers. I might as well have taken money from the witch."

Daddy went on and on. I started to understand there was more to that moment in the woods than I had thought. I was almost a teenager by then, but the motivations behind adult behavior still occasionally escaped me. It became clear that something was meant to happen between me and Bobby, and that Mrs. Willoughby was the instigator behind all of it. Bobby was eighteen and I was not quite thirteen. The full impact of what Mrs. Willoughby had planned didn't sink in until I had some time to spend alone with Millie much later. She finally explained it to me. I later found out that Mrs. Willoughby assumed that if her son and I were together and I became pregnant, my dad would naturally want me to marry Bobby. She didn't know Daddy!

My head hurt as I tried to understand. Daddy knew what he had been doing to me for years. It made no sense that he would be so mad about the difference between my age and Bobby's. Why was he so mad about it?

The answer to that made me feel worse. As he ranted, I remembered that I was simply his property. He owned me, Nellie, and now Mary Anne. We were nothing more to him than a chair or a sack to hold cotton. Although Daddy's words sounded protective, I knew they had nothing to do with parental protection or love. Mrs. Willoughby had done something to defy him and tried to take what was his. That was why he was spitting mad.

"Pack up this trash," he bellowed. He spun on me. "Did you ever touch that boy? Did you kiss him?"

"No, sir," I pleaded. "Never. I'd never!"

"You *better never!*" He mocked me. "You won't ever get a chance to touch *any* boy! You're just like your mama! I ought to kill you!"

He slapped me across the face again, hard. My ears rang, and I felt dizzy as I stumbled back and slammed into the wall.

"Get your sister," he growled at me.

I ran out the door, rushing to find Nellie. She was out front leaning on a tree trunk and reading a magazine. Nellie had a way of removing herself from the people around her. It wasn't that she didn't care. She just found a way to avoid getting attached or involved.

"Come on, Nellie. Daddy's on the warpath."

"Now? Why?"

"Just come on, please."

Movement caught the corner of my eye. It was Mrs. Willoughby's car returning to camp. I felt an almost undeniable tug to run to her, jump in the back of that truck, and escape. Daddy bellowed from inside. His face appeared in the doorway, the shadows adding a demonic cast to his angry expression.

Mrs. Willoughby's car rolled closer. I could not move. My mind wrapped around one thought: *Why did she take me into the woods?* If she wanted me to be with Bobby, there had to be a reason. I loved Mrs. Willoughby and wanted to talk to her badly.

"Get in this house, now!" Daddy screamed.

I moved, breaking the trance. I could just make out Mrs. Willoughby's face through the window. She appeared to be staring right at me. I ran into the house, Nellie right on my heels.

Daddy packed our belongings in the back of his car. We were leaving.

"Field is still full," Nellie said. "We ain't never left a full field before. Not unless Daddy's been in trouble. Did he get in a fight again?"

I shrugged. I could not tell Nellie what I knew. We were leaving because of Bobby and Mrs. Willoughby. Daddy was going to get us away from that family. He would make sure we never saw them again. If Nellie found that out, I knew she'd blame me for it. So I stayed quiet and bit my lip, trying not to cry.

Daddy came back into the cabin. Sweat dripped from his brow, although it was cool outside.

"Get out to the car," he ordered.

I grabbed Mary Anne from where she sat across the cabin, and along with Nellie made it out to the car. We climbed in without saying a word. We knew that anything could set Daddy off again. Even Mary Anne seemed to understand that.

He and Millie got in, then he started up the car.

"Tramp," Daddy hissed. This time, he wasn't talking to me.

I looked up when he said that and saw Mrs. Willoughby standing off the road up ahead, her arms crossed over her small chest. Bobby was not with her. She seemed to stare right through Daddy, who revved the engine. The car lurched forward, pointed directly at her. She did not move. Only yards before hitting her, Daddy cursed and straightened it out. We rolled past where she stood.

In that instant, my eyes locked with Mrs. Willoughby's. There was sadness there, and something else. Failure, maybe. When I looked at the expression on Mrs. Willoughby's face, my mind cast a vision of Millie cleaning after I came back from the clearing. It struck me why her actions seemed so familiar. They reminded me of Mama when she was nervous about Daddy's anger. In a strange way, Mrs. Willoughby standing there did the same thing.

I waved to her, but she turned away as if hiding her face. Our car pulled out of camp, and that was the last time I ever saw her.

Chapter 23

Spiders

After leaving the migrant camp in Arkansas, we took a departure from the series of jobs Daddy had lined up. He avoided any farms we had worked in the past. I believe he was avoiding any chance of running into the Willoughbys. Instead, we worked small jobs from one Southern town to the next, and we spent most of the spring and summer living in the car. Just when I thought things couldn't get much worse, Millie announced one day that she was pregnant.

While the baby in her belly grew, her personality seemed to shrink. Food became scarcer, but Daddy always seemed to find a way to get drunk. As the heat pressed on us like a smothering blanket, he lost his temper more and more often. I would try to leave the campsite early in the evening on the days he got really drunk, and I always found an opportunity to take Mary Anne with me. We would find a tree near where Daddy had parked the car and climb up to the highest branch we could manage. Perched comfortably in the branches, I would tell her fairy tales. Sometimes she made up stories of her own. She would add a funny twist to "Jack and the Beanstalk" or make Cinderella a teenage rock star. She had a good imagination, and I encouraged her to exercise it. Sometimes we stayed up there all night. I always hoped the car would be gone in the morning, but it never was. Daddy didn't ever remember us sneaking out. He never remembered anything when he sobered up.

As the baby's time neared, Daddy found work at a new cotton camp in the South. We moved into the usual small shack. One night, as soon as the sun went down, Daddy sent Nellie, Mary Anne, and me outside, telling us to stay near the cabin and not to come back until he called. Millie was screaming, and I assumed they were fighting. I tried to get Mary Anne as far away as possible. I didn't find out that Millie's baby had been born until we were ready for bed. Daddy delivered his son that night. They named him Broadus. Millie was back to work in the fields the following day, pulling a long cotton sack behind her with her infant son sleeping at the end with a diaper over him for shade. I don't remember Millie's son very well, but I do remember that saying his name troubled me because he was named after Daddy. Daddy did not allow Mary Anne to play with or hold him. Mostly I left him alone, and so did Mary Anne.

When the cotton had been picked, we moved again and again. November slipped into December, and the air took on a chill as we drove northwest. Daddy found some odd jobs, but they did not last long. Because the new baby was so tiny and vulnerable, the situation turned desperate quickly.

By late December we were all cold, hungry, and worn-out from traveling. It seemed as if we drove aimlessly. The heater in our old car barely worked, and the baby cried constantly. One evening at dusk, we were traveling down an icy road near Joplin, Missouri. Five months had passed since Millie's son was born.

"The gas is low," Daddy grumbled from the front seat. "We got to find some place to get in for the night or freeze."

I held on to Mary Anne. She was shaking from the cold and making soft moans. Nellie was on the other side. She stared out the window.

"The baby's cold," Millie said.

"Shut up," Daddy snapped.

I could hear the tension in his voice. We had been driving for two days, and he had no money for alcohol. He was on a dangerous edge, and I worried for Millie and her child, more because of Daddy than the cold.

The baby started to cry, and the sound scared me. Maybe it was the acoustics of the tight space of the car, but his wails sounded hollow and empty. My thoughts returned to another night long before, when my new baby sister cried out in the same way. Mary Anne and I huddled together, and I shivered, giving her what warmth I could.

Daddy pulled off the highway and down a two-lane road. The arch of his headlights passed over what looked like an abandoned shack tucked some distance off the road, behind a copse of trees and at the top of a snow-covered hill. A narrow path led up to the shack.

Daddy saw it and veered the car off the road. By the light of the high beams, the entire area took on a bluish tinge and the trees became an army of shadowy soldiers flanking the hill. Something about the sight made me afraid, but I was so cold that I ignored the feeling in hopes that we would find warmth inside.

The path up to the shack was about three hundred feet off the highway and had not been cleared. A layer of hard snow, maybe six inches deep, ran up to the front porch. Daddy tried to get the car to drive up the hill. He mashed the accelerator, but the tires dug deeper into the snow. He cursed and tried again, but it was clear we were going nowhere.

"Okay, everybody out. We're gonna walk," he said.

Millie bundled up her son and stepped out onto the snow. I opened the back door, and Mary Anne grabbed hold of my hand. Together we started across the ice and snow. Before getting out of the car, Millie gave me a diaper to tie around Mary Anne's head like a scarf. None of us had hats, and our coats were thin and tattered.

Mary Anne's teeth rattled, and I tried to keep her warm, but it was no use. Instead, I focused on getting us up to that house. Nellie followed behind us, complaining loudly. For once Daddy ignored her, probably because she was so far behind him and he was freezing. Our destination appeared to be an abandoned old hunting shack, long deserted and left to decay. The front porch sagged and threatened to crash down at any second. Leafless vines grew up one side and disappeared through a broken window into the dark interior. The full moon shone through the windows, giving a little light.

"I'm cold," Mary Anne whimpered.

"It's okay. We'll be warm inside."

The snow softened the closer we got to the house. Mary Anne struggled to walk, sinking in the snow up to her knees. I held her tight and tried to follow the steps Daddy and Millie had left on their way up. An eerie silence pervaded; the only sounds were our heavy breathing and the crunching of the snow under our feet.

We made our way onto the porch decking, picked our way around large holes, and went through an open front door that dangled on one hinge. Inside, I could see the white snow through more holes in the flooring and through jagged breaks in the outer wall. It was a little warmer in there, but not much.

"We need a fire," Daddy said.

He trudged back to the car, leaving us inside. Mary Anne followed me as I walked around the cabin. In the full moonlight reflected off the snow outside, I could see pretty well. The cabin had three rooms. Two were completely empty of furniture, and a single, sturdy wooden table sat in the middle of the main room.

"I'm cold," Mary Anne cried again.

I tried to comfort her but couldn't do much. It was freezing in that house, and I felt as though we would never be warm again. Daddy pulled an old rusted-metal dishpan into the middle of the room and poured gasoline he'd siphoned from the car into it. Then he dropped a lit match inside. I flinched, expecting an explosion, but instead, a layer of flames danced atop the liquid, casting waving shadows across the room.

As I stood mesmerized by the flames, my hands started to ache. That fire warmed the shack quickly, and our frozen skin began to thaw. Even the baby quieted down, and Mary Anne let go of my hand and found a place on the floor to play.

Daddy went back out to the car and brought in a pile of blankets and clothing. He threw them on the floor. I inched away from him, my stomach turning as it always did at the sight of those blankets. At the same time, the chill was leaving my body, and I felt better than I had all day. Daddy and Millie started talking, and I dragged a blanket to a corner as far away as I could and lay back, watching the light play off the shadows under the sagging roof.

I felt sleep coming close. The longer I looked, the stranger the dark lines on the wall and ceiling seemed to me. It was as if they skittered across the roof beams and trailed down the walls toward the floor. I blinked, trying to clear away the discomfort I felt on seeing that movement, but it only made it clearer. It was as if the walls had legs, lots of legs!

Something large crawled out of a hole in the floor right beside my hand. It was an enormous, hairy black spider! I screamed and pushed myself away from the hole.

That's when I noticed the others. Spiders were everywhere—on the walls, ceiling, floor—and they kept pouring into the shack from every direction. I jumped up, barely avoiding another one that was an inch from crawling onto my leg. I screamed again when I saw the red hourglass on the back of that spider. Black widows! Hundreds of them!

Mary Anne, either reacting to me or the spiders, joined in the screaming. She was latched onto my leg in a matter of seconds. I tried to get her loose, eyeing what looked like a big Missouri tarantula racing toward my feet.

I had one thought: *Get up on that table!* I lunged for one of the sturdy legs and yanked Mary Anne off the ground, pushing her up and climbing behind her. Nellie was already on top of the table and was screaming and dancing up and down, tears rolling down her face.

From up high, I could see just how bad it was. The spiders must have been hibernating in the cold, nesting in the floors, ceiling, and walls. They seemed to be drawn in by the heat and were coming in from every hole or opening in the cabin. Millie stood in place, jumping up and down and screaming like a wild woman. She snatched her son up and shook him in the air as if trying to shake unseen spiders from him. I saw one of them rising over the edge of the table. I kicked at it and sent the thing flying through the air.

As we screamed, Daddy grabbed an old rag of clothing, wrapped it around a log, and rushed to the fire. He set the edge aflame and whipped that torch back and forth like a sword, burning up spiders. When he whipped it toward the ceiling, spiders rained down on us. One landed on my head. I whipped my hair around like mad, screaming until it dropped off. Little Mary Anne was hysterical, but I was busy slapping spiders off the table—our only refuge in the house. The revulsion I felt was overwhelming, and I felt sick to my stomach from the fear. Time lost its meaning as we floated in a living nightmare that I thought I might never wake up from.

"They're dead," Daddy finally announced. But I did not believe him. I could still see spiders all over the floor, thousands of legs twitching.

"Get off the table, now," he ordered.

We were all too afraid to move. I looked at Nellie and Mary Anne, not wanting to be the first one down.

"Get down from there," he growled, this time angry.

There was no arguing. We were just as frightened of his anger as we were of the spiders. As I climbed down, I saw that the spiders that remained were all singed or stomped to death. The smell of burning hair filled the cabin. Daddy told us to get to sleep. He may as well have told me to sprout wings and fly. When I did close my eyes, all I could see were squirming, wriggling spiders. I sat up until dawn, that scent filling my nose and the nightmare etching an indelible fear into my mind.

Chapter 24

Mr. Spencer

I often wonder if the fear of spiders stuck with Nellie as it did with me. I am still deathly afraid of them. But Nellie was strong and tough, more like Daddy than any of us. Although he had us all cowed down, she had a shell around her, a hard determination that seemed to keep her from feeling too deeply. At least that is how she appeared to me. Memories of that night flooded my mind as I sat in my home, years later, with Wayne.

As if sensing my thoughts, Wayne came and sat beside me on the couch, wrapping an arm around me. He had continued a valiant search for my family members even as my relationship with Jimmy grew. I had been told that Nellie had died long ago. Wayne knew this but never believed it. He always told me that he felt in his heart that she was not dead.

One day early in the spring, a few months after we found Jimmy, Wayne came home with a phone number. It was for one of Nellie's daughters. It took courage, but I dialed the number. Nellie's daughter told me that my sister was very much alive and gave me her contact information. I reached out to her that same day. We spoke, and it was as though we had not missed a day. She was as easy to talk to as she'd ever been, and her voice even had the same sound as it had when we were kids. At the end of the conversation, I knew that all the pieces were coming together.

"We should plan a reunion," I told her. "I've been talking with Brenda and Jimmy and our cousins. We could gather all our families together, meet again, and catch up on our lives."

"That sounds like a wonderful idea," Nellie said.

I felt like a marathon runner who sees the finish line less than a mile away. My soul stirred at the thought. My family was finally going to come back together! Even through the elation, my mind wandered back to how it had all ended, how I had lost every one of them and had been left behind, the last of us to escape Daddy's evil.

Needless to say, we stayed but one night in that spider-infested shack. Daddy moved us on from there, heading north. We did not stop until we reached Niles, Michigan. There Daddy met a farm owner named Mr. Spencer. That meeting became the fuse that started the final dismantling of what was left of my family. Mr. Spencer also saved my life.

Mr. Spencer owned a farm covering hundreds of acres. He grew apples, grapes, and blueberries, as well as many other crops. During the prime harvest season, he employed dozens of workers. They lived in the twenty or more small cabins that he built on his land. He cared about his workers and treated them with fairness and honesty.

He was in his late forties and had married late in life. His wife, Jackie, was only twenty-six, and she had already been married and had three children. She and Mr. Spencer had one son of their own, whom Mr. Spencer adored. Farming was Mr. Spencer's life, and he was as childlike and trusting as a young boy. He often joked that before he'd met Jackie, his farmhands had been his family.

In addition to the smaller cabins, he built a nice little house that the foreman stayed in during the harvest. Thanks to Daddy's special arrangements, it was ours! The foreman's house had been neglected and needed much work, but it seemed a castle to me. It had three rooms aligned like train cars, including such luxuries as a small kitchen with a stove, a sink, and a table with chairs. It also had electricity and running water in the kitchen; a small pump was stationed at the sink. The kitchen door had a pane of glass that allowed the sunlight to brighten the room. I'd never been in a farm shack that let in so much light, especially one that had no holes in the walls. The middle room was used as the bedroom and opened into the front room with a solid door for the entrance.

It was such a nice place, compared to our usual living arrangements. At first, I thought we weren't supposed to be there. When we pulled into the camp, I could not believe it when Daddy passed the small cramped cabins and stopped in front of this little house. I stood by the car and stared at the slightly sagging tin roof and the large front porch with its loose floorboards, and it looked amazing to me. With the grapevines that spread out from one side of the house and the woods that shaded the other, it all looked so much like a home that it was hard to imagine being allowed to live there.

I was told to help carry our belongings inside, and the sense of being an intruder lessened. It felt good to be a part of a real house with electricity and even a stove that looked like what other people used to cook. At fourteen, I was beginning to notice things like that more often.

Daddy gathered Millie, Nellie, and me into a group.

"Mr. Spencer made an arrangement with me. We can stay here through the winter, in the foreman's house, if we help take care of the grapevines and I fix the place up. Don't you think you're gonna be shirking your work, you hear?"

After the shack with the spiders, this house was like heaven, and

I was grateful to be allowed to stay. I had no argument with cutting back the grapevines and doing anything I could do in order to live in such a clean house with real furniture.

Not only did Mr. Spencer let us live in the foreman's house, but he also paid Daddy a salary for the work he did. For the first time that winter, we were warm and not as terribly hungry as we had been. Unfortunately, the extra money also gave Daddy the opportunity to take up his drinking again. We settled into the typical dance: him getting drunk, and me doing everything I could to avoid him and protect Mary Anne.

Mr. Spencer lived a few miles down the road from our new home. His two-story farmhouse sat at the end of a gravel drive. He lived there with Jackie and their four children, who were all much younger than me. I found myself over at their house helping with the children and housework on occasion, and I got to know them pretty well. I especially liked Jackie, who insisted we call her by her first name. Right away I realized they were different than most folks we'd come across in our travels. Jackie was very generous, and Mr. Spencer was eager to make our lives comfortable, offering an extra heater or a day off if the weather was very cold.

I escaped our home often, trying to avoid the fights between Daddy and Millie. They were getting more violent, and I did not have the heart to see Mary Anne watch her mother suffer more abuse. She was little, and she had been so bubbly and sweet when we met her. I could see her personality changing right before my eyes. She was broken, and she flinched whenever anyone came near. She never spoke unless we were alone. It hurt to see what Daddy had done, and I often wondered what would become of her.

Strangely, as the abuse continued, Millie seemed to grow closer to Daddy. I noticed that a change had come over her one night while Daddy was out drinking. She spoke to me and Nellie.

"You two are getting older."

Nellie nodded, and I just listened while playing paper dolls with Mary Anne on the floor. I noticed she was paying attention, too, and I remember thinking she looked worried. I had become to her what Brenda had been to me, and I knew I was oftentimes the only buffer to keep her from harm.

"You know," Millie said, "it's about time for you girls to head out on your own. I think you're both old enough to make it alone."

Nellie sat still, silently nodding her head in agreement. I just listened as she continued.

"I think things would get better between Broadus and me, and Mary Anne, too, if you went on your way."

I looked at Mary Anne to see what she thought. She acted as if she hadn't heard her, but I could see she had and didn't like the idea.

Nellie sat at the table. She did not look up. Instead, she scratched a fingernail along the tabletop.

"He won't just let us go, you know."

"You could run off. You're old enough to make it on your own now."

"I could," Nellie said, still not looking at any of us. "I could start a new life. Get a job and take care of myself. He can't stop me."

"No, he can't," Millie agreed.

Later that night, Nellie and I lay in the darkness, trying to sleep. Nellie started whispering to me, and I noticed right away that her voice sounded different.

"I think I'd get a job in town somewhere. Maybe at a movie theater dishing out popcorn. Or at a place ladies go to get their hair fixed. I'd be good at that."

I sat quietly, my stomach turning. With each word she said, I grew more and more afraid. I pictured Daddy storming into the room, grabbing us both by the neck and squeezing the life out of us. I think he might have done it, too, if he heard Nellie talking like that. We had lived under a mountain of fear for so long that I could not believe that

Nellie had climbed so high as to actually think about trying to run away. Nellie was sixteen at the time, and I was fourteen.

She is much stronger than me, I thought. *At least she can dream about it.*

As the weeks passed, though, her stories got more frequent and more detailed. Even I could sense that they weren't just words anymore. She was planning her escape! At the same time, Millie found a way to get us out of the house at least some of the time. She lined us up to babysit for the Spencers' children. We loved it, and it gave Millie time alone with Daddy.

Jackie was a good mother and fun-loving young woman. She didn't seem all that much older than Brenda was when she left. Nellie and I quickly took to her, and Jackie returned the feeling. I loved going up to the house right from the start.

"How is life in your house?" she asked us one of the first nights we went up to sit for her kids.

"Good," Nellie said.

Jackie looked at us for a long minute. I fidgeted in my chair and Nellie gave me a warning look.

"Are you mistreated?"

Nellie shook her head. I did too. I remember being a little bit surprised by that. The fear had not totally left Nellie yet. She would still not confirm Jackie's suspicions.

Jackie sat with watchful eyes, gauging our reactions. With a slight shake of the head, she smiled.

"Come on in the back room. I have some clothes I want you to try on."

She took us to her room and pulled a handful of blouses and dresses out of the closet. She held a few up, measuring them by sight.

"Frances, you try this one."

She handed me a dress. My fingers touched the fabric; it was cotton, and it felt so clean and smooth. My heart ached for the time we'd spent at Connie Maxwell. I pressed the dress against my face, smelling the fresh fabric, and I cradled it tenderly.

"Here you go, Nellie."

She handed my sister a blouse. Nellie's eyes lit up. There was no sadness there, only a kind of fiery determination. We changed right there on the spot. It felt so good to be wearing something ironed and clean.

The work we did for Jackie, cleaning and cooking and tending the children, felt like a vacation to me. She played music on the radio all day, and I memorized every song as I ironed her clothes, washed dishes, and made the beds. Before we left that day, she gave us a small cardboard box with a few pretty dresses for each of us. She gave Nellie a pair of shoes!

When we arrived home, Daddy was there. It had been too cold to work the grapevines, so he spent the day fixing up the house. He was kneeling on the floor in the front room, hammering in a loose floorboard, when we came through the door.

"Where'd you get those clothes?"

Nellie answered without hesitation. "Mrs. Spencer made us wear 'em while we were in her house."

"She think she's better'n us," he cursed, returning to his work. "What did you do, sit around and talk all day?"

"No, sir," I said. "She had us working hard up at the house."

"They better pay me for that."

Truth be told, it was barely work with Jackie. Often, her sister Sandra would come by, and we'd visit all day, playing with the children and eating fresh-baked cookies. Jackie must have known the truth about our lives because she went out of her way to make us feel safe and happy. She often tried to get us to admit how bad it was, but Nellie never let on, at least not in front of me.

I especially enjoyed the radio. I loved hearing music so much and never tired of it, even if the same songs played over and over again.

While I went about my work, I would sing along. It was such a wonderful place.

I was happy, and Daddy started to notice it. He became suspicious of what we did all day that made me so happy. I knew that the music was part of the reason I was so joyful, but I dared not tell him. He questioned us every night. We tried to make it sound like hard work, but his questions became more and more pointed.

One night, I stepped into the house humming a song I'd heard that day on the radio. Daddy was there. He pounced.

"Where'd you hear that song?!"

I froze, my throat tightening up. I shrugged and lowered my eyes.

"I think Mrs. Spencer was listening to music with her sister while we was working hard," Nellie said. "Frances musta overheard it."

"You been talking to that woman?" he asked for the hundredth time.

"No," Nellie said.

I glanced at her and noticed something odd. She had changed somehow. When she said no, she had her arms crossed and she looked him straight in the eye. Her feet were planted, and she did not sound timid at all. She was sixteen now, and I saw a flash of the adult she was to become.

Daddy eyed her up and down. It was like lightning crossing between them.

"I wonder," he said.

Nellie finally flinched. Her eyes lowered, and a dark, evil smirk crossed Daddy's face.

Not long after that night, Daddy found a way to steal our joy again. We woke up early in the morning, excitedly expecting to go clean house, babysit, and get away from Daddy's iron fist. He watched us get dressed and brush our hair. As we started toward the door, he stood up and barred the way.

"You're not going over there anymore."

He seemed to gain strength from our disappointment. The look on his face was one of pure joy, and my heart sank. I walked away from the door and he followed.

"You won't be goin' up there again," he said. "That woman don't want you up at her house no more."

I was devastated. Jackie had returned some light to my life. Daddy knew that, no matter how we tried to hide it from him.

"What?!" Nellie said.

She was still standing by the door. I was shocked by her reaction. I looked at her, willing her with everything I had to stay quiet. Daddy looked as surprised as I did.

"You ain't goin' up there no more. And if you don't shut your mouth, you're not gonna be able to shut it."

"Jackie *never* said that," Nellie snapped right back at him.

Daddy took a step toward her. Nellie turned and ran from the house. To my shock, he did not follow her. Instead, he turned on me.

"Get out of my sight," he said, backhanding me across the head.

Then, inexplicably, he walked away, so I got out the door as quickly as I could. I saw Nellie disappearing into the vineyard. I followed after her, trying to step in the tracks she left behind in the snow. The cold cut through my thin dress, but I had to catch up with my sister. When I did, Nellie barely paid me any mind.

"I knew he'd do it," I said.

"I hate him," she hissed. "I hate his guts!"

"Maybe Jackie will come looking for us," I offered.

Nellie kept walking. She had to be as cold as I felt, but she showed none of it.

"Do you want me to get your coat?" I asked.

Nellie said nothing. The cold was too much for me. I ran back to the house and got my coat and Nellie's too. Then I grabbed some of the pruning tools and headed out to the orchard. The cold and hard work was better than being around Daddy. More than that, though, I sensed something new and dangerous in Nellie. I had an almost overwhelming fear that she would disappear into that vineyard and I would never see her again.

I followed after her tracks, but they ended on a patch of rocky ground where the snow had melted away. I stood there for some time, staring out into the woods, feeling empty and alone. I must have gone back to work, but the day passed in a haze. When I got back to the house, I realized I had carried Nellie's coat with me all day.

I prayed to see Nellie inside the house, but she was not there. Mary Anne latched onto me the second she saw me, and I spent an hour or so playing with her. I saw my own fears mirrored in her eyes; I felt guilty for staying away from her for so long.

Finally the door opened, and Nellie appeared. She looked cold, but not as much as she would have had she been outside all day without her coat. I wondered if she had been to see Jackie against Daddy's orders. She ignored me and glared at Daddy. Her lip curled up, and she openly snarled at him. I was glad he was so drunk that he was almost ready to pass out. I don't know if he had not seen her snarl or chosen not to react. Either way, nothing happened. Nellie stomped into the back room and went to bed.

My sister's change grew more pronounced the longer we stayed at the Spencers' farm. As the weeks passed, she became more brazen. I often cringed when she muttered under her breath or shot a scowl in Daddy's direction. It was as if someone had placed a time bomb in the house. I could hear it ticking every second, but I had no idea when it was scheduled to erupt.

One day, as spring threatened to push winter north, the sun shone so brightly off the snow that I felt almost blinded when I walked outside with Nellie and Daddy. We headed out to the vineyard to care for the grapevines. Nellie and I stayed away from Daddy whenever we could. That day, Nellie stayed far away from me as well.

When our work was done and the sun began to set behind the tall trees to the west, we returned to the house. I stepped over the ax Daddy used to split wood. It was lying on the porch beside a pile of logs and an old tin half filled with lighter fluid.

"Watch where you're walking, you fool," he snapped at me.

Millie, who stayed behind to care for her baby son, Broadus, and Mary Anne, was busy fixing dinner. Daddy sat down in one of the chairs, snapped his fingers, and pointed down to his boots. I hurried over to loosen the laces. I was so used to him ordering us around in any manner he saw fit that I thought nothing of it. As I tugged on one boot, I glanced up at Nellie. She was staring right at me. The look on her face confused me. It was as though she was mad at me.

I started when Daddy slammed his open hand down on the tabletop.

"Get me my bottle!"

He was clearly talking to Nellie. There was a challenge to his tone that I had not heard before. It was as if he had waited until that moment to address the tension that had been building since we had arrived in Michigan after leaving the Missouri spider shack. I held my breath, as I imagined Millie did as well.

Nellie made no reply. She turned and looked him in the eye. The hatred on her face was like a snake coiled to strike, and she looked at him in pure disgust. It was totally, slap-you-across-the-face clear she considered him as revolting as a bug she had squashed under her foot.

My heart beat in my chest as if it were trying to force its way out. The moment lengthened to the point of unbearable tension. When Nellie's lips parted and the words formed in her mouth, I felt as though the entire world had erupted around me.

"*Get. It. Your. Self!*"

Daddy's face turned to stone. "What did you just say to me, girl?"

"I said, *Get it yourself!* What are you, deaf?" she mocked him.

My mouth hung open. Panic gripped me. I could not believe what I was hearing. All my life, I knew that defying Daddy would be rewarded by the worst fate on earth. I was certain this would lead to one ending: Nellie would die. She had to apologize at once! I prayed hard that he hadn't heard her words. I prayed for God to strike Daddy deaf or Nellie mute! But he *had* heard, and I could tell by his twisted, red face, that she would not get away with it. I held my breath and waited for the murder, or worse, that I was certain would unfold in front of my eyes. I wanted to run, but I was frozen in fear.

Chapter 25

Alone

Tension sparked like an electric shock between Daddy and Nellie. Neither of them would turn loose. This would be a battle to the death for one, and I knew deep in my heart which one it would be. I sucked in my breath as Nellie started to curse Daddy. This couldn't be happening with her allowed to remain standing! I felt as though I was going crazy, and nothing made sense. She cursed his drinking and his mason jars full of home brew that cost every cent we worked for. She cursed his temper, his sadistic, horrible bullying, and his conscienceless acts toward all of us. She did not hold back. Reaction to the years of abuse poured out of her in a rushing sewage of rage.

"I will never obey you again. I don't care what you do to me. You've done it all already. Why would I care? You're a perverted, filthy old child molester! You're not my daddy!"

Stop! I screamed inside my head. *Lord, strike her mute!* I could barely stand it. Nellie kept on screaming curses at Daddy until finally he stormed toward her, fists clenched, eyes bulging in his red face. I held my breath and prayed.

What happened next could have been comical if I did not know how truly dire a situation Nellie had put herself in. Amazingly, she held her ground as he lunged at her. His hand cocked back. I knew the force of the strike he had ready for her. I wanted to close my eyes, hide from it, but they refused to shut.

As the fist came crashing at Nellie, Daddy's full weight and the momentum of his lunge behind it, one of the floor planks he'd been working on buckled. He lost his balance and stumbled as Nellie took a strangely calm step backward. Daddy fell flat on his face right at her feet.

I stared at Nellie as Daddy bellowed like an angry bull. He struggled to regain his footing, and for an instant, Nellie just stood there.

"Run!" I screamed.

Nellie's eyes widened. It was as if she suddenly realized what she had done. Her cheeks turned white as snow. A second later, she was out the front door. I saw her jump off the porch and land in the front yard. My heart sank, though, when she planted herself there and turned to face the house. Daddy shook his head, snorting, as he pushed himself up from the floor. Nellie started to shriek at him from the front yard.

"I dare you to come out here you stinking, filthy pervert! You coward! Come on out here, Broadus! Ain't got the guts!"

She continued to curse him. He shook his head again, as if trying to wake up from such an unexpected dream. I watched his face turn a deeper red, and volcanic rage bubbled to the surface. A strange, eerie stillness filled the cabin. He was unusually quiet as he moved silently toward the door.

I knew he had zero control over his rage. Often, when angry at one person, he would lash out at the nearest one just to let out some of the steam. So, I grabbed Mary Anne's hand and put myself between her and Daddy.

Nellie spouted every filthy and obscene word she had learned from him. I was afraid to breathe for fear of attracting his attention, but he did not look at either Mary Anne or me. His attention was locked on Nellie. He stood in front of the door glaring but made no move to go after her. Although I could not believe what I was seeing, I did not trust that this tense calm would last. With an arm around her skinny shoulders, I hurried Mary Anne into the bedroom. Millie joined us there, and we watched the front room in silence. At last, Nellie's screaming ceased for a moment. The silence hung over us like thunder clouds. For a precious short while they were both quiet.

Suddenly, Nellie renewed her barrage, louder and with even more venom. That seemed to break Daddy out of his stupor. Instead of walking toward her, though, he turned and marched into the bedroom past Millie, Mary Anne, and me as though he did not see us standing there. A minute later he stepped out the front door carrying the small cardboard box full of Nellie's belongings. Slowly, he walked out to the front porch, watching her like a cat might toy with a mouse. When he reached the end of the porch, he dumped everything Jackie had given her on the edge of the porch. She could see clearly what he was doing. She stopped yelling for a minute, watching intently. He picked up the tin of lighter fluid and, staring Nellie in the eyes, doused her new clothes.

The two squared off over the small pile. In it was everything Nellie owned. In a way, it was her life there on the porch floor. They stared at each other, neither blinking. Then he struck a match and dropped it. The pile burst into flames.

Nellie erupted in a fury!

"*You dirty, lying perverted horror from a snake pit!*" she screamed. Nellie was totally out of control now, jumping up and down in the front yard, fists shaking, eyes blazing. "He's a liar, Millie. He's a liar! Our mama is *not* dead. He's a filthy, stinking liar! He rapes his own children! Our mama is alive, and he's a bigamist that broke out of prison!"

On and on she pounded, jumping up and down, shrieking like a banshee until she had spit out every secret she'd held inside for sixteen years! I could not see Daddy's face, but I know Nellie's words cut him to the bone by exposing him in front of Millie. He moved as fast as a weasel. Jumping over her smoldering clothes, he reached down and jerked up the long-handled axe that still rested by the woodpile on the edge of the porch.

He lifted it high above his head, slinging it round and round as he leapt down from the porch and raced after Nellie. He was insane with rage and revenge, and I was sure she would die for it. I prayed for God to give wings to her feet as she raced across the yard! Daddy had already attempted to murder us once. Back on that dark highway in Texas, we had done nothing to defy him. Now, Nellie had not only refused his orders, but she also named the dark secret of Daddy's degradation right in front of Millie. I knew he would kill her with that ax as easily as I had seen him chop a chicken's head off to fry up for dinner.

Raw survival instinct overtook Nellie in that moment. I have never seen a human move as fast as she did. She sprang forward as gracefully as a deer, spinning around and racing away. Daddy had no chance of catching her. After running about fifty feet, he realized that. As a last effort, he threw the ax end-over-end toward her back. It struck the earth, and Nellie disappeared into the woods. I breathed for the first time in what felt like an hour.

When Daddy finally turned back toward the house and headed inside, I scurried with Mary Anne and Millie back into the kitchen, as far as we could get out of his reach. We left the door open a crack and watched him. He sat in the chair where he kept his whiskey bottle in the front room. His face was still beet red, and his eyes were bloodshot and bulging. The veins in his neck looked as if they would explode. I knew we were not safe.

As quietly as I could, I inched over to the kitchen door and looked out the window. I scanned the backyard, looking for any sign of Nellie. Millie motioned at Mary Anne to get into bed and stay silent. I turned my attention outside. As night fell over the farm, I watched for Nellie. All the while, Daddy drank from his jug of whiskey and spat out curses.

"I'll bury that ungrateful harlot!" he yelled from the front room.

He continued to curse Nellie, but as the hours passed, his voice became slurred and his outbursts more infrequent until I was sure he had finally passed out. The house was deathly silent. I crept into the living room. Daddy had fallen off his chair, drunk, and he lay in a heap on the floor. Millie and her son were asleep with Mary Anne in the bedroom. I knew nothing short of an earthquake could wake him up now, so I walked just past him, eased open the front door, and stepped out onto the porch.

The night air was bitter. I took a deep breath and could smell the stench of burned cotton and wood coming from the charred mark on the porch. I sat down beside it. The stench was almost overpowering, but I didn't want to move. I was afraid to take a step off that porch. If I did, I was afraid my entire family, the only family I had ever known, might disappear from the world, and I would be totally alone. I felt that Mama, Brenda, Susie, Nellie, and even I would cease to exist. The fear did not make sense; it did not even seem rational to me, but it was more than real. Every person I loved had left.

I sat in the night watching for any sign of Nellie. She had to come back, at least to say good-bye. She could not leave me here alone forever. It was hard enough when I lost Brenda and Susie. I had never been as close to Nellie, but her flight cut just as deeply as all the others. And of course, losing Mama had been worse than anything. Mama had promised and crossed her heart to come back and get us, but she never did. I couldn't allow myself to think about losing the last piece of family. The longer I sat on the porch, the clearer it became. I was alone, the last of us caught in Daddy's evil grip. I knew I would never get away. This would be my lot.

Nellie, please come back! I wept, the tears rolling down my cheeks in steady streams. A tiny crack inside my heart had started the day

Brenda and Susie left. That crack widened when Robbie was adopted and Mama turned her back and walked away from us at Connie Maxwell Children's Home. When Nellie ran into the woods, it ruptured into a gaping hole. I was left empty inside, totally alone and hopeless.

My eyes could not stay open. The eastern sky lightened, a deep purple replacing the blackness of the night. I was caught somewhere between sleep and the real world. The trees seemed to grow up and tower over me. The porch roof became a wave of earth trying to swallow me up and drag me down. Shadows played with my mind, filled with evil things that took the shape of Daddy.

Still, wrapped in my coat, I did not move. I could not let Nellie go. I refused to give in to the overpowering sense of loss, loneliness, and fear that threatened to swallow me. Instead, I sat on the porch and forced my eyes to open again, to see the world for what it was.

That is when I saw it. At first, I thought it was another trick of my exhausted mind. A shadow moved out of the woods, crawling toward an old chicken shed beside the house. As it neared, I knew it was Nellie. She had come back!

As quietly as I could, I crept back into the house. Daddy snored on the floor, his empty whiskey bottle resting beside him. I feared waking him, but still tiptoed slowly into the kitchen. I wrapped up a piece of cornbread in a rag and then went to the middle room, where I very quietly gathered the quilt from the corner that we used for sleeping. Then I crept back outside through the kitchen door, fearing that Nellie would be gone again before I reached the coop. But then I heard a rustle inside. I climbed in, and Nellie was huddled there. The tears came flooding back, and I handed her the food and blanket. She took it gratefully, wrapping the quilt around her shaking shoulders.

"I ain't never going back," she said through chattering teeth.

I put my arms around her. Although I was chilled from my night outside, I willed what little heat I retained into her shivering body. Her shaking finally stopped, but my tears did not.

"I'm going into Niles to stay with Sandra, Jackie's sister. She can get me a job at that restaurant where she works. They think I'm eighteen so it ain't gonna be no problem. Daddy lied to them about both of us. They think you're sixteen instead of fourteen, so you can work too."

Nellie wiped away a tear that stained my cheek. She reached into her dress pocket and pulled out a tattered strip of brown paper. On it was scribbled an address.

"That's where I'll be. Memorize it, then burn it up. Don't you dare let *him* find it. Sandra gave it to me. She said if I ever get away, that she'll take me in. I'm going there today. You got to get away, too, Frances. When you do, go to that address. I'll be there. Okay?"

I broke down, sobbing. Nellie held me for just a second, then pulled away.

"Let me come with you," I begged through my tears.

Nellie's face changed. Her mouth turned down and she pulled farther back from me. She did not look me in the eyes when she spoke.

"Sandra's struggling hard enough with her two kids and no husband. She can't afford to take both of us in right now. Give me some time to make some money, then maybe you can come."

I knew she didn't want me to go with her. Nellie wanted total freedom. She needed to be on her own, and she wanted to go by herself. My greatest fear became reality in that moment. She was leaving me with him. I would be the last to get away, *if* I got away. Worse, I knew he would take his anger out on me for her rebellion. He could just as easily kill me in her place.

The hole inside me widened into an open gorge. I felt what was left of my heart break and sink into a dark, lonely place where no hurt could ever touch me again. I dried my tears and stood up, looking away from her.

"That's all right." I forced my voice to stay strong. "Daddy would never let us both go anyway. I'll stay and make sure he doesn't find you."

Nellie gave me a quick hug. "I love you, Frances."

I hugged her back. "I love you too."

Nellie left me the blanket and crawled out of the shed with the cornbread. I followed and watched until she disappeared into the woods, hoping the thin coat she wore would be enough to keep her from freezing. She waved one last time and was gone. At that moment, I vowed I'd never leave Michigan with Daddy. I wouldn't travel another road or be forced to lay down on that filthy quilt beside him. No matter what! That night, I decided I would choose death if I could not get away from him.

Chapter 26

Courage to Run

When Nellie left, I knew she was better off, but at the same time I had been left behind again. I knew I hated this man we called Daddy, the man who had done everything possible to ruin and destroy everyone around him. Talking to Nellie so many years later, this grown, free woman with kids of her own, brought back the deep sadness I'd felt the night I'd last talked to her, even though it was a joyous occasion.

When I finally hung up the phone with Nellie, Wayne smiled at me and asked if I'd like to consider a family reunion now that so many family members had returned to my life. It made me smile.

"Honey, guess what? That is exactly what we had in mind!"

"Okay, we'll do it," he decided.

Wayne went to the computer to make plans for the reunion. I watched him go. Although I was thrilled, I could not stop thinking about what happened after Nellie escaped.

Daddy's rage over Nellie leaving did not explode as it used to. Instead, it festered. His drinking became constant, and he beat anyone who seemed to get in his way. I did my best to keep Mary Anne safe, but it was impossible to avoid his anger.

The weather seemed to match his mood. The hint of early spring vanished days later, replaced by a blanket of new snow and dreary clouds. The temperature plunged, making it hard for us to work the grapevines on a consistent basis. Mr. Spencer stayed away as well. On occasion, he'd stop by during the day when the weather was nice to find Daddy and me working the grapevines. Daddy made sure to show a good face, but the second Mr. Spencer left, he cursed him, claiming that he'd been the one responsible for taking Nellie away. At the same time, he made no effort to find her. Of course, Mr. Spencer was clueless. I did not know at the time, but Jackie and her sister knew what was going on with Nellie, and they had made a vow not to tell anyone where she was hiding.

Daddy made sure that I did not learn from Nellie's example. He drove me like a slave master, beating me at the first sign of defiance. He used my love for Mary Anne against me as well. If he thought I was a step too slow, he would strike her for it. I withdrew inside myself, the pain becoming so unbearable that I had to refuse to admit it was even there.

At night, I would lay by myself and think about freedom. I prayed for Nellie. *Please hold Nellie in your arms and protect her. And please God, show me the way out of here.*

I cried constantly, wishing I had left with her but knowing that her only chance for freedom was to make it out on her own. I had to stay behind for her sake. I knew there was no other way.

One morning, Mary Anne found me. She looked up at me, and I could see the worry in her big, dark eyes.

"Are you mad at me?" she asked.

"Of course not, honey," I said.

I tried to smile, but it was forced and it slipped off my face sooner than I meant it to.

"Do you want to play jacks?"

"Sure," I said.

I felt so sorry for her. She did not deserve any of this, not any more than me or Nellie had. I tried to make her smile, but the effort was almost more than I could endure. I played with her but hurried out when it was time to get back to work.

That night, I got Mary Anne settled away from Daddy's notice. He drank and drank, eventually passing out at the table again. Millie and her son hid in the other room. Once Daddy was unconscious, I got up and walked out to the porch. I sat down as I did the night Nellie left, gazing out into the quiet night. This time, though, it was different.

"I don't want to live," I said to the stars.

I meant it. I was fourteen and I had not done any of the things a normal teenager does. I'd never seen the inside of a high school or been to a ball game. I didn't know how to talk on the phone. I didn't know how to talk to *people*. I was tired of being hungry and afraid all the time. I felt so empty. And I was shamed by what Daddy had done to me. I did not know how I could continue to live with that. Things would never be what they should have been. I truly believed that there was no more life left in me. I was alone.

I stood up and walked back inside. I did not try to be silent or worry about Daddy catching me up walking around. I just did not care anymore.

Life went on like that for a month. It was as if someone else was living my life, and I couldn't feel anymore. Daddy beat me. He beat Mary Anne. He had horrible, bloody fights with Millie. He drank every day. Life went on, and I endured it in silence.

I believe Daddy noticed. At the same time, I think he mistrusted Mr. Spencer from the day Nellie left. I existed in an empty stupor until one morning Millie stopped me as I was heading out to tend the grapevines. There were acres of them, and they needed to be pruned.

"Your daddy is getting ready to leave," she said, pulling me toward her and whispering close in my ear.

"What?"

I stared blankly at her, not comprehending. Then it hit me. She meant *we* were getting ready to leave.

"Shh. Listen, he's planning on heading to Arizona to find warmer weather."

A little bit of my soul reawakened when she said that. I remembered the vow I made. *I will not leave Michigan without Nellie.* I would not let the last piece of my family fall away and disappear forever. I dared to hope.

"I think it would be better if you got off by yourself before we go. Things would be easier with Mary Anne and me. We could be a family, you know. I know you want to get off by yourself. I can help you. I will help you if you want to leave."

I stared at her. There was a desperate tone in the way she spoke.

"If you want to stay here and try to find Nellie . . . I can help," she repeated.

Excitement made my heart flutter. A part of me did not trust Millie. She was a good person, but she was as cowed by Daddy as we all were. I knew the strange things someone could do or say when they were being abused, but the thought of finding Nellie overwhelmed that.

"How would I do it?" I asked hopefully.

"After we pack up, I'll set your box of stuff down behind the car. When it's time, I'll distract your daddy while you fetch it and get out."

"When is he going to leave?"

Millie's voice dipped lower. "Tonight."

"*Tonight?* You're leaving *tonight*? Why didn't you tell me before now? I don't know where to go. I don't know what to do. How will I do it? I'm afraid."

Millie blinked. "I'll help you. Just be ready."

Daddy hollered from outside.

"You better go." She pushed me toward the door.

I headed out, my stomach in a knot. I could not believe all this was happening so quickly. I was very afraid to leave. Even with Nellie gone, the years of threats and abuse from Daddy kept me bound like a prisoner of war. Millie's words, though, changed something inside of me. I had vowed not to leave Michigan. Did I have a choice? Would Millie really help me?

That day I was barely able to stand still. I caught Daddy glancing at me from the corner of his eye a few times. I think he must have noticed something different, considering I had totally withdrawn a month before and had walked around like a zombie until that moment.

That day felt like a month. When snow started to fall just after noon and Daddy called me in for the day, I could barely contain myself. All I could think about was the possibility of failure. Failure meant death.

Inside the house, I tried to corner Millie. I needed more details, but she avoided even looking at me. All I had was her word that she'd help. It was enough though. I was committed the second she told me that Daddy was leaving that night.

For the rest of the day, Daddy never mentioned that he intended to leave. The sun began to set, and I saw him and Millie quietly start to pack. I felt every nerve in my body tingling with fear and anticipation. Would she remember to set my little box out? Would I be able to grab it before I ran? I didn't want to lose the few clothes Jackie had given me.

When it was totally dark, Daddy finally let me in on the plan. He turned and barked at me, "Go help Millie pack. We're leaving here tonight."

A small bit of courage stirred in me. *Oh no* we're *not*, I thought. My hands were shaking as I joined Millie in the small kitchen. I inched closer to her than I needed to be, hoping she would whisper to me more about her plan. I pleaded with my eyes for her to tell me something, but she avoided looking at me.

"Finish gathering up the pots and pans," she said.

That was it. Nothing about our earlier conversation. Doubt crept into my body, chipping away at my resolve. *Can I do it? Will she help me? I can't do it by myself.* Outside, Daddy kicked up an enormous racket.

"What is that noise?" I asked, afraid.

"He's loosening the bolts on the butane tank."

"Why's he doing that?"

The butane tank held the gas that fed the stove in the kitchen. It belonged to Mr. Spencer.

"He's planning on taking it with us so he can sell it down the road," Millie said.

"He's stealing it?"

She just nodded and picked up another box. That really made me mad. Mr. Spencer and Jackie had been so good to all of us. I didn't understand how he could steal from them. Millie walked out to the car without another word about it. When she was gone, I searched out my small box of belongings. It was already packed and sat on the floor beside the front door.

Millie came back in and scooped up another armful. She headed back to the car, and I followed empty-handed. I did not pitch in because I wanted to delay leaving as long as I could, hoping that Millie would give me some sign that the plan was going forward.

Once Daddy secured the stolen tank in the trunk of the car, he called out to us.

"Get in the car, now."

He seemed nervous and in a hurry, as if he expected Mr. Spencer to show up and find him stealing his property. Millie, carrying her son, ushered Mary Anne into the backseat. I stood watching.

"Hurry up," he quietly said, giving me a warning look and taking his place in the driver's seat.

Although there was threat behind his tone, he spoke softly, as if afraid someone would hear him. "I'm coming!" I shouted as loud as I dared.

I saw Daddy cringe and pull his head down. I shouted again. "I forgot the pots and pans!" My voice was louder than usual in the still night, and he was getting frantic.

I turned around and rushed back into the house before he could say anything. I grabbed the box and walked out, purposely jiggling the contents. The clatter echoed over the fresh layer of snow covering the yard, sounding like cymbals clanging together.

"Quiet down," he hissed.

"What did you say?" I hollered back as loudly as I could.

Each ring of those pots filled me with courage. I was defying him, and nothing was happening! I was alive, and I tasted freedom for the first time since being taken from Connie Maxwell.

Daddy glared a warning at me, but he didn't want to make any noise, so he stayed quiet. If looks could kill, I would not be here today. I could see his anger building, but he tried not to show it. And something else. He was afraid!

"Frances, hurry up now," he said in a syrupy voice. "The kids are getting cold."

I yelled to the top of my lungs. "You want me to hurry?" I could see the internal fit raging inside him. He was paranoid that Mr. Spencer would be driving by, or anyone for that matter. His fear of the police was not logical. This time he wasn't in control of the situation; for once, he was on the receiving end of fear. Each time he urged me to hurry, I yelled back louder. He shrank down like a shadow behind the steering wheel.

"*What did you say?*" I practically bellowed the words.

This was getting fun! I wanted this horror of a human being to feel fear for a change!

I still held the box of pots and pans in my hands. I met his eyes as he sat inside the car, and he stared helplessly as I lifted the box higher up into the air over my head. Suddenly, I dropped the box to the ground. The clanging of pots, lids, and pans was deafening. It sounded like an alarm going off in the night.

That's when he jumped out of the car. He ran toward me, but I stayed one step away. I knew he wanted to grab me around the neck and drag me into the car. If he did that, I'd soon be in Arizona, his slave for life. I could not let that happen. The die had been cast. I could not go back. I'd either be dead or be free this night.

Daddy realized this simple fact. It must have radiated from me like sunlight. In his deranged mind, this was his last stand. Nellie had gotten away clean. She had shown him for what he was. I knew he would not let that happen again, not in front of Millie. I saw a flash of his old strength, his old venomous anger, when he lunged for me.

I jumped back. The courage I had felt turned to panic. Murder was in Daddy's eyes. I bolted around the other side of the car. He slipped a little on the snow, and I was able to get the vehicle between us. We circled once, twice, three times around the car. I could not let him get his hands on me, or it would be over. Each time he raced to the passenger side, I outran him and made it to the driver's side. I was terrified that he would outrun me!

The next time I passed the house, I made a run for it. Leaping up onto the porch, I threw the door open. As I spun around to slam it shut, I saw Mary Anne spring out of the car.

"Fances, come back!" she screamed.

My heart broke in two. In that instant, I could see her future. I knew the suffering she would endure. I had been through it already. I had survived, but I wondered if she could.

"Mary Anne, I—"

Daddy's face appeared out of the darkness. He was moving lightning quick, and his eyes were afire with hatred. He loomed so close that I screamed in utter terror and slammed the front door shut. My hand found the lock and slammed the bolt home just as the door handle rattled. The entire frame shook; his curses filtered through the solid wood door. He was no longer concerned about quiet.

For just a second, I thought I was safe. Then I remembered the kitchen door was unlocked!

My mind screaming, I raced through the dark rooms and into the kitchen, where I caught a glimpse of Daddy's face in the moonlight just outside the kitchen window. I knew it was too late! His mouth snarled savagely, spit landing on the window as he bellowed at me. "Open this door before I rip your head off!" His eyes were bulging pools of pure unbridled fury. The veins in his neck strained. I was going to be locked inside an empty house with this madman! "Jesus, help me!" I cried out loud. I heard the windowpane shatter and felt slivers of glass spray my face as his thick fist busted through the window. As he reached inside for the doorknob, I turned, racing to the front of the house. I jumped off the porch and fled to the safety of the woods with Daddy right on my heels and little Mary Anne standing in the snow screaming, a sound that sent shivers down my back.

I was running for my life, and he was so close I could hear him breathing. I felt his hand touch the back of my hair and knew if he caught me, he would bury me in a snowy grave in Michigan that very night.

I dove ahead of him and into the woods, losing him behind me. He stalked back and forth like a hungry lion. Slowly and as quietly as possible, I inched through the deep snow to what I hoped was the direction of the main road. Suddenly, my foot slipped and I fell facedown across a huge hollow log. The front of my dress ripped as I fell on my knees across the rotted wood. I lay on the frozen ground, terrified, afraid to move and praying for a miracle that would make him go away. Then, like an answer to my prayer, Millie called out. "Come on, Broadus! Leave her out there. We gotta get goin' before somebody hears us." I shivered in the snow, watching and praying as tears slid down my face and turned to ice. The only thing between my body and the frozen ground was my tattered dress.

Chapter 27

Freedom!

"*Come on, Broadus,*" Millie called out. "Somebody's gonna call the law on you."

Daddy had continued to pace like a caged animal for what felt like hours. Finally, his shoulders sagged. His belt dragged in the snow behind him as he turned and slowly walked to the car. I could breathe again, and I even adjusted to ease some of the pain in my legs.

The engine roared to life and the headlights panned over my head as the car turned onto the main road. I shrunk back down again, afraid to be seen, but he drove off into the night. I saw his brake lights flash once, and then he was out of sight.

I dared not leave the cover of the woods. I crouched in the snow behind my log and waited. I knew he'd be back. Finally, the cold got to be more than I could bear, and I stood up. I winced when I touched the cuts on my leg, and my entire body shook.

I took one step, and lights suddenly appeared on the road. I jumped and scurried back to my log just as Daddy's car turned back from the highway. His lights shined right on me as he headed back toward the house.

The car came to a stop next to the porch. The engine continued to run, and the lights pointed directly on the branches over my head. I put my face right up against the packed snow behind the log and held my breath.

Maybe a minute later, the engine revved. The snow below my face fell dark again, and I peeked up over the log. His car had turned and headed back the way it came. He didn't slow this time as he drove away.

I wasn't sure what to do or where to go, but I was certain if I continued to lie in the snow without a coat, I would die of exposure out in the woods. I didn't know anyone except Mr. Spencer and Jackie. Plus, I was only fourteen, and I knew Daddy could force me to go back with him if he found me. I hoped that since he'd stolen the butane tank, he would never drive over to the Spencers' looking for me.

I decided to take my chances and make my way to their farmhouse. It was more than half a mile down the snowy gravel road just to get to the road to their house. Once on the main road I would be in the open with no place to hide. I hoped I could remember the direction in the dark.

Having made up my mind to leave, I tried to raise my legs. It was so cold in one spot that my calf was stuck to the ice. I couldn't pull it free without tearing my skin. When I tried to yank it loose, it felt like a knife was cutting my flesh. I couldn't move! I was shivering, crying, and near freezing. I rubbed my hands back and forth, trying to warm the area on my calf that was stuck to the log.

The friction was finally enough to warm my calf to the point where I could move my leg, but the cold had caused it to go almost numb. I got up slowly, limping away toward what I hoped was the main road as fast as I could. The more I moved, the easier walking became. Soon I was able to run at a trot out of the woods.

God led me to the main road leading to the Spencers' farm. Once I was out in the open, I expected to see Daddy's car lights appear out of the darkness at any second. My breath came out in raspy gasps, and my eyelashes were frozen stiff. I frantically prayed for someone, anyone, to drive by and stop for me before Daddy could find me on this deserted highway.

I had never hitchhiked, but when I saw headlights coming up behind me, the cold and pain overcame my fear, and I walked out into the middle of the road. It didn't occur to me at the time these headlights could be the ones I was running away from! I was standing in the middle of the road when it hit me that I did not know if this approaching car was Daddy's. Still, I stood there waiting, knowing it was too late to run. As the lights got closer, I realized it was not a car at all but a semitruck. The truck driver pulled his rig up beside me and rolled down the window.

"Hey there, do you need help, young lady?"

It was a man's voice, deep and strong. He opened the passenger door and let me climb into the warm cab.

"Can you take me home?" I asked, my teeth chattering.

The truck driver looked at me, his eyes narrow. I was a fourteen-year-old girl, alone and bleeding in the middle of the night on the side of the road.

"My boyfriend tried to hurt me. I just want to get home," I said.

"Sure, I'll take you home. I have a daughter about your age. You get on home where it's warm and safe."

The driver turned his heater up full-blast. It quickly warmed my frozen feet and hands. I have always believed that God sent that truck driver to me in the middle of the night.

"Thank you," I said as we pulled up in front of the Spencers' house.

"No problem." He smiled warmly at me. "You just be more careful from now on."

I don't think he had any idea that he had just saved my life!

Outside the Spencers' house, the chill returned worse than it had before. This was exactly where Daddy might come looking for me. I could not worry about that though. I just had to hope that the Spencers would take me in from the cold.

The house was dark. I knew they were all asleep, but I had no choice. I banged on the door as loudly as I could, yelling hysterically.

"Jackie! Mr. Spencer!" The strength seeped from me, and I reached out for the doorjamb to keep from falling over.

"Help!" I screamed.

Suddenly, the porch light came on. The door opened, and there stood Mr. Spencer. He barely seemed shocked when he ushered me inside and closed the door behind us. The warmth of the house embraced me, and I thought I would faint. My teeth were chattering as I tried to talk.

"I ran off and left my da . . . daddy," I said. "He's going to Arizona, but I can't go with him."

"It's okay, Frances. Jackie thought you might come for help. You're safe now. Come here and sit down at the table."

Jackie, awakened by the noise, joined us in the kitchen. She fixed me hot chocolate and wrapped a large flannel shirt around me. It was as if a dam broke inside me. My entire story, my entire life, poured out of me. For the first time, I told someone about our life, and Mr. and Mrs. Spencer listened to every word. I told them about everything except the sexual abuse; I could *never* tell anyone that. I told them how we were beaten and how Daddy kidnapped me and Nellie from the orphanage. I explained he had stolen their butane tank and it was in his car. I was so embarrassed about that, but I promised I would pay them back for it.

Mr. Spencer looked sad. "I'm not worried about the butane tank, Frances. You don't have to pay for the wrong someone else does." I had never been told that before. Up to this point I felt everything my daddy did was my fault.

My hands shook as I tried to drink my hot chocolate, and I could not stop stuttering. I felt I had to make them understand how mean and evil he was as quickly as I could before he came back for me. At that point I was pretty certain he would return, and I was terrified they would make me go back with him. The words, once free, had a life of their own.

"Please, can I stay here with you? I can't go back to him."

"You are not going back to him," Jackie said.

"Absolutely not," Mr. Spencer agreed.

"You don't know him though. Not like I do. If he comes here—"

Mr. Spencer interrupted me. "If he comes around here, we will deal with that then. For now, we need to care for you. You're blee—"

The sound of a car coming up the driveway interrupted him. I froze, panic rising inside me. An engine revved and then stopped. A door slammed and heavy footsteps came crunching over gravel. My heart felt as if it would surely jump out of my chest. Daddy had come to get me!

Chapter 28

One Last Battle

I must have appeared hysterical to the Spencers. When I heard that car stop outside, I jumped up like a startled rabbit. I stumbled, knocking over the chair as I rushed to get to the front door. I had to lock it and keep him out. There was no telling what Daddy might do. Barring the heavy wooden door with my body, I screamed, "No, no! He's not coming in here!" I tried to reach my hands across the door and tried to block their access to the door handle.

"It's okay, Frances."

Mr. Spencer's soft voice was calm. He approached the front door, and I looked up at him, not knowing what to do. I moved out of his way, praying silently that this kind, gentle, simple farmer would not be murdered while trying to help me. A psychotic, evil maniac was storming up their front walk, and I knew it was my fault they were in this situation. Mr. Spencer remained calm. I took a step to the side and hid behind the door, crouching by the crack between the door and the wall.

"Please don't open the door," I whispered.

Mr. Spencer turned on the porch light and reached for the knob.

"Tell him I'm not here. Please, please, tell him I'm not here!"

Mr. Spencer opened the door and stepped outside. Daddy stood on the gravel drive a few feet away from his car. I heard Mr. Spencer trying to calm him.

"Broadus, it's late now. You need to come back in the morning," he said.

Daddy ignored him.

"Where is she?" he yelled.

"You're going to wake my children," Mr. Spencer said. "Quiet down."

"Get out of my way! Send Frances out here now."

In his peaceful way, Mr. Spencer stood his ground. Through the crack between the door and the frame, I saw Daddy. His feet stomped, and he looked ready to lunge at Mr. Spencer. I had seen it many times in the past. He was sizing him up and ready, almost eager, for war.

"Frances, get out of that house!" he bellowed.

Daddy cursed me and the Spencers while I remained paralyzed in fear. I was sure we were all going to die this time. With everything inside me, I wished he would just tell Daddy that I was not there.

Again I begged. "Tell him I'm not here!" Mr. Spencer, however, would not lie. I had watched my dad beat men twice Mr. Spencer's size. When he reached down and picked up a small log off the grass, I knew Daddy would kill him if he stood in the way. I could barely stand the horror.

"Get his shotgun!" I whispered to Jackie. "Call the police! Tell him you're calling the police!"

Mr. Spencer did not flinch. I couldn't tell if Daddy could hear me, but I was frantic.

"Tell him you're going to call the police! He's afraid of the police!" My heart was in my throat and I could barely swallow. *Why won't they listen to me?!*

"Don't take another step with that weapon," Mr. Spencer called out to Daddy.

His voice never rose. He never showed an ounce of fear. Mr. Spencer simply stood up to Daddy with faith in his heart. It was an amazing sight, but one I knew could not last. Daddy had no faith. He did not have an ounce of love in him. When he took a step toward Mr. Spencer, all the bloody battles passed in front of my eyes.

My urging got louder. "Tell him you've called the police!"

Daddy took another step forward; the log looked bigger the closer he came. "Please, oh please, tell him you've called the police!"

That is when Jackie reappeared. In my hysteria I hadn't heard her coming, but suddenly she passed me and walked out onto the porch. She carried a loaded shotgun.

Mr. Spencer did not take his eyes off Daddy. He gently took the gun from his wife's hands and pointed it at the ground.

I thought I'd go crazy! "Point the gun at *Daddy*!" I whispered.

"Get on out of here, Broadus," he said. "Unless you want to talk like a man."

I could see the rage filling Daddy's face. His entire being seemed to quiver with malice. He took another step forward and lifted that log out in front of him.

In response, Mr. Spencer raised the barrel of his gun and leveled it at Daddy's chest. Daddy did not stop. He took another step, and then another. I was sure either Mr. Spencer would shoot or Daddy would club him down. In the meantime they would have to take me to the hospital for heart failure!

"Jackie," Mr. Spencer said, as calm as when this all started, "please go on in and call the police."

It was as if Mr. Spencer had known all along the power of that one word. It was the only thing Daddy ever truly feared. When he heard "police," the fight left him. The log fell from his hand, and he backed off.

I heard Jackie making the call from behind me. There was no way Daddy could have heard her talking, but his pace quickened. He fumbled with the door latch for the car. He got in, and I heard his car start up.

"I'm going to kill you all," he yelled out the window. But there was nothing behind those words. His hold over me broke that night. He would rather lose a fight than deal with the police. If a man like Mr. Spencer, one full of kindness and peace, could stand Daddy down, then I knew I could as well. God gave me the courage, and Mr. Spencer showed me what power there is in staying calm. Although I was not to be free of Daddy's memory for many years, I was finally free of his evil. Daddy could never hurt me again.

Chapter 29

Forgiveness

Physically, I was free, but Daddy's ghost was not as easy to escape. He followed me through years of my life, haunting my memory and chipping away at any attempts I made to find happiness. I sank very low; I lived hard and was unable to shake the ugly memories of my past. Then God sent a friend and calm presence into my life. His name was Wayne. I had asked God for a man I could pray with who would read the Bible and go to church with me. More than anything, I desired to pray together with my mate—to be with someone who was not ashamed to pray in public.

God lifted me up from wretched depths I won't describe in this book. He gave me a great love for Him and an inner peace that I didn't understand at the time. I wanted to live for Him the rest of my life and share His love with a man that felt the same.

Meeting Wayne changed my life. After many long talks on the phone and one dinner, we decided to go out again. He took me to a nice restaurant, and I sat down across from him, a little nervous. Looking into this handsome man's gentle eyes, I realized how much he did not know about me, or about my lost family. Wayne had a wonderful family, and they were all close. I wondered if he could understand my past.

Through all the battles of my life, one awesome presence had always stayed by my side. I turned to Him at that moment. I would know if Wayne was the one if he prayed with me. From across the table, I looked deeply into Wayne's eyes.

"Will you pray with me and thank God for our dinner?"

Wayne, who was not yet a Christian, nodded eagerly. We joined hands, and I thanked God for our food. After we said amen, I looked at him. He was very serious. I learned later that he had also asked God for someone to pray and go to church with. He had faith, believed in God, and wanted to learn more, but had not yet totally trusted God for salvation. This was a man who would pray with me out in public and not be bothered by people looking at us. He was hungry to learn as much as he could about Jesus.

That moment had a major impact on me. It was a sign, but the years weighed heavy on my heart. It was not until we were married that I fully opened up to Wayne.

"My life has not always been so nice," I said.

"Nobody's life is *always* nice," he answered.

"My dad was not a good man," I began.

I continued on, telling him the story up until I escaped with the help of Mr. Spencer. I was concerned about how Wayne might react, but I couldn't stop. The story ran out of me like rain falling from a heavy gray cloud. When I stopped talking, Wayne took my hand.

"I'm glad you didn't give up," he whispered.

For some reason, I found it harder to finish the story from there. It was a whole new tale that needed its own time and place.

"I'm not sure I didn't," I said.

"You're here now, with me."

I had struggled when I left the Spencers. I found work, but I was young, inexperienced, and had no skills at all. I got involved with a man, the father of my two children, who was not much different than my father. He was a mean, controlling alcoholic. He threatened to take my children away from me if I didn't do exactly as he ordered. I felt completely alone, and he pushed alcohol on me until I began to drink along with him. I finally found the strength to divorce him, but the habits stuck, and fear engulfed my life.

"I believe that God brought us together," Wayne said softly.

I smiled at him. "After my son went into the army and my daughter went to college, I moved to Tennessee."

He grinned at me from across the table. "I'm sure glad you did!"

"I was so lost, and I remember praying one night, asking God to allow me to find a house close enough to a preacher so that I could learn more about God. With all my heart I wanted to learn how to be saved, and I felt if I lived within a few blocks or even a mile or so of a preacher, it would not be a burden on a man or woman who knew the Lord to tell me about Him too. When I looked for a house to buy, I searched a long time. After months of searching I finally found the house I felt I could make into a home.

"When I was following the Realtor back to her car to sign the papers, she looked over at the house next door and said, 'You'll like your neighbors. The pastor of First Baptist Church lives right next door.' She didn't notice that I had stopped walking!"

"I prayed a similar prayer," Wayne confessed shyly. "How were you saved?" he asked.

Our food showed up then. I smiled at him.

"That's a real long story."

On a morning years later, Wayne came to our kitchen table with a serious look in his eyes. While he had searched for my family, he was also searching for something else. I knew this, but I never let on that

I did. It was not something I wanted him to find. It was something I wanted buried in the past and never brought back again.

While he was searching for Brenda, he had brought the topic up.

"I think we need to find your dad's grave."

"No, I don't think so," I said.

"You've found love, Fran, but you can't be totally free until you find forgiveness too."

I shook my head. "I forgive."

"Not your father," he said.

He was right. I was already saved, and I tried to live a life in touch with God, but I still had not truly found the strength to forgive the one who had torn my family from me and ruined years of my life. I resented everything about my dad, and I felt I had every right to.

"I don't think this is the right time, honey," I said to Wayne, and that was the end of that. Or so I thought.

A few years later it came back up. This time, though, Wayne knew more.

"I found your dad's grave," he said that morning as I sat at the table drinking coffee. I almost choked.

"How did you do that?" I asked. I was shocked and on guard. "I don't think I want to know where he's at."

Wayne ignored me. "He is in an unmarked grave in Cowpens, South Carolina." Cowpens was only three hours from our home. "Fran, I think we should go down there and put a headstone on his grave."

I looked at my husband for a minute. "Why on earth would I want to do that?"

"Because no grave should go unmarked." I thought about what he said.

"And I want you to do one more thing."

"What else?" I didn't think I was going to like this.

"I want you to think of something you want to say to him. Then we'll have the stonecutter write it on his stone."

He sounded so sincere about it that I decided not to put up a fight. I could do this for my husband, for the man who had shown me that true kindness and love still existed. So he took me to a shop that sold grave markers. When we arrived, I chose a small stone.

"What do you want engraved on it?" the man working there asked.

I took a deep breath before answering. "Matthew 6:15," I answered.

"What is that verse, if you don't mind me asking?" The man looked kindly at me.

"But if you do not forgive others their sins, your Father will not forgive your sins."

"Oh. That is nice. Come back in a week and we'll have it ready for you."

A week later we returned. The man told us to pull around back and open the trunk. Two very large men appeared and placed the stone in the back. The car bounced when they let go of it.

"That is heavy!" I said.

"Weighs about three hundred pounds, ma'am."

I looked at the stone. It was only about two feet high and two feet across. Wayne started the engine, and we drove off. Not a block away, I turned to look at him.

"How are we going to get that thing out of the trunk?" I asked.

He shrugged. He recently had back surgery and could in no way lift that stone. A part of me was relieved. If there was no way to remove the stone, there would be no need for me to go through with this. I didn't say anything else as we drove off to Cowpens.

We came to a stop at a tiny cemetery right in the heart of town. The grass was green with large patches of brown. Some of the graves looked unkempt, but others appeared as if someone came each and every day to care for them. My heart rose up to my throat when Wayne opened his door.

"Come on, honey," he said.

I got out and walked around to the trunk. He had it open.

"What now?" I asked, half hoping we would go back home.

He paused, scratched his head, and looked around. Suddenly, he pointed behind me. I turned, and through a line of tall oaks, I saw a family having a backyard barbeque. There were about two dozen people scattered across the lawn. Wayne would not give up. He walked us over to the yard. Not knowing what else to do, I approached an older man and introduced myself.

"I have not seen my father in over thirty years, and I just found his grave," I explained. "It is unmarked, so we brought a stone."

I did not even have to finish my story. Three young men sitting nearby jumped to their feet. They offered to help and followed us back to the cemetery. They reached in and took out the stone as if it were made of cork and placed it exactly where I asked.

"We have money. I can pay you," I said.

They laughed and said no. Nodding to us, they walked off to rejoin their party. I watched them go and then turned to Wayne.

"The Lord sent us help," I said. "I guess it is His will."

Wayne nodded. "Without them, we'd have never gotten it out of the trunk."

That was when I finally turned back and really saw the stone standing on Daddy's grave. A weakness came over my body, and I reached out. The small marker had his name and the dates printed on it, as well as the Bible verse, Matthew 6:15. Wayne took my hand, and together we stood there, looking down.

Some might wonder how anyone could forgive a man like my dad. In that moment, it was not my mind that forgave him but the power of the Lord working through me. I could never have done it through my own power. There was no thinking about it. Instead, my heart opened up, breaking free from the weight that burdened it. Layers and layers of anger, built up over so many years of abuse, shed away. I was left raw and facing Daddy one last time. As I stood there by his grave, I realized I wasn't angry. All I felt was sorry that a life had been wasted. Then, like a giant balloon that had been released into the air, my bitterness rose up out of me. I did not forget, and it took time to get past many of the hurts, but the process of forgiveness started the day we set that stone on his grave. Wayne and I stood still, looking down at his stone and holding each other for a long time.

I had survived, although it was not always easy. I found love, although it took me half a lifetime. I was rebuilding a family torn apart. What had Daddy found?

He never cared to know love, or he would never have treated his children as he had. He lost everyone in his family, and never would they return to his side. He had survived in his way but had ended up in an unmarked grave.

I felt sad for Daddy. Not for what he did; there is no excuse or understanding for that. I felt sad for what he did not do—love, enjoy life, embrace God. In that moment, with my heart wide-open, my soul reaching out, and tears running down my cheeks, my mouth opened and words spilled out.

"I forgive you, Daddy." Tears ran down my cheeks.

Wayne's arm wrapped around my shoulder. He pulled me close to him, and I rested my head on his chest. The sun set behind the line of oak trees as wisps of pink and purple crossed the sky. A light breeze touched my face, and a gaping wound inside of me finally healed. I was free at last, and it was as if I could see Daddy's ghost float out into that sunset, gone but never forgotten—forgiven but never understood.

Chapter 30

The Reunion

Our car turned onto the winding road leading into Lake Greenwood. Through the high, straight trunks of the giant pines that surrounded the park, I saw the water. It shimmered in the afternoon sunlight as millions of tiny ripples floated on its surface.

"Look how beautiful," I said to Wayne, who was driving.

He looked at me instead of the lake. "Are you nervous, honey?"

I let out a huge breath. My stomach was turning like a clothes dryer, and my head felt lighter than air. My insides seemed out of order, as if something huge was building up where there had been nothing but emptiness.

"Just very excited," I said.

He laughed. "I am too."

We turned along the bend in the road, and that's when I saw the parking lot. It was filled with dozens of cars! I could not believe it. These people were kin to me. They were part of my family; a family I never believed I would have this side of heaven. Wayne found a spot and parked the car. He turned off the engine, but I made no attempt to get out.

"They're waiting for you," he said gently.

"What if they don't like me?"

Wayne placed his hand softly on mine. "You know that won't be the case."

"But I don't recognize them. I don't *know* them."

"Well, you're *gonna* know them in just a few minutes. Let's go!" He smiled.

"Okay, I'm ready."

I looked into his eyes, and an overwhelming sense of love swept through me. It replaced the nervousness and fear I felt. Wayne was always the calm, soft voice of reason.

"I could not have done this without you," I told him.

"You would have found them eventually," he said. "I'm just the tool God used."

I ran my hand softly over his cheek. "I mean, I couldn't have found them and learned how to forgive without you."

"That wasn't me," he said.

I nodded, understanding what he meant. God had brought him into my life for a reason. Wayne, the calming light that helped me find true freedom, was my soul mate. He came when I most needed him and showed me the meaning of forgiveness.

"Let's go," he said again, a huge smile on his face.

"I can't believe that I'm going to see them all again."

"You *won't* see them if you don't get out of this car." He laughed.

I laughed with him. His humor gave me the courage to open the door. I stepped out of the car and immediately heard the distant sound of laughter and children at play coming up from the lakeshore. Taking Wayne's hand, I followed that sound. That joyous sound seeped into my soul with each step. It filled me.

As I topped a gentle rise, the sound of guitar, keyboard, and tambourine mingled with the laughter of children. At the top of the grassy hill, I froze. Down below me, a family spread out under a giant tree. I saw people sharing pictures and heard others telling stories. I watched as groups of people laughed and hugged.

Overwhelmed, I turned to Wayne. I had a large lump in my throat.

"Can this really be happening?"

"It can." He hugged me and whispered in my ear. "This is your family, honey!"

With a deep breath, I walked toward the reunion. The faces below became clear and more familiar. A small group of children raced toward us, engrossed in their own game of tag. I had never met them before, but I could see my family reflected on their cherubic faces.

"Frances!" someone yelled.

I looked up and saw Jimmy walking quickly toward me. He took me in his strong arms and hugged the air out of my chest. He shook Wayne's hand and clapped him on the back.

"This is a miracle," I breathed.

The smile on his face said it all. It was as if he were glowing from the inside.

"Come on," he said. "Everyone's waiting for you."

Jimmy led me to the park shelter. We passed several long tables covered with dishes of food. There were black-eyed peas, potato salad, fried green tomatoes, macaroni salad, deviled eggs, fried chicken, catfish, hush puppies, and some of the most beautiful pies and cakes I'd ever seen. My stomach rumbled when I took in the smell.

I spied Brenda immediately, sitting in a chair at the end of the first table. She was handing out chips and cookies to passing children like a mother bird feeding her young. The tenderness I remembered from our childhood radiated from her like a warm, loving hug. All the children felt it too, and they flocked around her.

"Hi, Sissie," I said.

My sister rose to her feet and spread her arms. I hugged her for what felt like an hour. Our embrace only ended because the children were restless. They wanted their treats. Brenda laughed, and the sound was like music to my ears.

I sat beside her and we visited, talking as we had at her house, only this time she was smiling! Happiness and contentment radiated from her eyes. Jimmy and Wayne sat with us. Everyone seemed at home, as though we had never been apart. The band struck up another song, and I noticed Brenda swaying to the music. Nellie walked over and joined us. We were all together again at last.

To my surprise, when that song ended, Brenda walked over to the band. She whispered to them and they nodded. I was shocked when she picked up the microphone; Brenda is a very reserved person in public and is not one to call attention to herself—ever. When the tune started, though, my heart missed a beat. It was a gospel song my mama used to sing to us when we were children.

"Farther along, we'll know all about it . . ."

I stood up, as did Jimmy and Nellie, and listened to Brenda sing. Her voice embraced us. She sounded so much like Mama that it was as if my mother were there with us. We were a family again.

My eyes brimmed over, and a tear slid down my cheek. That was the moment that the whole inside of me filled to overflowing. It filled with Brenda's lovely voice, with Jimmy's strong presence, with memories of Susie and Mama. It filled with people of my blood, a family I had lost so long ago. It filled with love and forgiveness.

I reached out behind me, searching. A familiar hand found mine. I squeezed and looked up into Wayne's eyes.

"Thank you," I said out loud.

He looked down at me and smiled. "Don't thank me."

I smiled back, feeling the warmth of his embrace. "I wasn't thanking you, Sweetheart."

Acknowledgments

I would like to acknowledge and thank Brian Hampton and each person at Thomas Nelson whose talent, patience, and wisdom shaped *Cruel Harvest* into the book we prayed for. The creativity and editorial skills of Kristen Parrish and Janene MacIvor are priceless! I am in awe of your talents.

I want to thank Joel Miller, whose faith and insight pushed this book forward. I am certain that God worked through Joel Miller to birth *Cruel Harvest.*

Lori Lynch, Julie Faires, Jennifer McNeil, Chad Cannon, Katherine Rowley, Brenda Smotherman, Kristi Henson, Debbie King, April Dupree, Lisa Schmidt, and so many others behind the scenes at Thomas Nelson deserve a medal! Your kindness and patience seem limitless. Thank you all!

I want to thank everyone for their prayers during the years that it took to write this book. You know who you are. Your encouragement and faith is deeply appreciated.

I would also like to acknowledge the Helen Reese Agency.

And a special thank you to Wayne Grubb, my husband and friend, who held my hand and prayed faithfully beside me, never doubting for seven years as I wrote and rewrote page after page. Your contribution is priceless.

Most of all I want to thank Jesus Christ for allowing me the privilege of knowing Him and for finding the perfect home—the home *He* chose, for *Cruel Harvest.* Thank you, Lord!

Author's Note

Wayne and I wanted very much to find Mary Anne, but we never learned Millie's maiden name or if Mary Anne took the name of her real father, so, sadly, we were unable to find either of them.

Wayne searched the Internet for my mama and learned she had died several years after my dad died. She is buried in Spartanburg, South Carolina, in her sister's family plot.

Mr. Spencer, Jackie, and I remain friends.

About the Author

Fran Grubb travels across the southeast United States with her husband, Wayne, singing her way into the hearts of her listeners and speaking at churches, tent revivals, prisons, women's shelters, children's homes, drug or alcohol rehabilitation centers, or any place there is need. Fran and her husband are founders of Feed the Hungry Children, a nonprofit working with the hurting in Kenya.

For more information see www.frangrubb.com.